# Theology and Religious Studies
# in Higher Education

**Continuum Advances in Religious Studies**
Series Editors: Greg Alles, James Cox, Peggy Morgan

# Theology and Religious Studies in Higher Education

## Global Perspectives

Edited by

Darlene L. Bird
Simon G. Smith

continuum

**Continuum International Publishing Group**
The Tower Building                 80 Maiden Lane
11 York Road                       Suite 704
London SE1 7NX                     New York NY 10038

www.continuumbooks.com

**British Library Cataloguing-in-Publication Data**
A catalogue record for this book is available from the British Library.

ISBN-10: HB: 1-8470-6311-X
        PB: 1-8470-6312-8

ISBN-13: HB: 978-1-8470-6311-3
        PB: 978-1-8470-6312-0

**Library of Congress Cataloging-in-Publication Data**
A catalog record for this book is available from the Library of Congress.

Typeset by Newgen Imaging Systems Pvt Ltd, Chennai, India
Printed and bound in Great Britain by MPG Books Ltd, Bodmin, Cornwall

# Contents

# List of Contributors

**Darlene L. Bird** is currently Lecturer in the Centre for Academic Practice at Queen Margaret University, Edinburgh, UK. She holds a PhD in Literature, Theology and the Arts from the University of Glasgow and is the former Subject Coordinator for Theology within the Subject Centre for Philosophical and Religious Studies, University of Leeds, UK. Her publications include *Bodies in Question: Gender, Religion, Text* (Ashgate, 2005) and *Believing in the Text* with David Jasper and George Newlands (Peter Lang, 2004).

**Erik (E. P. N. M.) Borgman** is full Professor of Systematic Theology at Tilburg University, the Netherlands. From 2004 to 2007 he was Director of the Interdisciplinary Heyendaal Instituut for Theology, Sciences and Culture at Radboud University, Nijmegen, the Netherlands. His research concerns the relationship between religion and contemporary culture.

**James L. Cox** is Professor of Religious Studies in the University of Edinburgh, UK. He has held prior academic appointments in Westminster College, Oxford, the University of Zimbabwe and Alaska Pacific University. His recent publications include *From Primitive to Indigenous: The Academic Study of Indigenous Religions* (Ashgate, 2007) and *A Guide to the Phenomenology of Religion: Key Figures, Formative Influences and Subsequent Debates* (Continuum, 2006).

**Shannon Craigo-Snell** is Assistant Professor of Religious Studies at Yale University, USA where she teaches Modern Christian Thought and writes about feminist theologies, Karl Rahner, and performance. She is the author of *Silence, Love, and Death: Saying 'Yes' to God in the Theology of Karl Rahner* (Marquette University Press, 2008).

**Denise Cush** is Professor of Religion and Education and Head of the Department of Study of Religions at Bath Spa University, UK. Her teaching and research interests include religious education in international perspective, Buddhism, Hinduism, Christianity and Contemporary Spiritualites.

Recent work includes research on teenage interest in witchcraft and Paganism, co-editing an Encyclopedia of Hinduism, and co-writing a commissioned report on the state of religious education in schools, initial teacher training and continued professional development in England.

**Gavin D'Costa** is Professor of Christian Theology, Department of Theology and Religious Studies, University of Bristol, UK. His book, *Theology in the Public Square*, Blackwell, Oxford, 2005, discusses the nature of theology and religious studies more extensively. His forthcoming work, *Disputed Questions in the Theology of Religions*, Blackwell, 2009, traces the way 'religion' and 'inter-religious' dialogue has been shaped by modernity's discourse on 'religion'.

**David F. Ford** is the Regius Professor of Divinity at the University of Cambridge, UK. He is the Founding Director of the Cambridge Inter-Faith Programme, Co-founder of the Society for Scriptural Reasoning, and an Academic Member of the Council of 100 Leaders for West-Islamic World Dialogue in the World Economic Forum. In addition, he is a Member of the Advisory Board of the John Templeton Foundation and a Trustee of the Center of Theological Inquiry in Princeton. He is the author of many books, including: *Christian Wisdom: Desiring God and Learning in Love* (Cambridge, 2007), *Shaping Theology: Engagements in a Religious and Secular World* (Oxford, 2007), *The Shape of Living* (London, 2002) and *Theology: A Very Short Introduction* (Oxford, 2000).

**Janet Jarvis** is currently a lecturer and the discipline coordinator of Life Orientation in the School of Social Science Education within the Faculty of Education at the University of KwaZulu-Natal, South Africa. Her recent Masters thesis focused on teachers' understanding of the human right to 'religious freedom'. She is currently engaged with doctoral research.

**Ursula King** is Professor Emerita and Senior Research Fellow at the Institute for Advanced Studies, University of Bristol, UK, and Professorial Research Associate at the Centre for Gender and Religions Research, School of Oriental and African Studies, University of London. Educated in Germany, France, India and England, she has lectured all over the world and published numerous books and articles, especially on gender issues in religions, method and theory, modern Hinduism, interfaith dialogue and spirituality, and on Pierre Teilhard de Chardin. She has held several visiting chairs in the United States of America and Norway, and been awarded honorary doctorates by the universities of Edinburgh, Oslo, and Dayton.

**Kim Knott** is Professor of Religious Studies at the University of Leeds, UK. She is Director of the AHRC Diasporas, Migration and Identities Programme; and General Secretary of the European Association for the Study of Religions. Professor Knott is author of *The Location of Religion: A Spatial Analysis* (Equinox, 2005) and *Hinduism: A Very Short Introduction* (Oxford, 1998), and is currently working on spatial and geographical approaches to the study of religion, and directing a project on 'Media portrayals of religion and the secular sacred'.

**Thomas A. Lewis** is the Vartan Gregorian Assistant Professor of Religious Studies at Brown University, USA. He is the author of *Freedom and Tradition in Hegel: Reconsidering Anthropology, Ethics, and Religion* (University of Notre Dame Press, 2005) and numerous articles in the philosophy of religion, religious ethics and methodology in the study of religion. He is currently completing a book on religion, modernity and politics in Hegel.

**Mattias Martinson** is Associate Professor in the Department of Theology, Uppsala University, Sweden, and Honorary Research Fellow in the Department of Theology and Religious Studies, University of Glasgow, UK. He has written extensively on the foundational problems of theology in a post-modern and post-Christian situation, and his works include *Perseverance without Doctrine: Adorno, Self-Critique and the Ends of Academic Theology* (Peter Lang, 2000), and more recently (in Swedish) under a title that translates *Post-Christian Theology: Experiments and Interpretative Attempts* (Glänta Produktion, 2007).

**C. A. E. (Tony) Moodie** holds degrees in science, psychology, education and theology. He taught psychology, education studies and social theory for 25 years, first at the Edgewood College of Education and then at the University of Natal (later UKZN). He is currently the principal of the Theological Education by Extension College in Johannesburg, South Africa.

**Hugh Pyper** is Professor of Biblical Studies and Head of the Biblical Studies Department at the University of Sheffield, UK. His recent publications include *An Unsuitable Book: the Bible as Scandalous Text* (Sheffield Phoenix Press, 2005) and *The Joy of Kierkegaard: Kierkegaard as a Biblical Reader* (Equinox, forthcoming in 2009).

**Simon G. Smith** is Co-Director at the Subject Centre for Philosophical and Religious Studies based in the Department of Theology and Religious Studies at the University of Leeds, UK. Simon's academic background is at the meeting point of Buddhist Studies and social theory where his research has included the developing nature of the self since the Enlightenment. Prior to his work for the Subject Centre, Simon was a lecturer in Religious Studies at the University of Leeds.

**Stephan van Erp** is Senior Researcher and Assistant Professor for Systematic Theology at the Radboud University Nijmegen, the Netherlands. He is Chief Editor of ET-Studies, the new journal of the European Society for Catholic Theology. His research concerns Fundamental Theology and Constructive Theology, in particular the doctrines of God and Revelation.

**Mohammad Sadegh Zahedi** is Assistant Professor of Islamic Philosophy and Theology at the Imam Khomeini International University, Iran. His academic interests include comparative philosophy and theology, Islamic mysticism and Islam and modernity.

# Introduction

This volume marks the proceedings of a conference organized by the Higher Education Academy Subject Centre for Philosophical and Religious Studies (PRS)[1] entitled 'Theology *and* Religious Studies and/or Theology *versus* Religious Studies?', held in Oxford, England on 6–7 July 2006. The conference came about as the organizers, and editors of this volume, through their work for PRS, considered the United Kingdom to be in a somewhat unique position in having a sizeable number of university and college departments that accommodated both theology and religious studies, often incorporating other subject areas such as biblical studies, sociology of religion and church history. Despite this they found that there seemed to be very little interaction between disciplines beyond the environment of the department, and even then to a limited extent. This would seem to suggest that the disciplines of religious studies and theology have sought to define themselves without necessarily considering other arguably related areas of study involved in the teaching and study of religion and religions. This has led to a number of tensions between theology and religious studies over the years partly, we would suggest, because of this lack of formal engagement.

The conference sought to address some of these tensions and question whether it was possible to establish an idea of teaching and studying religion in higher education in a manner that draws on elements from the different disciplines, and how this might assist us in gaining a greater understanding of historical and contemporary forms of religion. As a result we sought perspectives from theology, religious studies and biblical studies scholars; drawing on the unique viewpoint of the United Kingdom as well as inviting international contributions. This resulted in a diverse and fascinating conference that provided an interesting and stimulating debate on the role of religion in higher education not only in the United Kingdom but in many countries around the world.

In order to contextualize this the first chapter of this volume is written by Denise Cush after the conference as a reflection of it and a response to it. It provides a very personal account of her 'conversion' from theology to religious studies. Here Cush draws on three decades of teaching and researching in both theology and religious studies to consider their developing and enduring relationship with each other. She sums up her experience thus:

> I participated in the . . . conference full of hope that the time was ripe for Theology and Religious Studies to work more fruitfully together . . . I left the conference convinced that the time was not yet there.[2]

Cush contextualizes this point by providing some helpful definitions of theology, something we as conference organizers and editors have not sought to do in order not to stifle debate. She argues that theology has always exerted hegemony over religious studies. The latter emerged from the former and this persists through theology's more obvious vocational element and in having connections with particular traditions. Cush asserts, 'Theology often has access to forms of advocacy, patronage, and even funding that . . . Religious Studies does not have.'[3] Having established this she provides a useful take on the development of religious studies, drawing largely on the work of Ninian Smart, and concluding that religious studies possesses what she calls an 'epistemological humility' which arises from a 'refusal to come to premature conclusions about the truth and value of religious traditions'.[4] And while this lays open claims from theologians that religious studies lacks analytical depth, in reality the two disciplines tend to steer clear of each other by 'assigning' Christianity to theology, and other religions to religious studies. Indeed she suggests that only in resolutely 'Studies of Religion' departments, like her own, can this distinction be overcome. Religious education too, rooted though it is in Smartian phenomenological approaches, may be seen as a good place for theology and religious studies to meet, given the aim of some educators to develop 'religiously literate' students. But, she argues, this is not enough:

> Theology does still retain its overtones of confessionalism, theism, Christianity, and privileging written doctrine over lived praxis, and perhaps more significantly, thinking about questions raised by religions from one particular perspective, rather than trying to take into account of as diverse a range of perspectives as possible.[5]

Thus is the gauntlet thrown down to theology to have the confidence, garnered through the continuing perceived hegemony over religious studies, to risk moving closer to it and, using some approaches employed within religious education, perhaps to return to what we would see as a more academically inclusive teaching of religion in higher education.

David Ford, who Cush cites in seeking to define Theology, also sees the merit in bringing together Theology and Religious Studies in the contemporary context:

> for Universities in early twenty-first century Britain the combination of theology and religious studies makes good sense and has a promising future, but that there is some urgency in the need to think about its own rationale in order to develop itself . . .[6]

Like Cush, Ford begins with a useful historical perspective on the development of religious study in universities, and suggests that religion has become more important since the turn of the century and that academics should stop fighting the battles of the twentieth, or even the nineteenth, centuries. He argues that we need to think more clearly about the field of religious study, but that this does not necessarily mean a homogenous approach. Rather he sees an interdisciplinary approach as succeeding in meeting the needs of the teaching and study of religion in contemporary society.

> The combination of theology and religious studies encourages the fulfilment and interrelation of three key transgenerational responsibilities: towards universities and their range of disciplines . . . towards religious communities and disciplines . . . and towards societies and public understanding.[7]

Thus, Ford suggests, there is a good fit between theology and religious studies in considering the issues that religion raises in contemporary society. But, like Cush, he wonders whether the disciplines are in a position to capitalize on this. Drawing on the development of the Berlin model of the University he argues that while there was a tension between the religious and secular in its formation this complex settlement 'was not continued and creatively reshaped in the twentieth century, leading to a serious imbalance and inadequacy in academic engagement with the religions'.[8] He suggests that it is possible to ameliorate these issues and concludes with a series of recommendations that he believes will help to both reinvigorate the relevance of the teaching and study of religion in the contemporary university. Ford's is something of an inclusive model, somewhat removed from that suggested by Gavin D'Costa.

D'Costa also questions the nature of the university with regard to theology 'at this cultural scene in our history'.[9] He wishes to see theology in its position as 'queen of the sciences', but regards this as opening up a critique of the modern university and its role in society. He argues that the Enlightenment project led to tradition and telos becoming 'secondary and eventually unnecessary to the discipline of "theology"',[10] whereas, quoting Paul Griffiths, 'religious learning . . . requires explicit appeal to authority in ways that consumerist pedagogy does not'.[11] Like Ford, D'Costa draws on the Berlin model of the university, suggesting that while theology made it into the university it was stripped of its transcendental, non-rational perspectives. Here theology becomes subsumed under other disciplines, something that led to the emergence of religious studies. He questions, therefore, whether theology should seek a return to its pre-Enlightenment state. In doing this he postulates the need to found, from the public purse, a Catholic University. While this is unlikely, and for many unpalatable, it is a bold statement that seeks to emphasize his point that theology should be theological, and that it is in religious studies that the question of truth may finally emerge.

So while Ford is offering an inclusivist approach, D'Costa is arguing for a far more exclusivist approach to the teaching and study of religion, one in which religious studies seems to have the role of, at best, riding on the coat tails of theology.

Theology as the future of religious studies is something for which Erik Borgman and Stephan van Erp argue. They suggest that the manner in which theology and religious studies have been distinguished since the latter's emergence from the former means that 'its separation of facts from norms seems to have adapted to academia's demands and as such could be regarded the true heir of theology in a post-Christian and post-colonial situation.'[12] Borgman and van Erp, however, suggest that while theology can be seen as being part of religious studies it is also the future of religious studies 'in as far as theology studies the embodied practices of faith in the world'.[13] This leads them to a much more inclusivist position for the role of theology in the university than D'Costa and they explain how this has been achieved at their institution in the Netherlands. This has happened as the result of a change in the way in which theology is considered in a number of leading Dutch higher education institutions, especially in dividing theology and religious studies. They seem to suggest that such a move tends to force theology into a position not dissimilar to that outlined by D'Costa, that of a church-bound, normative and authoritative-prescriptive discipline. Borgman and van Erp argue that this need not be the case and that theology can still engage with the contemporary world without an abdication from Christian doctrine. This is often not the case, however, and they use recent theological research into the relationship between religion and medicine as an example of how theological study is divorced from the sphere of human behaviour: an approach they refer to as 'colonialism writ small'.

Instead they suggest that 'before and beyond phenomenology, theology has provided a tradition of reflection on the hermeneutics of experience'.[14] This is a key point in their argument which seems to suggest that religious studies has abandoned the ground that led it away from theology in the first place. This would seem to chime to a certain extent with Cush's suggestion that theology and religious studies can meet in a religious education rooted in phenomenology. In this sense Borgman and van Erp also look towards a return to teaching and studying religion in a less segmented manner, but through a more inclusive form of theology. This would reflect a resurgence of interest in religion in society seen through reducing assumptions of secularization, as they state:

> To do justice to religions, they should be presented as what they claim to be: traditions of justifiable forms of understanding the world and human existence, in relation to and in discussion with other forms of understanding in our current situation.[15]

Borgman and van Erp's approach is one that is recognizably theological, yet takes on many of the developments found in religious studies over the last 40 years and posits an approach which seems to suggest a teaching and study of religions itself in a manner that does so in the context of contemporary society. Mattias Martinson also sees the way ahead in the teaching and study of religion to be regarding religion as being a living and changing cultural phenomenon.

Like many other contributors to this volume, Martinson sees the problems of trying to find positions for theology and religious studies within the university, let alone in relation to each other. Like Borgman and Erp he wants to make a case for the relevance of theology in an academic setting. Indeed he wishes to go further than them by arguing for 'the importance of a committed critical form of theological reflection at the core of *any* serious notion of religious studies . . . without lapsing into a narrow defence of Christianity as a sheltered and timeless objective of theology'.[16]

To illustrate this Martinson draws on Don Wiebe's notion that academic theology, because of its relationship with secular reason, is bound to explain away the very essence of its religious significance. As Martinson suggests

> This course of 'dysfunctional' involvement in religious faith constitutes what Wiebe understands as 'the irony of theology'. Momentarily, theologians act as if they stood firmly on the side of scientific reason, but throughout their work they succumb to a displacement which jeopardizes theology's identity as a secular academic endeavour (through its basically religious intent) as well as undermines its *raison d'être* (through failing as religion). As such, it cannot be upheld as a reasonable form of religious studies.[17]

However, Martinson seeks to challenge Wiebe's assertions by turning the argument round on religious studies. He argues, along with other contributors to this volume, that religious studies has essentially emerged from Christian understandings of religion. How then, he questions, can religious studies 'ever function as a progressive intellectual force in a time when religion once again . . . has become a new and very tangible cultural factor'?[18] Martinson provides evidence for this from his experience of religious study in Sweden, using Islam as an example. From this he concludes that while, in Western Europe at least, we are moving to a post-Christian milieu, we are also seeing a rise in the claim that we are also in a post-secular situation (where secularism has often been fundamentally a Christian sentiment) and as such 'we must rather approach religion as a constantly shifting expression of a divergent cultural praxis.'[19] Here religious studies is exposed as needing to engage critically with the theological aspects of any belief to be taken seriously. But it will also show that 'the flawed spirit of a Christian secularism at odds with the religious reality of our time'.[20] Like Borgman and van Erp, Martinson is suggesting that there is a future for theology in the study and teaching of religion in the academy if it has something of a reality check on the cultural context of the twenty-first century. These factors are something that Thomas Lewis regards as being problematic in his chapter. Nevertheless, he does see the normative claims that theologians make as being important to the essence of what theology is.

Lewis considers whether theology belongs inside the academic study of religion. In doing this the key point for him seems to lie in the assumption that while theologians make normative claims, those engaged in religious studies should not do so. He suggests that religious studies scholars should take a leaf from their own methodological book and ensure that the object of study should be clearly distinguished from the study itself. In doing this he acknowledges the difficulties inherent in holding normative positions when studying religion, where these are regarded as matters of 'faith'. Nevertheless, he argues that while such claims are inevitable they are used as grounds for excluding theology from the academic study of religion. For Lewis this should not be the case and while he acknowledges the difficulties inherent in a normative approach, he does regard them as being important to theology's role in the study and teaching of religion. This, he seems to be suggesting, requires a willingness of those making normative claims to engage in dialogue. This, he believes provides considerable scope for the study of theology in religious studies. He states

> Focusing on normativity and the willingness to offer justification for normative claims redirects the debate towards substantive issues at stake and away from some of the dead ends that leave us wondering exactly how far the debate has come since the 1960s and 1970s.[21]

Lewis clearly sees a place for theology in religious studies, one that requires some movement from both sides, as his call for dialogue would suggest. For James Cox, however, this very much depends on how one defines religion, and he wishes to define it in a manner that would place religious studies amongst the social sciences thereby, to his mind, distancing it from theology.

For Cox the way religion is defined comes in two parts that respectively focus on the community's benefits and experiences, and on religion as an authoritative transmission of authority. So for Cox the first part restricts the study of religion to 'identifiable communities', meaning that religion is always a 'social fact'. He adds

> Theories about religions . . . are also social facts, which means that scholars of religion must also conduct their research in a self-critical, reflexive and transparent manner.[22]

For Cox the scholar of religion cannot study the experiences themselves but an empirical observation of them, 'this means that academic work is concerned with what communities postulate rather than the object or objects on which their postulations are made.'[23] This allows the scholar of religion to study religion in a scientific and transparent manner.

The second part of Cox's definition, religion as an authoritative transmission of authority, is his attempt to counter Timothy Fitzgerald's assertions that the category of 'religion' must be dropped as a legitimate field in the social sciences since it 'hides within it a theological assumption that defines religion always in relation to a transcendental referent'.[24] Cox seeks to do this by drawing on the ideas of Danièle Hervieu-Léger, not so much through her work on secularization, but in her consideration of the boundaries between the religious and non-religious. This is something, he suggests, that is more problematic now than at any time in history given the increasingly complex nature of contemporary society and culture. In order to overcome this

> Hervieu-Léger contends that the problem cannot be resolved by siding either with a substantive or functional approach to defining religion, but by turning the focus of defining religion towards a sociological perspective.[25]

Here Hervieu-Léger sees 'acts of believing' as being something that outlines the relationship between the one who believes and the object of belief. The key issue to this approach, however, is not the questioning of the validity or religion *per se* but a question of legitimation of the acts of believing, again quoting Hervieu-Léger who states that religion is an

> [I]deological, practical and symbolic framework which constitutes, maintains, develops and controls the consciousness (individual or collective) of membership to a particular heritage of belief.[26]

Bringing these two parts together, Cox argues that he is able to come to a definition of religion which is 'empirical, socio-cultural, non-theological and non-essentialist'.[27] This definition, Cox believes, challenges theologically inspired definitions of religion and while it is not without its difficulties it does show that the academic study of religion can be regarded as something that is not theology, but not strictly belonging to other disciplines either. Theology, therefore, is just one of the fields that provides data for the scientific scholar of religion, and allows religious studies to exist fully separately within the academy.

Along with Cox all the contributions considered so far to some extent look at theology and religious studies in relation to each other within a context of the study and teaching of religion in higher education. Many, if not most, seem to be staking a claim for their own 'home' discipline within this context in a manner not wholly dissimilar from politicians debating over the 'middle ground' of the political spectrum. Kim Knott seeks to clarify this, albeit from her position as a scholar of religious studies, by presenting a socio-spatial analysis of the relationship between the disciplines.

She states that no discipline exists in a vacuum and all define themselves in relation to what they are not. In order to demonstrate this Knott looks at some of the data provided by scholars and their subject associations in considering where the disciplines of theology and religious studies locate themselves. Using Knott's data we can come to similar conclusions by using the evidence presented to us in this volume:

> One discipline can be portrayed as wholly containing the other; they can be seen as distinctive and separate disciplines . . .; they can be envisaged as largely separate but partially overlapping; they can both be contained within a large meta-discipline . . .; one can be distinguished from the approach that pre-dated it; one can embrace the other; or the embrace can be mutual.[28]

Knott takes her investigations further by looking at Tony Becher's work on academic tribes, and maps his typology onto the definitions provided by theology and religious studies scholars. This leads her to conclude that the territory of the study of 'religion' and 'God' is a contested one marked by continuous struggle, as she states the two disciplines 'are like twins, ever bound to one another though sometimes striving to be free and to experience themselves as separate and distinctive'.[29] Knott's analysis is useful as it does not seek to make any claims for theology and religious studies as such but rather considers how they are seen in relation to each other from both without and within.

This notion of theology and religious studies being inexorably linked together is also considered by Ursula King who argues that theology and religious studies are part of the same spectrum, what we have been referring to as 'the study and teaching of religion'. Like most contributors to this volume King acknowledges that there are grey areas between the two. Yet scholars from both sides can become entrenched in their own areas which do not reflect the nature of the faiths that they are seeking to study:

> Some debates about theology and religious studies are couched in static and essentialist discourses that seem to reflect a real fortress mentality where the surrounding walls of clearly demarcated territory are represented as high and solid . . .[30]

King goes further than most in advocating that theology and religious studies are an integral part of each other, interwoven to form part of the same cloth. She acknowledges that this is difficult enough within the context of a single academic tradition, such as the British context, but even more so when we are faced with the global challenge in the study of different theologies and religions. This, she believes can be achieved through interfaith encounter and dialogue, but also through considering new paradigms of religion such as those re-imagined by a growing number of female scholars who are bringing previously marginalized perspectives into the mainstream.

What King presents is an increasingly complex and diverse environment in which the study and teaching of religion exists. In order for religion to survive in the academy, and even reclaim lost ground, we must recognize and celebrate this diversity and allow theology and religious studies to become more than the sum of their parts.

This is something that has been explored by Shannon Craigo-Snell, who considers how theology and religious studies can be taught in the context of interdisciplinary theology. Drawing on her experiences of teaching at Yale University she argues that neither theology nor religious studies alone can meet the diverse expectations of her students stating that what her course offers is 'the blunt reality that Christian talk about God permeates our world and has enormous influence on art, politics, economics, science, sociology, literature etc.'[31] The students find that there are many connections between theology and other disciplines, and are encouraged to see 'theological performances' in everyday life, and then make their own theological arguments through a genre of their choice. Craigo-Snell provides a number of fascinating examples of how this was achieved by students and argues that through doing this theology is able to have a much broader role in the University. It also addresses issues between theology and religious studies since it does not support the traditional dualism between confessional and non-confessional approaches. Through her courses Craigo-Snell helps students to see theology in the world around them, bringing the study of religion back into the centre of discussions about contemporary society without seemingly loosing the intellectual rigour of more traditional courses.

Jarvis and Moodie provide a useful addition to this discussion considering the relationship between theology and religious studies in a South African milieu, both in historical and contemporary contexts; principally from the perspective of religious education. Before discussing higher education in particular Jarvis and Moodie provide a historical background to religious education in South Africa, underlining the changes that have occurred since apartheid, including the closure of departments teaching religion, and in some cases the amalgamation of departments of theology and religious studies. They cite the case of the University of Pretoria as one which has shown how changes in the study of religion can mirror changes in society as a whole, where a single theology faculty now exists that welcomes students of all backgrounds and encompasses denominations that were previously at either side of the apartheid divide. They suggest that, in South Africa at least, theology, religious studies, and religious education are collaborating more than ever before.

Zahedi also provides an interesting and useful perspective on the place of theology in Iranian universities. This serves as a reminder, mentioned elsewhere in this volume, that theology is not necessarily Christian but can relate to other religious traditions, in this case Islam. Zahedi suggests that theology in Iran is often studied in either 'traditional' or 'modern' forms. The former is very much text-based, mainly Shiite, drawing on a canon of commentaries in addition to primary text. Modern theology is a much more recent development and is much more akin to a religious studies approach as described elsewhere in this volume with two main strands respectively drawing on theological and philosophical concerns, and engaging in more social science-based approaches. This has resulted in a greater critical engagement with religious ideas than has previously been the case, the key issue now being how this can be maintained in a confessional context. This is something that Hugh Pyper seeks to address, also through textual means in his chapter.

So far the positions taken in this book have been those between theology and religious studies. As Pyper reminds us, however, this is not the whole story and there are other areas of study which do not sit easily in this relationship, and which are often forgotten. Coming from a position in biblical studies, Pyper looks at the reasons behind what he sees as the marginalization of biblical studies in the study of religion in UK higher education and draws upon what he sees as an uneasy relationship between theology and biblical studies. He suggests that textual studies of the Bible are becoming increasingly less popular partially because of language requirements and a concentration on more practical areas of theological study; also it is seen to be at odds with post-colonialist approaches to religious studies. However, rather than being a fringe subject, Pyper suggests that it could be regarded as providing the solution to some of the issues inherent between theology and religious studies. He argues that 'the methodological debates that characterize the divide between systematic and dogmatic theology, biblical theology, the history of the Near East and the study of religions have their roots in debates over the bible.'[32] Pyper suggest that the Bible has been subjected to the many reading strategies encompassed within theology and religious studies and as a result asks:

> Could we unify the theological and religious studies enterprises in a unified department by starting students with a biblical text and showing them how a systematician, a literary critic, an anthropologist, an archaeologist and a historian of religion would read it?[33]

Pyper goes on to show how this would be possible and closes with a suggestion that biblical studies can be seen as providing both theology and religious studies with a way of making sense of religion in contemporary Western society and offering an anchor point from which both can set themselves in context.

Certainly the study of religion faces questions about its importance, but also has a better opportunity to show its relevance for the first time in at least a generation. We would argue that despite their differences theology and religious studies (as well as biblical studies and other areas of religious study) can have an enormous effect on the way in which contemporary and historical religious phenomena is viewed. How they achieve this in relation to each other is another question. In discussing this the views represented in this volume offer a useful overall analysis of the relationship between theology and religious studies. They are both hopeful and sceptical of whether a meaningful way can be found to study and teach religion in a manner that brings together their key approaches; and they offer exclusivist and inclusivist perspectives. Perhaps the one common theme running through the volume is that, while some contributors do advocate a dialogical approach, no one at root seeks to move out of their own academic background, but advocates using their own favoured approach as a basis for teaching and studying religion.

This would suggest that Cush is perhaps right that despite some very useful analysis in this volume and at the conference from whence it came, the time is not yet right for scholars of theology and religious studies to develop a single approach. As such there seems to be a call for a multidisciplinary approach to the teaching and study of religion, rather than an interdisciplinary one. Nevertheless, in bringing them together we would argue that we have re-ignited a debate that considers the differences and tensions, as well as the similarities and points of contact, between and within theology and religious studies, and would hope that this book will further stimulate debate and lead to at least a consideration of more inclusive approaches.

# Notes

1. See http://prs.heacademy.ac.uk last accessed 27/08/2008.
2. Denise Cush, 'Religious Studies versus Theology: Why I'm still Glad that I Converted from Theology to Religious Studies', Chapter 1 of this Volume, p. 16.
3. Ibid. p. 19.
4. Ibid. p. 22.
5. Ibid. p. 27.
6. David F. Ford, 'Theology and Religious Studies for a Multifaith and Secular Society', Chapter 2 of this Volume, pp. 31–32.
7. Ibid. p. 34.
8. Ibid. p. 40.
9. Gavin D'Costa, 'Theology and Religious Studies OR Theology versus Religious Studies?', Chapter 3 of this Volume, pp. 45–46.
10. Ibid. p. 46.
11. Paul J. Griffiths, *Religious Reading: The Place of Reading in the Practice of Religion.* Oxford: Oxford University Press, 1999, p. 68.
12. Erik Borgman and Stephan van Erp, 'Theology as the Past and Future of Religious Studies: An Incarnational Approach', Chapter 4 of this Volume, p. 55.
13. Ibid. p. 56.
14. Ibid. p. 64.
15. Ibid. p. 67.
16. Mattias Martinson, 'The Irony of Religious Studies: A Pro-theological Argument from the Swedish Experience', Chapter 5 of this Volume, p. 74.
17. Ibid. p. 75.
18. Ibid. p. 77.
19. Ibid. p. 83.
20. Ibid. p. 84.
21. Thomas A. Lewis, 'The Inevitability of Normativity in the Study of Religion: Theology in Religious Studies', Chapter 6 of this Volume, p. 95.
22. James L. Cox, 'Towards a Socio-cultural, Non-theological Definition of Religion', Chapter 7 of this Volume, p. 101.
23. Ibid. p. 104.
24. Ibid.; Fitzgerald, T. (2000), *The Ideology of Religious Studies.* New York & Oxford: Oxford University Press), pp. 17–18.
25. James L. Cox, 'Towards a Socio-cultural, Non-theological Definition of Religion', Chapter 7 of this Volume, p. 106.
26. Hervieu-Léger, D., 'Religion as memory: Reference to Tradition and the Constitution of a Heritage of Belief in Modern Societies', in J. G. Platvoet and A. L. Molendijk (eds), *The Pragmatics of Defining Religion: Contexts, Concepts and Contests.* Leiden: Brill, 1999, p. 88.
27. James L. Cox, 'Towards a Socio-cultural, Non-theological Definition of Religion', Chapter 7 of this Volume, p. 108.
28. Kim Knott, 'A Spatial Analysis of the Relationship between Theology and Religious Studies: Knowledge-power Strategies and Metaphors of Containment and Separation', Chapter 8 of this Volume, p. 130.
29. Ibid. p. 134.

[30] Ursula King, ' "A Coat of Many Colours": Interweaving Strands in Theology and Religious Studies', Chapter 9 of this Volume, p. 140.

[31] Shannon Craigo-Snell, 'Interdisciplinary Theology: Bridging the Theology/Religious Studies Divide', Chapter 10 of this Volume, p. 152.

[32] Hugh Pyper, 'The Bible: Fringe or Hinge?', Chapter 13 of this Volume, p. 187.

[33] Ibid. p. 188.

Chapter 1

# Religious Studies *versus* Theology
## Why I'm still Glad that I Converted from Theology to Religious Studies

Denise Cush

## Introduction

Rooted in my personal experience of both disciplines, this chapter will examine the relationship between Theology and Religious Studies, and argue that the latter still needs to distinguish itself from the former. Although the two subjects may draw upon a similar range of methods, we often differ in aims and content. There are still problems of unequal power and prestige, Christian hegemony continues, and issues of gender are not irrelevant. The chapter also contains reflections on and responses to a number of the papers given at the Oxford conference in July 2006, and considers the light shed on the debate from issues arising out of religious education in schools. The discussion is rooted in the English context.

The relationship between Theology and Religious Studies has been for me more than an academic debate, but one that has affected my whole adult life, both professionally and personally. This chapter therefore will be somewhat more personal than usually found in academic texts, but the recognition of the relevance of personal biography is one of the many contributions of feminist scholarship. This chapter thus discusses the question as it appears to me in my particular context, without making any universal claims. Its sources are the various texts listed in the bibliography, reflections on the conference entitled 'Theology *and* Religious Studies or Theology *versus* Religious Studies', July 6–7, St. Anne's College, University of Oxford, and my own experience of over three decades of Theology, Religious Studies, teaching and researching in Religious Education and educating teachers for Religious Education.

In order that my particular perspective is put in context, a brief biography is required. My inherited tradition was Roman Catholic Christianity, and my schooling was in Roman Catholic voluntary-aided state schools. My first degree, in the early 1970s, was Theology at Oxford, which majored in Biblical Studies, including Hebrew and Greek, but also the history and doctrines of Christianity up to 451CE and contemporary Systematic Theology. I enjoyed my studies, though the milieu was rather male and Anglican, but did think that I ought to know something about other traditions. I then drifted into a PGCE (Postgraduate Certificate in Education) and found to my surprise that I enjoyed teaching. I also discovered the work of Ninian Smart who seemed to be articulating everything that I was thinking about the limitations of my Theology degree in both content and approach, and experienced a road-to-Damascus conversion to the Smartian approach to studying and teaching about religions. This led me to Lancaster, where in the MA programme I focused on Phenomenology, Buddhism and Hinduism (probably as the 'most different' traditions from the Christianity I knew). I then spent 9 years teaching in a sixth-form college (where I was responsible for both academic Religious Studies, Biblical Studies and Philosophy of Religion as well as confessional Religious Education, carefully distinguishing the two pursuits), followed by 21 years at Bath Spa, where I have taught Religious Studies as well as, in previous years, training teachers for primary and secondary RE (Religious Education), and have for the last 8 years been running the Department of Study of Religions (not Theology).

At various times over the decades I have found myself defending Buddhist, Humanist and Pagan perspectives, not because those were my personal faiths, but because they appeared to be getting a poor deal in a particular context. I have even been known to defend Christianity, for the same reasons, in some contexts. I am currently involved in teaching Religion and Education, Buddhism, Hinduism, Christianity and Contemporary Spiritualities. Decades of teaching a diverse range of faiths has had an evitable effect on my personal beliefs and values.

In 1999 I wrote an article exploring the relationships between Religious Studies, Religious Education and Theology entitled 'Big Brother, Little Sister, and the Clerical Uncle: The relationship between Religious Studies, Religious Education and Theology?' My conclusions included that Religious Education was not content to be patronized by her older 'male' relatives, and that Theology and Religious Studies should stop squabbling. Given that in the decade following, both Theology and Religious Studies in England have thought more deeply and critically about their aims, content and methods, I participated in the 2006 conference full of hope that the time was ripe for Theology and Religious Studies to work more fruitfully together. However, I left the conference convinced that the time was not yet there, more than ever pleased that I discovered Religious Studies and knowing why I am continuing to work within a Religious Studies rather than a Theological or hybrid department. The following reflections may explain why.

## Reflections on the nature of Theology

As ever in academia, some of the problems arise from the diversity of definitions of the key terms involved, and 'Theology' is no exception. Apparently first used within the Christian tradition to refer to the teachings about God, by the twelfth century it had expanded to refer to the complete collection of Christian teachings (McGrath 2001: 138). Generally within the European history of the use of the term, the Christian God is presumed to be the God under consideration, so that 'Theology' is the term for 'the systematic study of the Christian faith at university level' (McGrath 2001: 138).

There are many ambiguities and questions surrounding the term. Does it necessarily imply that there is a God to study – in other words, is it a confessional activity, engaged in by 'insiders' only? Does it imply that God is male? Does it imply that the important dimension of religion is belief or doctrine? In a European or UK context, does it mean in practice, Christian Theology? Can there be Buddhist Theology?

The major question in relation to Religious Studies is whether Theology is necessarily confessional. Some definitions do tend to suggest or even directly claim this, for example:

Adrian Thatcher (1997: 75) 'the systematic reflection on God and belief in God, by Christians for Christians'.

John Macquarrie 'the study which, through participation in and reflection upon a religious faith, seeks to express the content of this faith in the clearest and most coherent language available' (cited in McGrath 2001: 138).

Karl Rahner 'the conscious and methodical explanation and explication of the divine revelation received and grasped in faith' (cited in McGrath 2001: 139).

David Tracy (1988) 'the intellectual reflection within a religious tradition' (cited in Corrywright and Morgan 2006: 49).

On the other hand, there are those who seek to define Theology as an academic pursuit open to those of all faiths and none, or to be more inclusive of either non-Christian traditions or of everyone including atheists, for example:

Alister McGrath (2001: 139) 'the systematic study of the fundamental ideas of the Christian faith'.

David Ford (2005: 60) 'theology at its broadest is thinking about questions raised by and about the religions'.

Jeff Astley (1996: 67–68) 'reflective religious discourse . . . broad enough to cover reflection that involves a rejection of God'.

Indeed, in a later text, McGrath (2006: 111) gives two somewhat contrasting definitions: 'reflection upon the God whom Christians worship and adore' and 'the systematic study of the Christian faith at University level' which taken together seem to capture the ambiguity of the term.

The characterization of Theology as the insider's study of religion and Religious Studies as the outsider's approach is certainly therefore too simplistic. My fellow students even back in the 1970s included atheists and agnostics as well as Christian believers. However, although technically one does not have to be a believer to choose to study Theology, there is still a likelihood that one will be. Research undertaken by graduate students for the conference revealed that the majority of Theology students were Christians whereas half of their sample of Religious Studies students were agnostic (Quartermaine et al. 2006). In an English context, there is still a presumption that 'Theology' will be mostly Christian Theology. This is the case even from the most inclusive representatives of Theology, as is illustrated by Ford (1999). Topics studied, such as 'the problem of evil' do tend to be approached methodologically, if not actually, in a theistic manner (e.g. Ford 1999: 68–82).

An inescapable implication of the term Theology is that religion is centrally about God. This again was confirmed for me by Ford (1999). Other traditions might consider that religion is more centrally about surviving death, or how to conduct one's present life. Some scholars are happy to employ terms like 'Buddhist Theology', for example in the title of the volume edited by Jackson and Makransky (2000). While understanding why they wish to use the term, and that in so doing they may contribute towards a development in the meaning of the term, I do not think that the word has yet sufficiently escaped its etymology and history to be easily so used.

More generally than implying that religion is centrally about God, there is a presumption that religion is about beliefs and doctrines, again a very

Western, Christian idea. My own Theology degree was mostly biblical texts and systematic Theology, and again Ford (1999) confirms that this continues to be the case. The focus on beliefs and doctrines is linked with another problem with the concept of Theology, in that the texts and doctrines tend to represent for most of the history of Christian Theology until relatively recent times, and to some extent still continuing, a socially elite and male gendered perspective. Thus I found myself agreeing with Ursula King's paper (2006) that problems with Theology in our UK context can be the privileging of text and an elite male version of a tradition, as well as Christian hegemony and the ambiguity over confessionalism mentioned above. Finally, even the most pluralist and inclusive varieties of Theology, open to exploring ideas from all traditions, tend to do so from one perspective.

Turning to a more practical advantage which Theology has over Religious Studies in the current higher educational climate, is that Theology has a more obvious vocational connection, and work placements with Christian communities, in ministry, youth work etc. can be regarded as an obvious link. Likewise, in having connections with particular traditions, Theology often has access to forms of advocacy, patronage, and even funding that the non-aligned Religious Studies does not have.

## Reflections on the nature of Religious Studies/Study of Religions

Again there are problems of definition arising from critical questioning, including whether terms such as 'religion' are either useful or bear any relationship to reality. The discipline (if such it is) of Religious Studies grew out of Theology (as well as Oriental Studies) in the UK context, and has had to work hard to distinguish itself from the parent discipline(s). As Kim Knott (2006) has pointed out in her paper, although there might be internal disagreement over the nature of the subject, the one thing Religious Studies scholars would agree on is that 'it is NOT Theology', by which statement scholars are usually distancing themselves from the implications of confessionalism and a Christian content/perspective, and possibly also from a concentration on doctrines and texts. (The alternative term 'Study of Religions' was suggested by a student at Bath Spa University in the early 1990s, when Brian Bocking was Head of Department, in order to emphasize both the plurality of religions studied and the non-confessional nature of the approach).

It is somewhat harder to say what Religious Studies is, and there are doubts whether it really is a subject discipline or merely an area of human experience to which a range of disciplines can be applied. 'Religious Studies is generally wider, more comprehensive and less focused than theology' according to Whaling (1999: 230). Certainly a wider range of content is usually implied, drawing from a range of religions rather than predominantly one. Christianity is one of several religions rather that having a privileged place. Generally all dimensions of traditions are examined, including social and ritual practices, and anthropological and ethnographic approaches can be as important as, if not more important than, the textual and historical studies that form the basis of Theology. Religious Studies tries to capture traditions as they are in real life rather than in ideal portrayals, and, increasingly, to complement elite and/or male versions of traditions with the experiences of the 'ordinary' worshipper and women.

The history of the subject in the United Kingdom has been highly influenced by the 'Lancaster' approach of the 1970s which made much use of 'phenomenology' as a method of study. Over against Theologians, the attempt was made to be 'methodologically agnostic' and to *understand* religious traditions rather than either endorsing them as true or explaining them in terms that believers themselves would not recognize, as was often the case in the more reductionist versions of the social sciences. The ideas of trying to be impartial, 'bracketing out' one's own preconceptions and attempting to see things from the believers' point of view were very attractive to agnostics and pluralists, and to those working in fields where it was important to be seen as being fair to all traditions, such as in Religious Education and interfaith activities. I have often thought that in addition to the attractions of a 'non-confessional' approach to studying religions, phenomenology appealed because it seemed to supply the emerging discipline with an 'ology' to call its own – after all, to argue for being a separate discipline requires a particular content, founding scholars, and a distinct methodology – the latter always a weak point in Religious Studies' argument.

Since the 1970s, however, phenomenology has come under much attack, and there has been much more stress on ethnographic and other approaches both in Religious Studies and Religious Education. Apart from the more specific critiques of phenomenology per se, and its essentialist stance, which do not need rehearsing here, the claim of Religious Studies to be looking at religious traditions impartially has been undermined. Postmodern thinking has questioned the ability of scholars to be 'objective' when everyone is situated in and formed by a particular context. It is interesting that the countries that have pioneered non-confessional Religious Education in schools (e.g. Sweden, England, Norway) have not been secular countries, but ones with (at least until recently) a state church of a liberal protestant nature. Thus it has been easy to suspect Religious Studies scholars of a hidden agenda – perhaps endorsing the belief that there is a transcendent something (such as Eliade's 'sacred'), a universalist agenda that all religions lead to the same goal, that religion per se is a good thing, or at the very minimum that there is something out there in the real world that corresponds to the concept of 'religion'. Tim Fitzgerald has argued forcefully that the very concept of 'religion' is covert theology (e.g. 1995) and that the very title of the subject 'Religious Studies' has the ideological function of persuading us that there is something called religion (Fitzgerald 2006). Steven Sutcliffe (2006) argued that this is not necessarily the case, as the subject can be viewed as studying the construct or folk category of 'religion' rather than implying 'religion' as a natural category – nevertheless, the criticism of Religious Studies/Study of Religions implying there is such a thing as religion that is parallel to the criticism of Theology for implying that there is a God to study.

Again it is clear that the idea that Theology is confessional and Religious Studies neutral is an oversimplification. There are those who suggest that Religious Studies without Theology rules out questions of truth and value in its attempt to be impartial (e.g. D'Costa 2006, Ford 1999: 17). This has never been the case, as can be seen from an examination of the writings of one of our 'founding fathers'. Ninian Smart himself, way back in 1968, argued that although Religious Studies should 'emphasise the descriptive historical side' it should also 'enter into dialogue with the parahistorical claims of religious and anti-religious outlooks'; it must 'transcend the informative . . . in the direction of understanding the meaning of, and into questions about the truth and worth of, religion' (Smart 1968: 105–106), a quotation which had much influence on Religious Education in schools, being reproduced in the ground-breaking *Religious Education in Secondary Schools* (Schools Council 1971) and engraved upon my heart and those of many others of my generation working in Religious Education. In the decades since Smart's 1968 book, Religious Studies has become increasingly aware both of the impossibility of a neutral standpoint and of the need to engage with the issues of contemporary society. This 'engaged' aspect of Religious Studies is defended by Helen Waterhouse (1993) and Rosalind Hackett (2003). It is a caricature of the subject to see it as claiming to stand nowhere and refusing to pursue the truth. A great strength of the Religious Studies tradition in the United Kingdom is that what has been ruled out is not evaluation of religious traditions in terms of truth, value and spiritual usefulness, but the premature evaluation of other people's traditions by those who have not made sufficient attempt to clarify the facts and see them from the perspectives of the adherents. The refusal to come to premature conclusions about the truth and value of religious traditions I have termed 'epistemological humility', a phrase independently arrived at by David Chidester in South Africa (see Cush 2005).

A positive feature of Religious Studies in the English tradition is that it has attempted to study each tradition in its own terms, employing its own vocabulary. This, however, as pointed out by David Ford (1999: 6), risks the student/scholar of religions having 'a tourist smattering' of several languages rather than being literate in any. On the other hand, the alternative of first 'becoming literate in one language' risks that first language providing the categories, vocabulary and perspectives through which all subsequent traditions are viewed.

Turning to the practical advantage which Religious Studies has over Theology in the current educational climate is that it is, arguably, better preparation for becoming a teacher of Religious Education in state-funded community schools in England. The law requires syllabuses to take account of 'the principal religions represented in Great Britain' (1988 Education Reform Act 8.3). Teachers are usually expected to be able to include at least Buddhism, Hinduism, Islam, Judaism and Sikhism in addition to Christianity, and since 2004, 'other religious traditions and other worldviews' (QCA 2004: 7). The approach taken in the Agreed Syllabuses is non-confessional and inclusive, with the aim of enabling pupils to 'flourish individually within their communities and as citizens in a pluralistic society and global community' (QCA 2004: 7).

## Reflections on the relationship between Theology and Religious Studies

Theology still continues to be the senior partner in the subject area labelled 'Theology and Religious Studies' in the United Kingdom, as a glance at the list of scholars in the Association of University Departments of Theology and Religious Studies (AUDTRS) handbook reveals. It has an ancient history, prestigious established posts, the protection of a state church, clear links with a vocational outcome, and the majority of scholars. Its main problem is justifying its existence in a secular higher education system (see Smart 1995 for the case against). However, Religious Studies is still trying to justify its very existence as a subject, against those who see it as a form of Theology or an area within Social Science.

The above discussion demonstrates that the relationship is not the simple contrast of confessional Theology versus neutral Religious Studies, at irreconcilable odds. There is quite a lot of overlap in both content and the variety of subject disciplines employed. Both are trying to understand religious traditions. Both make use of a range of subject disciplines including historical, textual and social science methodologies. Theologians can make use of the findings of Religious Studies, and Religious Studies explore the teaching of theologians. Is the difference really neither confessional approach nor methodology, but merely content?

In practice there has been a tendency in the United Kingdom for Theology and Religious Studies to avoid confrontation by dividing up the field between them, so that Christianity is dealt with by Theology and Religious Studies deals with the rest. The phrase 'other religions' reveals much. At the 2004 conference of the British Association for the Study of Religions, I noted that whereas there were whole days or sections of days dedicated to Buddhist, Jewish, Islamic Studies, etc., there were none with the heading Christian Studies. Similarly, having a University Faculty of Theology, there is no perceived need for an Oxford Centre for Christian Studies to parallel those for Buddhist Studies, Hindu Studies, Islamic Studies and Jewish Studies. This tendency was labelled the 'fundamental distinction' by John Hull (1993) when discussing the wording of the 1988 Education Reform Act and subsequent official guidance on Religious Education, and this distinction has been noted elsewhere in Europe, for example by Tim Jensen (2004) in Denmark, and in the paper given by Mattias Martinson (2006) with reference to Sweden. These countries are some of the few worldwide that have pioneered non-confessional multi-faith Religious Education at some level of schooling, so the continuing distinction between 'Christianity' and 'other religions' is notable.

However, the division is not just of content. In a resolutely 'Study of Religions' Department, it has been sometimes a problem to find both staff and textbooks for students that deal with Christianity from a 'Study of Religions' approach rather than a Theological one, though there are some very honourable exceptions. What have I been looking for that I have found difficult to obtain? The answer to this might help to distinguish between Theology and Religious Studies. What is often lacking is a sufficiently wide overview of the tradition, parallel with those available for 'other' traditions: wide in the sense of looking at the full diversity of Christianity, at the huge variety of denominations, and derived new religious movements, geographical and cultural variations worldwide, but also in the sense of including all dimensions of the tradition – ritual and practice, ethics and politics, visual and material sources as well as textual, the experience of contemporary 'ordinary' (and female, and black) adherents as well as historical celebrated thinkers or 'great men', the tradition found in practice as well as in scriptures and systematic theology. Further than that, a Study of Religions approach treats Christianity not as a special case, but as one 'religion' among many, which has developed in an inter-religious context since its origins, and is not necessarily the tradition which forms the perspective of the student, as is increasingly no longer the case.

Both subjects have a tendency to want to include the other as a subset. Corrywright and Morgan argue that 'the phrase "religious studies" or "the study of religions" can claim to include theology or theologies', whereas Ford (2005: 66) describes how British university Theology Departments have come to 'embrace' Religious Studies. Ford (and others) have pointed out that whereas in the United States of America Religious Studies and Theology have kept themselves distinct, in the United Kingdom there has been less drawing of clear lines, with many Departments calling themselves 'Theology and Religious Studies' (in Ford's view [1999: 17], perhaps the 'best practice'). This reflects the different positions taken by the two countries on the relationship between church and state. The openness of Theology to include Religious Studies mirrors the attitude of the Church of England tendency that sees the church as there for everyone in the parish, which lives in tension with the attitude of 'members only'. Although this can be seen as an admirable inclusivity, it can also be seen as patronizing and colonizing from the receiving end, especially where there is an imbalance of power. As there still appears to be an imbalance of power between Theology and Religious Studies (note the word order) it would appear to be still important to distinguish between Religious Studies and Theology to avoid Religious Studies being integrated out of existence. Perhaps in a more equitable climate, a better relationship between equals can be devised.

Could the two subject areas agree to be taking different approaches but nevertheless work together? Perhaps the easiest area to see potential for co-operation is in the area of applying the insights of Religious Studies and Theology to the problems of the contemporary world – 'applied' Theology and 'engaged' Religious Studies may well find themselves covering similar ground (see Hackett 2003). Another possible area of co-operation might be in defence of distinctively religious perspectives on philosophical and ethical issues. The increasing popularity of papers on Ethics and Philosophy of Religion at A level is leading some students to choose to pursue these rather than either Theology or Religious Studies at university level, which may affect the viability of some programmes.

## What can be learned from Religious Education

One of the main criticisms of Religious Studies coming from the side of Theology is that Religious Studies stops short of questions of truth and value. This has been disputed above, but it is in this area that university level Religious Studies might have something to learn from Religious Education. Religious Education in state schools in England has developed a strong tradition of a non-confessional approach to studying religions. Heavily influenced by Smartian phenomenology in the 1970s, it has moved beyond phenomenology, while not rejecting its strengths, in the directions of ethnography, experiential and existential approaches, and an attention to philosophical and ethical issues. Religious Education in English schools is viewed as not only 'learning about' religions, but also 'learning from' – there is a strong emphasis on personal spiritual development and students being able to articulate their own informed views as well as understanding those of others (the terms 'learning about' and 'learning from' originated with Michael Grimmitt [1987] and are used as headings for the two 'attainment targets' for Religious Education in the *Non-statutory National Framework for Religious Education* [QCA 2004]).

The 'learning from' dimension enables students to evaluate what they have learned about religious traditions and ask questions of truth and value, without these questions and their answers being necessarily located in any particular tradition, but not ruling this out either. This is the only fair approach in classes that are composed of students of many different faith traditions and, increasingly, none. It is possible for students to 'learn from' or be 'edified by' (see Jackson 1997: 130) the study of a wide range of religions, without necessarily subscribing to one or any. Certainly students at school level are keen to explore and express their own views on religious and ethical questions – to quote a schoolboy in my hometown 'I like RE because other subjects tell you what to think – in RE you can say what *you* think'. My own approach to the evaluative side of Religious Studies at university level is to discourage the expression of 'personal opinion' in the first year in order to encourage the recognition of prejudice and stereotype, but gradually to encourage 'informed opinion' as students progress and can support their views with evidence. A similar progression is expected of students in schools, as can be seen from the eight levels of the 'Attainment Targets for Religious Education' (QCA 2004: 36–37).

In mapping the various ways in which scholars locate themselves on the Theology/ Religious Studies spectrum, Kim Knott (2006) suggested the notion of Religious Studies as 'Tertiary Religious Education' defined as including both experiential and personal elements. Whereas I initially interpreted this as a pejorative label, and have in the past been clear to distinguish the two, there may be some mileage in considering this possibility. After all, the benchmarks for *Theology and Religious Studies* (Quality Assurance Agency 2007: 4) do include the claim that the subject 'may contribute to a student's personal development'. In the end however, I would distinguish Religious Studies from Religious Education in seeing the former as a specialist academic discipline whereas the latter is a necessary part of the general and ongoing education of everyone (and to which specialist Religious Studies might contribute).

There are those who suggest that school students should view themselves as theologians (e.g. Astley 1996) and a common discussion in Religious Education circles is: 'someone who studies history becomes a historian, someone who studies religion becomes a . . . what? A theologian?' However, the label 'theologian' has been resisted by many for the associations with theism, Christian-centrism, and focus on belief/doctrine as the subject matter under consideration. Rather, teachers are aiming to produce 'religiate' persons, a term first suggested by Brian Gates (1975) or persons who are 'religiously literate', defined by Andrew Wright (1993: 64) as 'the ability to think and communicate intelligently about the ultimate questions that religion asks'(which is interestingly similar to Ford's 'broadest definition' of Theology above, and might suggest a point at which Theology, Religious Studies and Religious Education converge).

## Why I am still glad to have converted

So, although I see both value and legitimacy in both Theology and Religious Studies as academic disciplines within state-funded universities, and see interesting similarities and potential for collaboration, I consider the potential for confusion and assimilation to be too much of a danger to allow the edges to become too blurred as yet. There is still some force in the comment made by Brian Bocking (1994), 'If you don't know the difference between theology and religious studies, then you're a theologian' (*cited in* Corrywright and Morgan 2006: 50). Religious Studies still has to clarify its non-confessional nature and distinguish itself as different from Theology not as non-confessional, not as a matter of a division of content, not as employing different methodologies from other disciplines, but as a difference of general approach, and to do this without becoming just a subset of the social sciences or Cultural Studies. I find myself in agreement with James Cox that there is still a place for a *methodologically agnostic* approach to studying 'religions': 'a methodological middle ground between theology and culture' (2004: 263) and that this is at the heart of what makes Religious Studies a discipline in its own right as well as employing the methodologies of many other disciplines. Thus on Kim Knott's spectrum, in spite of having some sympathy for the idea of 'Tertiary Religious Education', I would locate myself on the far end of Religious Studies as a subject in its own right, distinct from both Theology and from the various other disciplines that it might employ. It is distinguished by both its content and its approach to that content.

## Conclusions and future possibilities

Words change their meanings and maybe Theology can become broad enough to encompass not only systematic religious thinking by Buddhists but also what we mean today by Religious Studies. However, we are not at that point yet. Theology does still retain its overtones of confessionalism, theism, Christianity, and privileging written doctrine over lived praxis, and perhaps more significantly, thinking about the questions raised by religions from one particular perspective, rather than trying to take account of as diverse a range of perspectives as possible.

Students in schools and universities (and even some teachers and lecturers) are increasingly coming to their studies, not rooted in one particular tradition, but with developing personal beliefs and values which have been influenced by a wide range of religious, spiritual and cultural traditions. The dangers of what has been described as a 'pick and mix' spirituality worry some, but in practice the communications revolutions have enabled the rich heritage of the human traditions we label 'religious' being open to everyone with access to a computer, library or bookshop. Although such non-aligned students may be characterized as global spiritual tourists, and at risk of ending up illiterate when compared to those who are immersed in one particular tradition, their ability to move between worlds with some facility may be an advantage. It has been noted that children brought up in diaspora situations need not be victims caught between two cultures, but can be skilled navigators of multiple cultural streams (Jackson 1997: 83). We are only just beginning to meet the generation of students whose world-views are formed from a wide variety of influences rather than the choice of accepting or rebelling against a heritage tradition. This is the generation for whom even 'new age' spirituality is something of historical interest that they associate with their grandparents.

Thus there are all sorts of possibilities for the re-imagining and recombining of our subject areas in the future by a generation of scholars whose formative cultural influences have been very different from the generation about to retire. Meanwhile, there is still a need for and a possibility of a subject in the space between Theology and Cultural Studies, as argued by James Cox, and the name of that subject is currently Religious Studies (or Study of Religions). However, while agreeing with James Cox (2006) that this subject studies 'identifiable communities with postulated alternative realities' (and wondering if that is also what the community of Religious Studies scholars is), I do not agree that it does not also include the study of 'transient popular individualistic movements' as these forms of spirituality appeal increasingly to younger generations, as for example in the attractions of individualistic forms of contemporary Paganism. What is true about both Theology and Religious Studies is that neither will stay static and, in the words of the QAA Benchmarking Statement that 'much of the excitement of the discipline lies in its contested nature' (QAA 2007: 5).

## References

Astley, J. (1996), 'Theology for the Untheological? Theology, Philosophy and the Classroom', in J. Astley and L. Francis (eds), *Christian Theology and Religious Education: Connections and Contradictions*. London: SPCK, pp. 60–77.

Bocking, Brian (2000), 'Study of Religions: the New Queen of the Sciences?', *BASR Occasional Paper* no. 21, pp. 19 (republished in a revised form in S. J. Sutcliffe (ed.) (2004), *Religion: Empirical Studies*. Aldershot: Ashgate, pp. 107–119).

Corrywright C. and Morgan P. (2006), *Get Set for Religious Studies*. Edinburgh: Edinburgh University Press.

Cox, J. L. (2004), 'Separating Religion from the "Sacred": Methodological Agnosticism and the Future of Religious Studies', in S. J. Sutcliffe (ed.), *Religion: Empirical Studies*. Aldershot: Ashgate, pp. 107–119.

—(2006), 'Towards a Socio-cultural, Non-theological Definition of Religion', paper given at 'Theology *and* Religious Studies or Theology *versus* Religious Studies', July 6–7, St. Anne's College, University of Oxford.

Cush, D. (1999), 'The Relationship between Religious Studies, Religious Education and Theology: Big Brother, Little Sister, and the Clerical Uncle?', *British Journal of Religious Education*, 21 (3), 137–146.

—(2005), 'Engaged Religious Studies' in *Discourse: Learning and Teaching in Philosophical and Religious Studies*, 4 (2), 84–104.

D'Costa, G. (2006), 'Theological Theology and Theological Religious Studies – A Modest Proposal', paper given at 'Theology *and* Religious Studies or Theology *versus* Religious Studies', July 6–7, St. Anne's College, University of Oxford.

Fitzgerald, T. (1995), 'Religious Studies as Cultural Studies: A Philosophical and Anthropological Critique of the Concept of Religion', *DISKUS*, 3 (1), 35–47. http://www.uni-marburg.de/religionswissenschaft/journal/diskus/ last accessed 27/08/2008.

—(2006), 'Theology, Religion, and the Invention of Secular Politics', paper given at 'Theology *and* Religious Studies or Theology *versus* Religious Studies', July 6–7, St. Anne's College, University of Oxford.

Ford, D. (1999), *Theology, a Very Short Introduction*. Oxford: Oxford University Press.

—(2005), 'Theology', in Hinnells, J. R. (ed.), *The Routledge Companion to the Study of Religion*. Abingdon: Routledge, pp. 61–79.

—(2006), 'Theology and Religious Studies for a Multi-faith and Secular Society' paper given at 'Theology *and* Religious Studies or Theology *versus* Religious Studies', July 6–7, St. Anne's College, University of Oxford.

Gates, B. (1975), '"Readiness" for Religion', in Smart, N. & Horder, D. (eds), *New Movements in Religious Education*. London: Temple Smith, pp. 59–75.

Grimmitt, M. (1987), *Religious Education and Human Development: The Relationship between Studying Religions and Personal, Social and Moral Education*. Great Wakering: McCrimmons.

Hackett, R. (2003), 'The Response of Scholars of Religion to Global Religious Violence', *British Association for the Study of Religions Occasional Paper* no. 26. Leeds: BASR.

Hull, J. (1993), 'The Fundamental Distinction: A Review of the DFE Draft Circular X/94', unpublished paper.

Jackson, R. (1997), *Religious Education: An Interpretive Approach*. London: Hodder & Stoughton.

Jackson, R. and Makransky, J. (eds) (2000), *Buddhist Theology: Critical Reflections by Contemporary Buddhist Scholars*. London: RoutledgeCurzon.

Jensen, Tim (2004), 'The Study of Religions in Denmark: Research, Teaching and Discussions', paper given at 'The Study of Religions: Mapping the Field', the 50th Anniversary conference of the British Association for the Study of Religions, Harris Manchester College, Oxford, September.

King, U. (2006), 'A Coat of Many Colours: Interweaving Strands in Theology and Religious Studies', paper given at 'Theology *and* Religious Studies or Theology *versus* Religious Studies', July 6–7, St. Anne's College, University of Oxford.

Knott, K. (2006), 'A spatial analysis of the relationship between theology and religious studies: the use of "insider" and "outsider" metaphors of containment and separation, and other knowledge-power strategies', paper given at 'Theology *and* Religious Studies or Theology *versus* Religious Studies', July 6–7, St. Anne's College, University of Oxford.

McGrath, A. (2001), *Christian Theology, an Introduction*. Oxford: Blackwell.

McGrath, Alister W. (2006), *Christian Theology: An Introduction*. Oxford: WileyBlackwell.

Martinson, M. (2006), 'The Irony of Religious Studies: An Argument from the Swedish Experience', paper given at 'Theology *and* Religious Studies or Theology *versus* Religious Studies', July 6–7, St. Anne's College, University of Oxford.

Qualifications and Curriculum Authority (QCA) (2004), *Religious Education: the Non-statutory National Framework*. London: QCA.

Quality Assurance Agency (QAA) (2007), *Theology and Religious Studies* available online from www.qaa.ac.uk last accessed 27/08/2008.

Quatermaine, Timothy Bridges, Dafydd Mills Daniel, Sarah Lincoln, Alan Smith, Jacob Waldenmaier (2006), 'A Response from Graduate Students', paper given at Theology *and* Religious Studies or Theology *versus* Religious Studies, July 6–7, St. Anne's College, University of Oxford.

Schools Council (1971), *Religious Education in Secondary Schools*. London: Evans Brothers.

Smart, N. (1968), *Secular Education and the Logic of Religion*. London: Faber & Faber.

—(1995), 'The Values of Religious Studies', *The Journal of Beliefs and Values*, 16 (2), 7–10.

Sutcliffe, S. (2006), 'What *is* religious studies? Disciplinary formation in comparative context', paper given at Theology *and* Religious Studies or Theology *versus* Religious Studies, July 6–7, St. Anne's College, University of Oxford.

Thatcher, A. (1997), 'Theology of Education and Church Schools', in Kay, W. K & Francis, L. J. (eds), *Religion and Education, Volume 1.* Leominster: Gracewing, pp. 61–99.

Waterhouse, H. (1993), 'A short critique of Nick Sutton's paper: "Issues Arising from the Distinctions Drawn Between Theology and Religious Studies"', *DISKUS* 1 (2), http://web.uni-marburg.de/religionswissenschaft/journal/diskus/#1_2 last accessed 28/08/2008.

Wright, Andrew (1993), *Religious Education in the Secondary School: Prospects for Religious Literacy*. London: David Fulton, p. 108.

Whaling, F. (1999), 'Theological Approaches', in P. Connolly (ed.), *Approaches to the Study of Religion*. London: Cassell, 226–274.

Chapter 2

# Theology and Religious Studies for a Multifaith and Secular Society

David F. Ford

## Introduction

The names given to the academic field that we are considering,[1] such as theology, religious studies or divinity, represent a long history in many countries and in diverse institutions. I will mainly concentrate on the present situation in universities in the United Kingdom, with a concluding look towards the future; but the fact that this situation is the outcome of a complex, often messy, process over many centuries is important for my position. It suggests that there is a need for careful attention to particular contexts, genealogies, conflicts, struggles, negotiations and power relations.[2] In addition, not only are the settings and institutional arrangements within which theology/religion/divinity are studied and debated the outcome of various settlements worked out over time; the very ideas in which we describe the field and these settlements are themselves 'past-entailing concepts', inviting a narrative and dialectical account of their development that is alert to multiple meanings sedimented over many years. This time-sensitive approach is critical of those that try to find either a single essence, whether of religion or of its study, or a single definition, unless that is broad enough and open to the historical particularity. It also resists tendencies to think that one might be able to stand outside history and begin again, working out a new conception of the field in line with such essences or definitions. So I start by trying briefly to describe and assess the state of theology/religious studies/divinity in British universities now. Ideally this would be accompanied by a historical account from the vantage point of the present, but that is precluded both by my time-limit and by the need for a great deal more research than I have done.

My own thesis is that for universities in early twenty-first century Britain the combination of theology and religious studies makes good sense and has a promising future, but that there is some urgency in the need to think about its own rationale in order to develop itself in the face of very different conceptions. This is a lively and fascinating field that is needed by universities, religious communities and society. Its history in Britain has brought it to the point now when it could be in a position to offer to the rest of the world a paradigm that has many advantages in responding intelligently to, educating people for, a global situation that, like Britain, is complexly both religious and secular.

## The field of Theology/Religious Studies/ Divinity in British universities

The field here has a wide variety of settlements, with the main emphases of particular departments ranging through biblical studies, theology of various sorts, religious studies of various sorts, and several types of combination of those. But I would suggest that the distinctive thing about the field in the United Kingdom is the extent to which it has theology *and* religious studies in its state-supported universities, often institutionally integrated in one department.

The distinctiveness is striking when the situation in two other countries is considered comparatively. In Germany the dominant university model is of confessional theology (Protestant and Roman Catholic), with roots in the Middle Ages, the Reformation, and especially in the nineteenth century pattern originating in the University of Berlin, founded in 1809. In the United States of America there is a divide between private institutions, often with religious roots, where theology may be taught, and state-supported institutions with departments of religious studies from which it is excluded, the roots of this being in an Enlightenment-inspired separation of church and state. In fact the American scene is far more diverse than that, especially in private universities that have divinity schools, and also in a few state universities such as the University of Virginia, but there is no combining of theology and religious studies on the British scale. And in the United States of America, as in the United Kingdom, the very labels 'theology' and 'religious studies' have become increasingly problematic: one of my reasons for liking the 'and' between them is that it builds in diversity and the recognition of a complex history of power struggles and negotiation, and resists a resolution of the debates in favour of one conception of one or the other.

The field in Britain has developed over centuries with successive waves of cultural, religious and educational developments leaving their marks. No one template, no one ideology, no one definition has dominated. As a member of one of the panels that contributed to the benchmarking document for the field some years ago, I remember being struck by how many different strands of history, religion and educational institutions there are. Even in terms of paradigmatic settlements, one would need at the least to list Oxford, Edinburgh, Aberdeen, Birmingham, Lancaster, King's College London, Heythrop and Kent – but even as I name these I can think of others that do not fit easily with any of them, and distinctive features that may seem insignificant to outsiders might from inside a department be important results of hard-fought battles and tough negotiation.

There has been no national policy by anyone trying to homogenize the field over the past 100 years, and state support for it through provision for universities has generally been channelled into departments shaped more by local histories than by central policies. As the balance between government and other sources of funding for universities has begun to shift towards the latter, new non-government stakeholders are emerging alongside the traditional ones of churches and other religious groups; and the government is also becoming far more interested in religion. One of the reasons why a volume such as this is significant is that those of us in the field need to become clearer about how we understand the field and what we want it to become if we are to be able to negotiate wisely with political, educational, religious and other stakeholders. Academics are always in danger of fighting a previous century's battles over again and ignoring new challenges: constriction and direction of the field due to religious hegemony is hardly the same threat as it was in nineteenth-century Oxford or Cambridge; but has the debate about the relation of theology to religious studies taken adequate account of new religious, political and financial stakeholders? Yet 'becoming clearer' need not mean becoming more homogeneous or opting for one master paradigm; indeed I will argue that it is vital to preserve and develop many niches in our complex environment if the best features of the field are to flourish.

What are those features? I would summarize them as follows:

- Overall, the combination of theology and religious studies at its best allows for the pursuit, through a range of academic disciplines, of questions of meaning, truth, practice and beauty raised by the religions, about the religions and between the religions. There is, it seems to me, no difficulty in arguing that pursuit of such a range of questions can be appropriately academic, but within the array of possible combinations of questions, disciplines and categories there are many different possible configurations of department.

- This means that the particular phenomena of the field can be richly and rigorously described, analysed and explained in ways that are often not possible where theology is studied apart from the range of academic disciplines that come under the heading of religious studies (cf. the recent Routledge Handbook edited by John Hinnells,[3] though that rather disturbingly does not include history).
- At the same time, it allows for issues of truth and practice, including normative practice, to be on the agenda in ways that are often not possible in religious studies settings. It might be that the most serious academic objection to the separation of religious studies from theology is that, without theology, religious studies arbitrarily limits its inquiries and outcomes. This especially applies to questions raised by and between the religions: it might be possible for religious studies to explore answers that have been given to these questions, but not to come to conclusions about their truth or goodness, let alone offer constructive proposals in line with, or in critique of, particular traditions. On the other hand, theology, like other disciplines such as philosophy and economics, can be a broker among disciplines, stimulating interdisciplinary inquiries, and challenging them with theological (or, in the other cases, philosophical or economic) questions, not the least concerning truth and practice.[4]
- The combination of theology and religious studies encourages the fulfilment and interrelation of three key transgenerational responsibilities: towards universities and their range of disciplines (a responsibility of excellence in the disciplines and towards the shaping of education and research according to the best norms); towards religious communities and traditions (a responsibility of educational, critical and constructive engagement); and towards societies and public understanding (especially the shaping of education, public policy and public discourse). Crudely put, theology alone (and I include here Hindu, Jewish, Muslim, Christian, secular and other tradition-specific bodies of thought, whether they call themselves 'theology' or not, as well as forms of theology that try to engage critically and constructively across traditions) can find some difficulties in doing full justice to the range of academic disciplines and to the demands for public understanding adequate to a religiously diverse society; and religious studies alone can have difficulties with the normative side of some academic disciplines, with the constructive requirements of religious communities, and with the normative and public policy aspects of public debate.
- The combination allows for forms of collegiality in relation to each of those responsibilities – collegiality within departments and universities,

between them, and within and between disciplines, religious communities, spheres of society and different societies. More will be said about this in the discussion of universities below.

- The combination offers a more diverse curriculum to a wider range of students, which in turn affects the richness of collegiality among students.

- Finally, the combining of theology and religious studies gives a setting where the future of the field can be discussed and worked out in practice with the participation of the main interested parties. There can be benefits for more specialized environments (either theology or religious studies) in learning from places where both dimensions are present and engaged with each other. A case can be made that it is generally beneficial for theology to become more open to religious studies and vice versa.

## University theology and religious studies for a religious and secular society

Each of those seven fairly general statements could be expanded upon and given historical depth, but I want, in line with what has just been said, to move on to my central proposal. This is in two parts: that there is an appropriate fit between the sort of society we are and the combination of theology and religious studies; and that this has consequences for our universities.

### Why theology and religious studies for a religious and secular society?

This is not the place to do a sociological profile of our society, but it is necessary to portray it in the very broadest brushstrokes. Whatever one's position on the secularization debate, it seems clear that at the very least Britain cannot simply be labelled religious, but nor can it simply be labelled secular. Rather, it is complexly and simultaneously both religious and secular, with intense debates about how this dual reality should be defined, described, explained and responded to. Religions, and the issues raised by being a multifaith society, are also, for various reasons, more prominent in the media and in public debate at the beginning of the twenty-first century than they were during most of the twentieth century. With this has gone new forms of recognition by the state of the importance of religions in shaping society, for example in the encouragement of faith schools and in sponsoring (and sometimes funding) projects and programmes aimed at 'social cohesion'. Perhaps more fundamental has been increasing recognition of the role of civil society, both nationally and internationally, in the flourishing of nations and regions (not least in their economic prosperity), and, within that, the significance of intermediate institutions, religious communities being among the most important.

The combination of theology and religious studies suits this situation well. It can engage with the range of religions; it can educate and inform about the religions, not only in universities but also in wider public life and within religious communities; some of its practitioners can also contribute definite positions on substantive public issues that require judgements about matters of truth and practice (an analogy might be economists who contribute to government and business as advisers, consultants or planners); it can create forms of collegiality and set up conversations and debates among students and among academics (and among both together) that pioneer the fostering of fresh understanding and peaceful relationships across religious boundaries; and it can act as a sign of hope and good sense amidst much bad news and nonsense. Neither theology by itself nor religious studies by itself could attempt all that. In short, the sorts of collegiality, education, research and debate that are likely to be of most benefit to a society such as ours can best be developed through theology and religious studies together.

## Theology and religious studies and the role of universities

Universities are also crucial intermediate institutions in our civil society, and they are the obvious location for a theology and religious studies which is concerned with that society in the ways just mentioned. It is worth considering the history of universities in relation to the religious and the secular.[5]

The modern university is a remarkable phenomenon. It has been called 'the European institution par excellence' and it has now spread all over the world. Its origins and development are complex, but two reasonable historical statements are that it originated in medieval scholarly corporations and that it underwent its major modern transformation through the spread of the paradigm of the University of Berlin, founded in 1809. Writing on 'the German university revolution' of the late eighteenth and the nineteenth centuries, Randall Collins says:

The period from 1765 to the present is institutionally all of a piece. The continuity may not be apparent at first glance; Kant and the German

Idealists seem epochs away from the themes of our own century. But Idealism was the intellectual counterpart of the academic revolution, the creation of the modern research university centred on the graduate faculty of research professors, and that material base has expanded to dominate intellectual life ever since. Kant straddled two worlds: the patronage networks of the previous period, and the modern research university, which came into being, in part through Kant's own agitation, with the generation of Kant's successors. The time of the Romantics and Idealists was a transition to our contemporary situation. University-based intellectual networks had existed before, but never with such autonomy for researchers to define their own paths and such power to take over every sphere of intellectual life . . . Idealism was the battle doctrine of the first generations of secularisers, a halfway house for wresting theology into secular hands; as the tide turned, Idealism became adopted as a defensive doctrine by religious thinkers.[6]

It was by no means inevitable that an institution with strong religious roots and control such as the university should become the leading research and higher level teaching institution of the contemporary world.[7] The French in 1793 replaced universities with a combination of academies and specialist government écoles. The Prussians were considering a similar *tabula rasa* approach at the beginning of the nineteenth century. But the combination of an extraordinarily creative set of thinkers and organizational innovators, together with appropriate historical conditions, led to Prussia reorganizing its educational system with the university at the top, and far more in continuity with the medieval university than was the French system. The university became not only the centre for formal credentials for state employment and a range of professions; it also had a good deal of academic autonomy, an increasingly differentiated set of specialist faculties, and what Collins calls a 'structural impetus to creativity', with professors expected to produce new knowledge.[8] It united research and teaching in pursuit of *Wissenschaft*, it gave considerable freedom in teaching, research and study, and its ideal was an all-round education of the mind, enabling the understanding to make sense of each discipline in relation to others.

The Berlin model spread in Europe far beyond Germany and also to America and elsewhere, and many of its key features are still characteristic of those universities that dominate intellectual life around the world. But it was a historical surprise, by no means an inevitable development when set in the context of its time, in which the French system seemed to have far more going for it.

What about religion in the Berlin model? Collins tells a linear story of one-way secularization: theological and ecclesiastical domination were ended as disciplines won their autonomy, and the state presided over the creation of a new system in which religion eventually played almost no part. In Collins' history the result of the process is that niches in the intellectual ecology previously occupied by theology are now colonized by other disciplines, especially philosophy, and religion has effectively disappeared. This is akin to the version of secularization theory according to which modernity brings with it the irreversible decline of religion in most areas, especially of public life. But what if a more complex, dialectical and historically accurate story is told, leading to a different conception of the contemporary implications?

Collins does not mention the religious-secular debate that took place over the constitution of the University of Berlin. Hans Frei's account of this emphasizes the differences between Fichte (its first Rector), who wanted to exclude theology because it was not sufficiently 'wissenschaftlich', and Schleiermacher (Fichte's successor as Rector and the author of the foundational paper which Wilhelm von Humboldt used as his inspiration for the constitution of the new university), who was both supportive of Wissenschaft and argued for the inclusion of theology as drawing on various disciplines with the overall aim of the professional education of clergy. Schleiermacher resisted any overarching systematic framework or theory of Wissenschaft for the University of Berlin since this could not do justice to 'the irreducible specificity of Christianity at the primary level of a "mode of faith", a cultural–religious tradition, and a linguistic community'.[9] Frei comments that Schleiermacher's

view won the day resoundingly. But that is in its way startling. Here was the university [sc. Berlin], the conception of which was most deeply influenced by a philosophical system, the idealist view of the rational and unitary character of study; the university, furthermore, that was to be the model for others in Western Europe and the New World. And it, of all institutions, found itself, from the start, unable to embody its own unitary idea, while the man who ended up defending both – the idea of the intellectual unity and supremacy of Wissenschaft and the university, and the actual as well as conceptually irreducible diversity of the institution of higher learning – was himself one of the leading idealists. It was a triumph of orderly eclecticism over system by a leading systematician. And he based the right of theology to a place in the university on the status of the ministry as one of the professions in the modern sense.[10]

Beginning from that account, the story of the historical surprise of the University of Berlin and its contemporary significance in the UK context might unfold differently. The continuing interplay of the religious and the secular, appropriately adapted to specific contexts, and refusing any overarching philosophy, ideology or religion, might emerge as part of its secret. Its genius was to create an institution that simultaneously did several things: it constructively drew on the two deepest roots of European civilization, the Hebraic and the Hellenic; it was sensitive to the context and needs (including religious) of its own society; it embodied creative responsibility for the future through teaching and research; it tried to safeguard freedom of intellectual inquiry and of belief; and it pioneered a type of environment in which a good deal of the most important intellectual inquiry and debate in both arts and sciences has continued to happen. One could also draw up the other side of the balance sheet, noting features such as the massive reliance on the state and its bureaucracy, the German nationalism that pervaded its universal ideal, the potential of disciplinary autonomy leading to fragmentation, the limitation of theology to a certain type of state-recognized Christianity, and the whole system's vulnerability to political manipulation (of which the Nazi and Communist periods were only the most extreme examples).

Looking today at the many universities around the world that owe a great deal to the Berlin paradigm, one sees various continuities and discontinuities. Most of the key elements are at the least under pressure – the unity of teaching with research, the interconnectedness of all disciplines, the ideal of Wissenschaft, the free responsibility of academics and students in teaching, research and study; and there are massive issues of political and economic domination, bureaucratic control and short-term strategies. How all the problems in these areas might be responded to is beyond the scope of this chapter, but they are not unrelated to my key concern now: how universities equip students and their societies to cope with a complexly religious and secular world.

The dialectical tension between the religious and the secular was anomalous even in relation to Berlin's founding concept of Wissenschaft, and in changed historical circumstances the tendency has been towards letting the tension slacken in the direction of an embracing, normative secularism. Even where this has not happened the form of the religious has been restricted to certain forms of Protestant and Catholic Christianity, with very limited concern for the rest of Christianity or other religions. On the whole, universities have been powerful supporters of secularization, whether in anti-religious or more neutral modes. This has generally meant (though arguably it need not have) that their attention to religious traditions, living religious communities, and to the questions raised by the religions, between the religions, about the religions, and between the religions and non-religious or mixed forms of understanding, belief and practice, has been marginal. *They therefore fail to do justice to huge swathes of past and present human culture, experience, thought, ethics, politics, economics, art and practice.* This leaves the educated elites largely ignorant, naïve or mis-informed about some of the most important dimensions of their own and other people's societies, and this inadequate and often distorted view of reality is widely disseminated through the media, schools and other institutions that are largely led by university graduates. It also leaves the religious traditions impoverished in the realm of informed, critical and construct-ive engagement in the public realm that might help them think through their self-understanding and their participation in society. And within the academy it not only leads to theology and/or religious studies being a small department, often relatively isolated from others or virtually indistinguish-able from others; it also cuts universities off from sources of wisdom they need to meet their current challenges.

My thesis arising from this account is that the 1809 University of Berlin, a creative continuation and reshaping of the medieval university, involved a complex religious and secular settlement that was not continued and cre-atively reshaped in the twentieth century, leading to a serious imbalance and inadequacy in academic engagement with the religions; but at the beginning of the twenty-first century there are good reasons and oppor-tune circumstances for pursuing the following question: *how might a univer-sity today be true to the core ideals of the Berlin paradigm, including its combination of the religious and secular, but in a way that is appropriate to the repair and renewal that that paradigm now requires?*

My brief answer is that the British model of theology and religious studies has a historic opportunity to develop a creative response to the twenty-first century situation and in the process to help, in a modest way, to reshape universities for the benefit of both academic life and of its responsibilities – towards religious communities and towards our religious and secular soci-ety. I will soon conclude with some thoughts about the future, but first want to comment briefly on some of the alternatives to my position.

## The secular option and the religious option

My position on theology and religious studies requires that a university acknowledge, at least implicitly, that ours is a religious and secular society and that it makes good sense in both academic and social terms to combine theology and religious studies in a university. This position is open to many types of departmental settlement, some of which are more in the direction of theology and some in the direction of religious studies. The ethos of a particular university might likewise be more in line with one or the other direction, and it seems to me an appropriate feature of a society such as in the United Kingdom that there should be diverse educational niches.

Further, the contention that universities should have a religious and secular character is a matter of legitimate dispute, and good cases (or at least cases that are persuasive to many intelligent people in our society) can be made for religious universities and for secular universities. In the twentieth century the main trend in new universities was towards the secular, but it is not inevitable that this will continue. In the United Kingdom, unlike the United States of America, religious universities have not been popular, but it is likewise not inevitable (and perhaps, as Gavin D'Costa argues, not desirable) that this will always be so. My argument is not that theology and religious studies in religious and secular universities should be the only option, excluding others. Rather, I am suggesting that it not only makes academic sense but also is best suited to contribute to the flourishing of a religious and secular society. such as in the United Kingdom. It can coexist happily – if sometimes polemically – with the other models.

## The future

I have argued that the mixed British ecology of theology and religious studies has a good deal to recommend it. It is good for the field academically; and it creates a place of collegial study and conversation that brings benefits to both the religious communities and the society as a whole. Moreover, it may have something to contribute to the shaping of universities. They face a great many changes and challenges, and they would be sensible to draw on wisdom from many sources, ancient and modern, multi-religious and secular. They need to provide 'mutual ground' for religious and secular wisdom traditions to engage with each other for the sake of better education, research and fulfilment of public responsibilities. If all this is granted, what might we in the field do in order to fulfil the promise of theology and religious studies in the future? I conclude with an agenda.

- Keep the 'and'.
- Produce rich descriptions of the field, both historical and contemporary, using the field's academic disciplines to do so.

- Develop rationales for the field, not just in the fairly general terms I have used, but also in Jewish, Christian, Muslim, Hindu, secular and other terms.
- Whatever the nature of the settlement in one's own department, make the case for it being open in both directions and supportive of the overall diverse ecology of the British settlement.
- Hold together the three transgenerational responsibilities towards universities, religious communities and societies, and build forms of collegiality around each responsibility.
- Seek the good of the whole university, and put intellectual and political energy into debates about its future in order to help it become 'mutual ground' (rather than 'neutral ground') for those of many religions and none.
- Seek endowments for the field: this is the best material way to ensure long term flourishing, and the early twenty-first century may well be a time when this is becoming possible in unprecedented ways in the United Kingdom.
- After we have done all that we might be ready to go back to change the first bullet point, replacing the 'and' with a forward slash, renaming the field **Theology/Religious Studies,** even perhaps adding/**Divinity**.

## Notes

[1] For a set of discussions of the field generally in line with what follows see David F. Ford, Ben Quash and Janet Martin Soskice (eds), Fields of Faith: Theology and Religious Studies for the Twenty-first Century. Cambridge: Cambridge University Press, 2005; other helpful accounts from different angles include: Ernest Nicholson (ed.), A Century of Theology and Religious Studies in Britain. Oxford: Oxford University Press, 2003; Walter H. Capps, Religious Studies: The Making of a Discipline. Minneapolis: Fortress Press, 1995; Ursula King (ed.), Turning Points in Religious Studies. Edinburgh: T&T Clark, 1990; Richard H. Roberts, Religion, Theology and the Human Sciences. Cambridge: Cambridge University Press, 2002; Miroslav Wolf, Carmen Krieg and Thomas Kucharz (eds), The Future of Theology: Essays in Honor of Jürgen Moltmann. Grand Rapids, Michigan and Cambridge, UK: Eerdmans, 1996; Journal of the American Academy of Religio, March 2006, 74 (1), 1–271 on the future of the study of religion in the academy.

[2] Cf. on this and the rest of this paragraph Timothy Jenkins, 'Anthropology, religion and time. An anthropological perspective on Theology and Religious Studies', unpublished paper.

[3] John R. Hinnells (ed.), *The Routledge Companion to the Study of Religion.* London and New York: Routledge, 2005.

⁴ Economics is an especially apt comparison. Many parts of people's lives are involved with and shaped by money and by economic systems, practices and understandings. When economics is studied academically there is no suggestion that staff or students should not be involved personally with money or other aspects of the economy. It is also common for universities not only to have economics departments that study (in ways analogous to a religious studies mode) the history, theory, statistical analysis and contemporary workings of economic systems, but also to have departments of applied economics that are closely connected with governments and business, and to prepare students in business or management schools directly for careers in business. In the course of pursuing applied economics and business studies many normative and practical questions must be not only raised but also answered, in ways analogous to theology's critical and constructive contribution to contemporary religious communities. The career-oriented aspect is paralleled by the training of religious ministers in some university departments of theology and religious studies or by the now widespread arrangements whereby universities validate qualifications taught by theological institutions run by particular religious communities.

⁵ Much of what follows is condensed from longer treatments in David F. Ford, *Christian Wisdom: Desiring God and Learning in Love.* Cambridge: Cambridge University Press, 2007, Chapter 9; 'Faith and Universities in a Religious and Secular World (1)' in *Svensk Teologisk Kvartalskrift*, 81 (2), 2005, 83–91 and 'Faith and Universities in a Religious and Secular World (2)' in *Svensk Teologisk Kvartalskrift*, 81 (3), 2005, 97–106.

⁶ Randall Collins, *The Sociology of Philosophies: A Global Theory of Intellectual Change.* Cambridge, Mass. and London: The Belknap Press of Harvard University Press, 1998, p. 618.

⁷ For what follows cf. Collins, ibid. pp. 640–645.

⁸ Ibid. p. 643.

⁹ Hans W. Frei, *Types of Christian Theology* Edited by George Hunsinger and William C. Placher. New Haven and London: Yale University Press, 1992, p. 114 – this is Frei's redescription of Schleiermacher's position.

¹⁰ Ibid. p. 112.

Chapter 3

# Theology and Religious Studies OR Theology *versus* Religious Studies?

Gavin D'Costa

## Introduction

I want to offer some reflections on the place of two disciplinary objects within our modern Western academy: 'religious studies' (which also goes under the name of 'religion', 'comparative religion', 'history of religions' and so on) and 'theology' which is my own discipline. I offer these reflections in the ongoing task of rebuilding what John Webster has called a 'theological theology'[1], by which I mean 'theology' that is ordered to its proper object: God; and this 'object' of study generating appropriate methodologies and presuppositions that are required for the discipline to properly operate. I shall be arguing that within the modern Western academy, painted with very wide brush strokes, theology has become increasingly assimilated to various disciplines within the humanities, social sciences and at an earlier period, the natural sciences, and in this move, replicates the development of the field: 'religion'. When this happens, I want to argue for the theology 'versus' religious studies part of our title. However, within the model of theology I am working with, broadly Thomist, there is much scope for a very positive critical engagement with the humanities, social sciences and natural sciences – and with world religions and alternative spiritualities. In this sense, I want to emphasize the 'and' of the relationship between theology and religious studies, but that relationship must respect first, the legitimacy of theological theology and secondly, its properly restricted claim to be 'queen of the sciences', a claim that does not question the legitimate autonomy of all sciences. Admittedly this is a rather difficult claim for other disciplines to swallow, but then that is to be expected at this cultural scene in our history – as I hope to explain in this chapter. Finally, I shall also be suggesting that such a view of theology generates a critique of the very university institutions within which it is embedded, opening up much broader questions regarding the nature of the university and its role in society. While this is not part of our study here, it should never be far from our concerns.

I will first offer a very scant genealogical picture of the modern university initially following Alasdair MacIntyre to chart the way in which the modern university has framed knowledge, and through this narrative, comment on how this relates to our two disciplinary areas, also paying attention to the nature of the university.[2]

## The genealogy of the modern university: modernity's paradigm of knowledge

In what follows I draw from the later MacIntyre, after he had become a Catholic Thomist, and specifically from his *Three Rival Versions of Moral Enquiry* (1990). The context of MacIntyre's enquiry is his attempt to show the collapse and bankruptcy of modernity, the parasitic nature of post-modernity, and the importance of an alternative, Aristotelian Thomism, that can both explain the modern situation as well as offer a diagnosis out of the moral collapse generated by modernity and postmodernity. He sees the modern liberal university as the structural establishment of modernity and also home to its parasitic offspring, postmodernity.

MacIntyre argues that the Enlightenment project, modernity, was doomed to failure:

> The Enlightenment project which has dominated philosophy during the past three hundred years promised a conception of rationality independent of historical and social context, and independent of any specific understanding of man's nature or purpose. But not only has that promise in fact been unfulfilled, the project is itself fundamentally flawed and the promise could never be fulfilled. In consequence, modern moral and political thought are in a state of disarray from which they can be rescued only if we revert to an Aristotelian paradigm, with its essential commitment to teleology, and construct an account of practical reason premised on that commitment.[3]

The Enlightenment project, in so much as it has dominated philosophy and moral and political thought, has inevitably affected theology and the intellectual institutions in which it has developed, the universities. This can be traced in at least three ways.

First, the impact of disembodied reason's central role meant that tradition and telos (that is, the authority of the Christian tradition in theological reasoning and its vision of the final end of men and women in union with God in the beatific vision) became secondary and eventually unnecessary to the discipline of 'theology'. This had a profound impact on the curriculum and the underlying goal of education. Paul Griffiths interestingly summarizes it thus:

> Pedagogically, modernity is the cafeteria-style university catalogue of courses from which consumers (provided they have paid their tuition fees) can choose what most pleases them; it is the row of paperback editions of sacred works from a dozen religious traditions jostling one another on the bookstore's shelves. Religious pedagogy [or what I am calling theology], by contrast, is the single curriculum, identical for all, like that in place in Nālandā in India in the eighth century, or at Clairvaux in France in the twelfth; and it is a single set of sacred works that cannot be placed on a par with (much less on the same shelf as) others. Religious learning therefore requires explicit appeal to authority in ways that consumerist pedagogy does not. The former wants to make choices for its learners, while the latter wants to equip them to choose for themselves.[4]

I'm in entire agreement with Griffith's quotation, except for his apparent shelving plans. I shall be arguing for a theological religious studies where theology requires interaction with the world religion's sacred texts and contexts. They need to be on a nearby shelf, mirroring our religious pluralist context.

Second, the notion that theology be understood as a unique 'science' as was the natural sciences or social sciences was equally undermined as theology's claim seemed predicated upon a number of authorities other than reason, thereby departing from modernity's canon of acceptable 'sciences'. This battle was finally fought (and lost) at the University of Berlin at the beginning of the nineteenth century. Berlin was designed to reflect the 'research university' along the lines of the Enlightenment vision of education.[5] In this respect, it intentionally defined itself against the earlier model of *paideia* which had characterized ecclesial forms of education and dominant forms of pre-Christian Greek education and instead emphasized a general critical, orderly, and disciplined science of research. That is, no texts or ways of reading them were to be seen as authoritative because of spiritual authority or traditions deeming them so. Rather, all texts were to be critically scrutinized, using methods that were accessible to all rational men (and eventually women), employing methods that could allow the repeating of tests to authenticate and establish results. In this sense, theology, whose authority rested on revelation, was an obvious problem for the University of Berlin and there was considerable controversy about its inclusion in the new research university.

It was only through the genius of Schleiermacher (1768–1834) that theology made it into the university, but on the purely pragmatic grounds that it was important for professional training, rather than arguing its status as a 'science', let alone queen of the sciences.[6] In this sense Schleiermacher conceded the most important point. He argued that just as medicine and law were included in the university as practical disciplines, the historical and philosophical study of theology was also justified, for these disciplines provided the materials for a theological training that was required for ministers of the church to practice their craft and thus serve the state. Hence, this meant that theology as a science would only find a home within other disciplinary shelters that had already established 'scientific' status. In the Enlightenment university history, languages and philosophy could claim this status. What made the situation rather precarious was the strong criticisms of theology from the very disciplines where it sought refuge: history and philosophy. Kant would only tolerate theology as the practical working out of the truths available in philosophy via universal reason in a transcendental mode, or in Fichte's case, an idealist philosophical mode.[7] Later 'philosophies' would simply replicate this pattern: phenomenology, Marxism, feminism, postmodernism, cultural studies and so on. Likewise, positivist history demanded theology be reigned in by its methods and findings – exemplified by Harnack and Strauss. Only recently is the bible escaping its reductivist positivist historical imprisoning.[8] Theology can of course learn from these disciplines – to claim otherwise for a Thomist would be an irrational argument, but, rather it cannot be ruled and conformed to these disciplines. Admittedly, judging the dividing line here is a very complex and difficult matter.

Third, given the institutional weight of science within the new research universities, many of theology's defenders tried to defend its field of truth in terms of this high-status discipline of scientific reason. Michael J. Buckley has argued in *At the Origins of Modern Atheism*, that theologians too often tried to defend theology from scientific criticism on scientific grounds or in purely philosophical terms, rather than Christological (or experiential) grounds.[9] This eventually had the effect of assimilating theology to science, and in this process, theology lost sight of its own unique method and object: 'Theology gives way to Cartesianism, which gives way to Newtonian mechanics. The great argument, the only evidence for theism, is design, and experimental physics reveals that design.'[10] This trajectory follows through post-Newtonian physics to atomic physics. The roots of atheism were partly planted by theologians, who failed to be theological enough, and thus reaped the bitter sweet apple that spelt their disciplinary demise.

In sum, modernity began to render and reconstruct theology within the grand-narratives of philosophy (Kant, Hobbes, Locke, Rousseau), history (Marx and Hegel), sociology (Comte, Durkheim, Weber) and science (both the natural and social sciences – Dawkin and Freud respectively). Within these narratives the world is best understood without God, and when God makes an appearance 'it' is positioned as the unspoken presupposition of freedom, a quick setting social cement, a heavy dose of opium, an out-moded National Health Service-like crutch, a big phallic father – and a variety of other idols.

Let us return to MacIntyre's project. For MacIntyre what united modernity and postmodernity was their rejection of the Aristotelian heritage and any underlying teleology. Eventually all that could be agreed was that people ought to be free to agree or disagree, and the birth of the modern nation state and liberal democracy was its social and political counterpart. However, with no common *telos* even this minimal consensus would eventually come into question. Nietzsche's insights were inevitable, given the irresolvable lacunae within the Enlightenment project that replaced the *telos* of the common good with the formal requirement of human freedom. Nietzsche saw that there could be no real foundation for ethics and consequently celebrated the will to power, which was always the repressed truth within the Enlightenment trajectory. For MacIntyre's own argument to work, he develops a further critique of the postmodern or what he calls the Genealogical 'tradition'.[11] As with modernity, MacIntyre is perhaps overly negative about postmodernity, failing to acknowledge some important achievements (e. g. women's suffrage in modernity and postmodernity's gesture towards transcendence). This negativity is not logically necessary to the position I am defending, nor I think to MacIntyre's position. The third tradition from which MacIntyre can reveal and narrate the genuine shortcomings of the Enlightenment and Genealogical traditions is Thomism, mediated by Pope Leo XIII's *Aeterni Patris*. Hence, at the end of the book, MacIntyre makes a startling suggestion. If moderns really value and seek true plurality, this would be better facilitated by 'rival universities':

> each modelled on, but improving upon, its own best predecessors, the Thomist perhaps upon Paris in 1272, the genealogist [postmodernist] upon Vincennes in 1968 [and one might add, the modern, upon Berlin in 1810]. And thus the wider society would be confronted with the claims

of rival universities, each advancing its own enquiries in its own terms and each securing the type of agreement necessary to ensure the progress and flourishing of its enquiries by its own set of exclusions and prohibitions, formal and informal. But then also required [*sic* – according to whom?] would be a set of institutionalized forums in which the debate between rival types of enquiry was afforded rhetorical expression.[12]

MacIntyre excludes other religions from his rival universities, but one can expound on MacIntyre's basic structure to include other religious universities, such as those that exist in the United States, Israel, Egypt, Turkey, Rome and other countries.[13] I shall return to MacIntyre's important suggestion regarding rival universities, but I now need to briefly relate the development of the field of 'religious studies' within this narrative. I have already noted the disciplinary eclipse of theology so that it becomes subsumed under the authority of other disciplines and precisely this, along with a number of other important factors, is the story of the emergence of the field of religious studies.

The European Empire led to many disciplinary construals of 'religion', of interest 'at home' and abroad. For example we find: Orientalism, knowledge for the purpose of domination and control, so well portrayed by Edward Said; Enlightenment study, so well articulated by its founding father and the founding father of comparative religions, Friedrich Max Muller – and the subsequent and further divisions of this study into philosophy, languages, ritual and anthropology, texts and literature, and in Weber's hands, sociological theory and so on. These traditions of enquiry were certainly part of the Enlightenment narrative. Indeed, the very notion of different 'religions', related to each other as species of a common genus, was itself a seventeenth-century invention, as Peter Harrison has so persuasively argued.[14] The construction of such a field ('religion') viewed from a perch above any specific religion is a project that is partly located in the Enlightenment's refusal to acknowledge the particularity of Christian revelation. Accepting this particularity would mean that all of history would require theological narration. Rejecting this particularity would require the 'creation' of an alternative (equally particular) secular history whereby different religions were organized within the Enlightenment's own overarching narrative and embedded within the categories of modernity's fields of discourse, rather than taking seriously the different organizations of time, space, history and power within the various religions. Such a taxonomy also failed to attend to the epistemological pre-requisites required for comprehension specified by some of the religions under examination.

It is time to draw together the threads of this brief narrative. First, the truth of the subject matter of theology within the modern university is easily conflated with the truth of the subject matter of various humanistic and social scientific fields, in part because the truth of God has been relegated to the status of private choice, rather like a penchant for cream cakes. Clearly such private preferences should not interfere with the public square. In the thirteenth century institutions of learning could assume God as the context of all learning. In the twenty-first century in Western Europe they cannot, or freely choose not to. Second, religious studies grows and flourishes under many disciplinary shelters including one with its own name. However, in its own shelter there is heated debate as to what precisely constitutes the uniqueness of the discipline with attractive bids to become assimilated to neo-phenemonology (Gavin Flood), cultural studies with a healthy dose of anthropology (Timothy Fitzgerald), feminist studies (Ursula King), scientific study (Donald Wiebe), and most ingeniously, with theology (David Ford). The other contributors to this collection of course add to this list in differing ways. Some of these bids are mutually exclusive, but certainly not all. Wiebe, for example, definitely wants to be rid of theology within the university. Ford wants them to live together in harmony, and even cross-fertilize. Fitzgerald's space for 'theology' is ambiguous in his otherwise carefully argued thesis.[15] But these debates are protected and encouraged: since inter-disciplinarity is funded by research councils the inter-disciplinary nature of religious studies is usually seen as its great attraction. Third, the question of truth that the religions raise are usually secondary to these other disciplinary interests that are dealing with them, or truth is dealt with in terms alien to the traditions being studied. This is precisely what we might expect: modernity's structural requiem to religious traditions; first Christianity, and now the world religions. Is this OK, and if not, where might the questions of truth these traditions raise be dealt with within the academy? This question has a shadow side: should theology be departing from the university and, paraphrasing Hamlet's famous words, be making its way back to a nunnery?

## Whose theology, which religion? Some concluding remarks

There is a nice irony within modernity – its Achilles heel perhaps. It seeks to be tolerant and open to plurality. MacIntrye's argument shows why it indeed enacts the opposite and it is only tolerant of those who agree with it. However, there is scope to argue that by the criterion of the modern university it should be open to intellectual plurality and indeed, should be hospitable to MacIntyre's suggestion for the setting up of 'rival universities'. From my Thomist position, in the English context, this would take me into an argument for the state funding of a Catholic university, not dissimilar to the state funding of Catholic schools. Admittedly, in England such a project is unlikely, but it is still worth flagging for the issues it raises.[16] In such an imaginary institution, let us call it St Thomas, one might expect three things, all relating to the issues I've been looking at.

First, theology and philosophy would be central to the entire curriculum, seeking to build a holistic and unified Christian intellectual culture, so that every discipline would be attentitive to the final telos of the human community. This would involve both methodological, substantitive and moral questions and these would vary enormously from discipline to discipline – and possibly even be irrelevant in some (as a colleague from pure maths has suggested, but I have no way of telling with my mathematical illiteracy). And in this conversation, theology would also be subject to questioning. Each discipline, including theology, might begin to learn its own lawful limits in such a conversation, underpinned by a basic fundamental trust in truth, rationality and the goodness of the created world. Such a programmatic sketch is developed in John Paul II's 'Ex corde ecclesiae' as well as 'Fides et ratio' (On Catholic Universities, 1990; Faith and Reason, 1998). Critics are right to fear clerical control freaks taking over religious intellectual institutions, but there is no good reason to base such fears from these papal documents that provide good arguments and reasoned justification.

This enterprise would also begin a task that started with Aristotle, got institutionalized in the thirteenth century at the University of Paris, but never quite attained its goal: the unity of the intellectual disciplines in service to God and thus, to the telos of the human good. In modern parlance: the institutional vision. Prudence Allen argues that the University of Paris's experiment would lead to a disastrous outcome, despite its own intentions, due to the poor implementation of a rich vision of an organic whole. In the practices of the University of Paris the parts were not held together. The four faculties of arts, theology, medicine and law were designed to operate in harmony, in the service of God, the church and civic society. However

once the institutional separation of branches of knowledge was made, a slow but steady rupture in the unity of knowledge began to occur.

Controversial questions began to bring the different faculties into conflict with one another. Ultimately, university education became more and more fragmented until philosophy became cut off from theology, medicine, or law.[17]

Eventually, Allen concludes as follows:

This process of fragmentation has continued to the present time. Universities now consist of a plethora of disciplines all vying for the central place in the determination of truth. Aristotle had correctly argued for the need to make significant distinctions in the search for truth. However, the institutionalization of Aristotle turned these distinctions into rigidly defined areas of knowledge that made a unified approach to the person nearly impossible. The shadow of the institutionalization of Aristotle haunts the corridors of the contemporary academic world like a ghost from the thirteenth-century University of Paris.[18]

Second, the question of truth in religious studies might at last emerge. Central to the study of any religion within a theological religious studies (paralleling what I have called a theological theology) is the assessment of the claims being made within say Hinduism, Buddhism, Islam, New Age movements and so on. While critics might rightly fear the emergence of Christian Orientalism, there is no logical necessity for such a phenomenon.[19] What is genuinely tolerant and pluralistic here is that the claims of Others are taken with proper intellectual seriousness, rather than simply bracketed off or assimilated and assessed by disciplines alien to the religion making such claims. This is not to say that historical, sociological, literary and other questions are irrelevant. They are clearly not. However, in imaginary St Thomas, they become related to a more holisitic engagement between two traditions of enquiry employing all the various disciplinary tools that are to hand.

Third, MacIntyre predicted that modernity's universities would be characterized by two marks: the growth of management and control over procedures; and the growth of subjects directly related to military and governmental requirements for pragmatic ends: power and wealth. Such an alternative university as St Thomas is well placed to ask the question of the meaning and purpose of knowledge and the university within society and to generate an important debate that has hardly begun.

Fourth, if as a reader you do not like the idea of a Christian University, shred or shelve that part of this chapter, but my arguments related to the disciplines of theology and religious studies still stand. Indeed, John Webster's critique of non-theological theology entirely neglects such a utopian turn as I have taken, but I think the logic of his argument is under-developed in this respect.

I hope to have argued that theology and its relation to religious studies is best promoted by moments of antagonism, an important 'versus' within certain sorts of institutional arrangements; but also moments of cooperation 'and' flourishing within alternative institutional arrangements. One thing is certain, if theology is not theological, it should abandon its name.

## Notes

[1] John Webster, *Theological Theology*. Oxford: Clarendon Press, 1998.

[2] I've tried to present this picture in more complexity in my recent book, *Theology in the Public Square*. Oxford: Blackwell, 2005. For a broader picture related to Muslim, Jewish and Christian universities and colleges see James Arthur, *Faith and Secularisation in Religious Colleges and Universities*. London and New York: Routledge, 2006.

[3] John Horton & Susan Mendus (eds), *After MacIntyre: Critical Perspectives on the Work of Alasdair MacIntyre*. Oxford: Polity Press, 1994, p. 3.

[4] Paul J. Griffiths, *Religious Reading: The Place of Reading in the Practice of Religion*. Oxford: Oxford University Press, 1999, p. 68.

[5] For the situation of the German universities at the time, see Daniel Fallon, *The German University*, Boulder: Colorado University Press, 1980.

[6] In 1808 Schleiermacher published *Thoughts on German Universities from a German Point of View* and in 1810, *Brief Outline on the Study of Theology*, trans. Terrence N. Tice. Richmond, Virginia: John Knox Press, 1966 [1811]. See also Hans Frei, *Types of Christian Theology*. New Haven: Yale University Press, 1992, where he carefully charts aspects of the debate generated by Schleiermacher's proposals in 'Appendix A: Theology in the University', pp. 95–132.

[7] See Kant, 'The Conflict of the Faculties', in *Religion and Rational Theology*, trans. Allen W. Wood & George di Giovanni. Cambridge: Cambridge University Press, 1996, pp. 233–239.

[8] See Stephen F. Fowl, 'Introduction' in ed. Stephen F. Fowl, *The Theological Interpretation of Scripture*. Oxford: Blackwell, 1997, pp. xii–xxx with the excellent overview of New Testament scholarship as falling into three camps: historical critical (Philip Davies, Werner Jeanrond, Heikki Räisänen), Christian theological (Peter Stuhlmacher, Brevard Childs, Francis Watson), and postmodern (David Clines, Anthony Thiselton, Stephen Moore).

[9] Michael J. Buckley, *At the Origins of Modern Atheism*. New Haven: Yale University Press, 1987, pp. 65–66, makes clear how theologians like Lessius and Mersenne rebutted atheism as if it were a 'philosophic stance towards life' rather than a 'rejection of Jesus Christ as the supreme presence of god [*sic*] in history'. I do not share Buckley's sympathy for 'experiential' grounds.

[10] Buckley, *At the Origins*, p. 202.

[11] Admittedly, this criticism is only focused upon Foucault and Deleuze, and de Mann's unmasking, and is hardly an exhaustive engagement with postmodern texts. Milbank, in this respect, is more thorough and more theological: *Theology and Social Theory*. Oxford: Blackwell, 1990, pp. 278–326.

[12] *Three Rival Versions of Moral Enquiry*. London: Duckworth, 1990, p. 234, my additional brackets.

[13] See James Arthur, *Faith and Secularisation in Religious Colleges and Universities*. London: Routledge, 2006.

[14] Peter Harrison, *'Religion' and the Religions in the English Enlightenment*. Cambridge: Cambridge University Press, 1990, and also Timothy Fitzgerald, *The Ideology of Religious Studies*. Oxford: Oxford University Press, 2000. Wilfred Cantwell Smith, *The Meaning and End of Religion*. New York: Macmillan, 1962, pp. 15–30, also shows the modern construction of the notion of 'religion'. However, Smith perpetuates this reification of modernity in his problematic notion of 'faith' as the common generic 'essence' of each tradition. See my: 'A Christian Reflection on some problems with discerning "God" in the World Religions', *Dialogue and Alliance*, 5 (1), 1991, pp. 4–17.

[15] Donald Wiebe, *The Politics of Religious Studies: The Continuing Conflict with Theology in the Academy*. Basingstoke: Macmillan, 1999; David Ford, *A Long Rumour of Wisdom: Redescribing Theology*. Cambridge: Cambridge University Press, 1999; Timothy Fitzgerald, *The Ideology of Religious Studies*. Oxford: Oxford University Press, 2000.

[16] An ecumenical Christian university, like Liverpool Hope University, is more likely.

[17] Prudence Allen R. S. M., *The Concept of Woman: The Aristotelian Revolution 750 BC–AD 1250*. Quebec: Eden Press, 1985, p. 417.

[18] Allen, *The Concept of Woman*, p. 419.

[19] I cannot further develop these remarks here, but have tried to address some of the issues in *The Meeting of Religions and the Trinity*. Edinburgh: T & T Clark, 2000.

Chapter 4

# Theology as the Past and Future of Religious Studies
## An Incarnational Approach

Erik Borgman and Stephan van Erp

## Introduction

The debate about 'religious studies versus theology' is said to be a symptom of a crisis of a different order than the debate seems to suggest. The American philosopher Peter Ochs has positioned this debate within the framework of a problem on a larger scale: 'the still unresolved relation of the Western academy to the civilizations it ought to serve, [. . .] [and to] religious traditions in particular'.[1] Ochs has characterized this relation as 'colonialism writ small'. The academy shows an unselfconscious tendency to act as if its categories and propositions, bound to a particular context and point of view, are part of the (religious) realities we deal with. In fact, we are imposing them on these realities. Both theology and religious studies, according to Ochs, manifest this tendency.

In our view, the current academic view of theology manifests a particular case of this 'colonialism writ small'. Theology is often defined as the study of one particular religion while religious studies is supposed to cover all religions in principle and the idea of religion in general. Furthermore, theology is seen as the study of a religious tradition from the inside, adopting and applying the normative viewpoints of the religious tradition it studies, while religious studies is regarded as the study of religion from the outside without a normative or doctrinal bias. The consequence of these distinctions between theology and religious studies is that the field of religious studies and its separation of facts and norms seems to have adapted to academia's demands and as such could be regarded the true heir of theology in a post-Christian and post-colonial situation.

Against this idea, we would like to propose not to consider theology as a biased form of religious studies, and in fact not to consider it as a form of religious studies at all. Theology does not have religion as its object, at least not – following a distinction made by Thomas Aquinas – as its *material* object. Instead of religion, theology studies the whole of reality from the viewpoint of a religious adherence to God. In other words, theology is substantially informed by the history and practices of particular religious traditions. It follows the religious dynamics instead of colonizing it. This entails that religious traditions must be studied, as they are in religious studies, but theology's aim is to articulate rationally the presence and transcendence of the God and gods these religious traditions address, trying to reflect on how this presence addresses itself to people, and how this is manifested in their lives.

Our thesis is that theology should be an integral part of religious studies, in as far as religious communities are embodiments of theologies. At the same time, religious studies should be 'succeeded' by theology, in as far as theology studies the embodied practices of faith in the world. In this sense, theology is the future of religious studies, because it reasons about the engagements with the world, of which not only religion but religious studies also are an expression. This is an important contribution theology could make to contemporary post-Christian, multi-cultural and multi-religious society. It would not have to be a form of religious colonialism or imperialism of reality, because a theology in the world, as any other academic discipline, is part of the university, and therefore of the broader cultural, societal and political debates about who we are, where we are, where we should be going and what truth could guide us there.

In this chapter, we will try to illustrate and account for this role of theology in the world, but only after we have described the theological context from which it emerged as a critical proposal.[2] Therefore, (1) we will describe the current situation of theology in the Netherlands and, in our opinion, the imminent failure of academic research, if theology will be all too strictly divided from religious studies. (2) Within this situation, we would like to propose an incarnational theology, which is a theology *sub ratione dei* that transcends and succeeds the emic/etic-distinction between theology and religious studies. (3) Next, we will illustrate this theological proposal with an example from a research project, which has been executed at the Heyendaal Institute for Interdisciplinary Research, in Nijmegen, the Netherlands, and at King's College, London.

At the Heyendaal Institute in Nijmegen, we have been developing research on the interface of theology and other clusters of academic disciplines. In this article, we will give the example of theology and the medical sciences. Its aim is not to develop a theology *of* medicine nor to develop a perspective on medical practices from a specific religious perspective. Instead, it aims to find and rediscover theology *in* medicine by locating religious views, understanding their relationship with religious traditions, and recognizing and furthering theological discussions in medical practice and the medical sciences based on these religious views, that emerge within the field of medicine itself. (4) Next, we explain how these point to the specific character of modernity as both secular and religious, forever at the same time secularizing and religionizing. (5) We reflect on the way in which we can deal with this situation as not just the situation of religion and theology, but as a religious and theological situation in which God as ultimate truth and goodness is present as the One who is addressing the situation and is searched for in the situation. We end with a brief conclusion.

## Theology versus religious studies: fault lines in the Dutch theological landscape

### a. Institutional (re-)allocations

In the past few years, a strong division between theology and religious studies has had significant consequences for the Dutch institutional landscape of the academic study of religion and faith. The attempt to merge three faculties for Roman Catholic theology – Dutch theological faculties are confessionally bound – has failed dramatically. The end result of a long process of negotiations between the three faculties of Nijmegen, Tilburg and Utrecht was, instead of one faculty, two faculties of theology, one faculty of religious studies and one department for religious studies and theology in a faculty of humanities. In that process, ideas on the differences between theology and religious studies have played a major role. The day, 1 January 2007 marks the start of a new ecclesially governed faculty for Roman Catholic theology in the Netherlands. The University of Tilburg closed its faculty of theology. In its place, a new canonical faculty of Catholic theology was founded, with branches in Utrecht and in Tilburg. At the same time, the Tilburg faculty of humanities incorporated part of the old theological faculty in a department for religious studies *and* theology, which has no formal relationship with the Roman Catholic Church. At the University of Nijmegen, a new faculty of religious studies has been founded on 1 July 2006. That university also kept its faculty of theology, which shortly after lost its canonical status. So, the intended foundation of a single Roman-Catholic faculty in the Netherlands, led to several institutions for religious studies separated from the ones for theology. Consequently, the profiling of these academic fields has been so competitive that the study of religion suffered greatly from these institutional divisions.

At the protestant faculties, they have known a distinction between *simplex ordo* and *duplex ordo* since the nineteenth century. The confessional faculties of Kampen and the Free University of Amsterdam followed the *simplex ordo* system. The state universities Utrecht, Leiden and Groningen followed the *duplex ordo* system, in which the so-called ecclesial theological sub-disciplines, like systematic and practical theology, were taught in a specific master programme for students who wanted to aspire to work for the church.[3] This has led to a marginalization of theology at state faculties, but at the same time these faculties saw an increase in – albeit it mostly implicit and unwanted – confessionally inspired philosophy and history of religion. Moreover, it has become increasingly difficult to account for the study of biblical texts and the history of the church within a separate faculty of religious studies, in contrast with the dividing and merging of religious studies in the humanities.

All these organizational developments have been accompanied with methodological considerations on the academic status of theology, its position within the university, the relationship between philosophical and confessional theology, and the relationship between theology and religious studies.[4] These debates on the status of theology were not new, but have been going on for decades, not least because of the Dutch confessional and denominational diversity of theological faculties, and the protestant division between a secular and an ecclesial curriculum.[5] Due to the foundation of new faculties of theology and religious studies, these debates have entered a new phase. After a period of drawing strict divisions between the two fields of study, future reflections will hopefully concentrate on shared tasks and collaborations between theology and religious studies, and on the interdisciplinarity and cohesion of sub-disciplines. These reflections are necessary to reformulate a field of research and education that has been so gravely partitioned and fragmented in recent times. Despite the recent institutional divisions, the emerged diversity of approaches and disciplines might offer new opportunities to further the tasks of theology and religious studies. To make that happen, former prejudices and rigid divisions as a consequence of faculty profiling might prove to be unhelpful however. Instead, further reflection is needed on how theology and religious studies share an engagement with understanding faith and religion in a multi-disciplinary and multi-faith society.

## b. The problem of strictly dividing theology and religious studies

The fact that there are many ways in which science, culture and religion are connected may have encouraged the discussion on theological method, but it has also confronted future education and research with important and as yet unresolved questions of content. What, for example, are the consequences of the radical split between theology and religious studies for the connection between theology on the one hand, and anthropology on the other? The connection between theology and anthropology, which has been conquered and studied intensively since the second half of the twentieth century, is at risk of being neglected when anthropology is perceived as being only part of religious studies and irrelevant for theology. Another example: To which field does moral theology belong? Will Catholic moral theologians at departments of religious studies have to bracket their faith and methodically limit their reflections to a methodological agnostic viewpoint?[6] Does the reduction to a historical or empirical approach do justice to the narrative, traditional and spiritual aspects of current moral issues? Is it true that the decisive and foundational arguments in moral theology are merely secular anyway nowadays? Yet another example: What are the consequences for exegesis when its connection to the history of theology and dogmatics is severed? Do cognitive and linguistic textual analysis allow for reflections on the theologies that lie behind intertextuality, editorial changes of texts and translations, or the influence of the theology of the gospel writers, the formation of a canon or bible translations on modern religion?[7]

These are but a few of the urgent methodological questions, which have arisen after the institutional division of religious studies and theology. They appear to indicate a fundamental yet unaccounted break with the recent past. The rise of phenomenology, anthropology and the social sciences and the position these have received in the field of religious studies, has caused severe problems for modern theology, which has become intertwined with these so-called non-theological disciplines. These problems have been intensified by the persistent use of dichotomies like internal versus external (or the related twin concepts of 'emic' and 'etic'), prescriptive versus descriptive, authority versus freedom and normative versus neutral.[8]

The *de facto* and methodological division between religious studies and theology tends to force theology back into a position from which it had distanced or in some cases completely freed itself in recent decades: that of an ecclesially bound, normative and authoritative-prescriptive discipline. Despite many criticisms and negative qualifications of these dichotomies that are supposed to theoretically support the difference between theology and religious studies, its representation and the development of theories in the Netherlands, are still determined by these crude and one-dimensional distinctions.[9] They have guided the separation of religious scholars and subsequently the separation has intensified the big yawning gulf between theology and religious studies.

## World and memory: an incarnational theology

If theology differs from the study of religion and is regarded as the study of reality as a whole in view of particular religious traditions, then the question arises how to reason and to speak theologically about reality, life, the world, power and politics, the human person, etc. within the academy. Does theology articulate a particular or traditional religious viewpoint in communication with others, or does it rationally (re-)construct such a viewpoint through the recognition of a singularity or unicity amidst shared views and common interests?[10] These questions are far more urgent than the issue of what can be regarded as specifically theological.[11] To our opinion, theologians could be less concerned with the demarcation of their field of study or the identity of their own tradition, and more with the world in which their ideas originate and to which they return them. This does not entail an abdication of theology or the church, and more specifically of Christian doctrine. On the contrary, we would like to argue that an engagement with the world has been the core interest of Christian doctrine, and it is through this engagement that theology is expected to find its incarnational authenticity.[12] It is this incarnational approach we would like to explore here tentatively.

According to David Tracy's definition of systematic theology, it has as its 'major concern the re-presentation, the reinterpretation of what is assumed to be the ever-present disclosive and transformative power of the *particular religious tradition* to which the theologian belongs'.[13] Similarly, Gavin D'Costa has argued for the place of theology within the university as a *tradition-specific* form of intellectual enquiry.[14] The particularity or specificity of a religious tradition emerges and changes through its ongoing relationship with God and the world that according to the Psalmist is God's, including the people with different world views that live in it (Psalm 24: 1). Consequently, questions as to what defines a religious tradition or how to distinguish between an insider's and outsider's point of view are continuously at stake in theology. Not only because the perspective of the theologian changes due to a changing cultural context, but also and more importantly because the community and its beliefs and practices she studies, are changing as well, and will continue to change due to that ongoing relation with God and God's ongoing concern with the world and the histories of people that inhabit it.

Theology should therefore be more than the intellectual articulation of a specific religious tradition from an insider's point of view, or its proclamation. Instead, it should also accommodate the reflection on emerging doctrines of faith, both inside and outside a particular religious tradition. Not only to critically enter into dialogue with different doctrines in order to respectfully and peacefully coexist in this world with others, but also to acknowledge that the divine truth dwells in all that is and that this is a given which reveals itself especially when particularities or individualities have lost their self-evidence, are violated, or appear to be insufficient in themselves.

To be able to critically recognize and reflect upon such a revelation, fundamental questions concerning methods and sources will continue to be on the theological agenda. Not because the list of sources – scripture, tradition, contemporary culture, experience – is as yet incomplete or needs to be updated. Not because theological methods are insufficiently accounted for, or incompatible with other academic disciplines. But to seek an understanding of the paradoxical fact that there is no set of ideas or doctrinal system that could be presented as a strictly demarcated insider's point of view, while no meaning or value is without a specific history but bears the memory of identifiable others. Not the history of religion or an a-theological type of religious studies, but an incarnational theology is the vital intellectual participation in that process of memory and representation, because it originates in and furthers the commitment with the stuff that religious doctrines are made on: God's engagement with the history of people and the remembrance of those who are connected through the history of hope and faith in a future when things will be better than they are.

## Finding faith in medicine: incarnation as practice

### a. Salvation between theology and medicine

To illustrate theology's engagement with the world and the memory of meaning, we will present an exemplary case. The example comes from current theological research into the relationship between religion and medicine, aiming to rediscover, rephrase and reconsider Christian doctrine within the realm of medical practice.

How to study the relationship between medicine and religion and faith? Traditionally, research on the relationship between religion and medicine was either anthropological, describing which specific religious traditions and practices are at work in medical practices, or ethical, evaluating the norms and limits of human care, compassion and responsibility. The number of academic publications on the subject of religion and medicine has grown exponentially in recent years. A selection of searches in the medical science database Pubmed/Medline on query combinations such as 'spirituality and health' or 'religion and health', returns thousands of publications, mainly from the last decade.[15] The scholars who are performing these research projects are mainly medical anthropologists and psychologists, who generally do not work within faculties of theology or religious studies.[16] The overall characteristic in current (mainly Anglo-American) research in religion and medicine is the instrumental approach of religion in relation to medicine. The main approach to religion and medicine is descriptive, the main focus is functional: where and how do people rely on religious ideas and religious practices in medicine – does prayer cure? – and what is their contribution to the process of curing or coping with what is incurable.[17]

Theologians have as yet entered the field of religion and medicine by claiming that any account of meaning in medicine was their terrain, and some even have critically suggested that the medical realm needs more awareness of the true responsibility and meaning of medical care. Theology then, it is suggested, could raise such an awareness or should even be regarded the guardian of true salvation, which at its best finds a certain expression in faithful medical care. Stanley Hauerwas for example has argued that any account of salvation necessarily includes questions of health, illness and disease, but according to him that does not imply that medicine can or ever should become the agency of salvation. He blames church and theology for failing to locate wherein salvation lies: in the sanctification of communal compassion for the sufferers, which is not defined by the will to survive, but by 'the truthful resignation to the givenness of life in the presence of God'. The regrettable consequence has been according to Hauerwas that many today seek an individual salvation through medicine instead of true salvation through communal solidarity with those who suffer.[18]

Hauerwas might be right in expressing his concerns about medicine itself becoming a salvific faith in contemporary culture by making claims about salvation that differ radically from Christian faith. The consequence, however, of that observation would be to support a strict divide between theology and religious studies. It would lead to a critical role of theology over against religious studies. Theology in Hauerwas' case critically approves of, but mostly dismisses, the situation that religious studies can only observe and describe. As if theology is not part of the religion religious studies study, and religious studies and the religions they study are not part of the reality theology views *sub ratione Dei*.

### b. The practice of theodicies

A different approach to the study of faith and medicine could profit from the insights of sociologist Max Weber (1864–1920). According to him, to understand doctrines of salvation one should analyse the ways societies respond to suffering. He placed such emphasis on the importance of suffering to a culture that he considered the whole character and style of different societies to be determined by their religious understanding of suffering, by what he calls their 'theodicies'. In his view, religions offer theodicies not simply as abstract solutions to intellectual puzzles, but as programs for action, or as substitutes for it.[19] Weber used the term 'theodicy' in a much broader sense than is usual. He did not confine his understanding of theodicy to the classical problem of how suffering can exist in the world if God is both omnipotent and all-loving, although he knew that this problem has been an important part of the human struggle to find a meaning for existence. Instead, he used the concept of theodicy to refer more extensively to the ways in which religions interpret the many inequalities that all people observe and also to the ways in which, based on those interpretations, religions create and legitimize different forms of society. In his *Sociology of Religion*, Weber first described the classical issue: 'the more the development tends toward the conception of a transcendental unitary God who is universal, the more there arises the problem of how the extraordinary power of such a god may be reconciled with the imperfection of the world that he has created and rules over.'

According to Weber, the human experience of inequalities is the problem factor that determines religious evolution and the need for salvation. He showed that the modern rejection of the God-idea was not motivated by scientific arguments, but by the difficulty in reconciling the idea of providence with the injustice and imperfection of the social order. In Weber's argument, all people experience great inequalities, which carry with them much suffering, unequally distributed. Why is this the case? According to Weber, religions pour explanation and meaning (i.e. theodicies) into the gaps of commonplace experience, and these theodicies create very different forms of society and of social behaviour. From the adopted theodicy

of a particular religion flow social consequences that give their characteristic shape and actions (or lack of actions) to society. Therefore, the
question what theodicy is, is of central importance, because theodicies are
embodied in current medical practices and forms of health care and have
great consequences on medical decision-making.

## c. Suffering and the call for theology

Weber's case proves that any understanding or reformulation of the origins and motives of medicine and public health is primarily an exercise in
understanding implicit and explicit theological views in contemporary culture and society. To recognize these views as the starting point for understanding the emerging theological views in medical practice and theory, a
phenomenological description of experiences of and views on illness and
disease is needed, so that these can be analytically compared and contrasted with theology. In doing so, the hypothesis is that it will become
clear that before and beyond phenomenology, theology has provided a
tradition of reflection on the hermeneutics of experience, which relates
the experience of suffering to culture, community and interpretation. This
tradition should not as much be presented within the medical realm as a
*depositum* of answers to questions of meaning that arise in situations of suffering, just as medical answers are not. Especially when addressing the idea
of suffering, which concerns not just the individual body, but also matters
of personhood and intersubjectivity, it will become manifest that neither a
neutral description of suffering by religious studies, nor a theology of individual experience, faith or mere opinion will suffice to understand suffering, let alone to confidently support certain medical decisions or further
the reflection on them.[20] Instead, the combination of phenomenological
description and a hermeneutics of experience will show that health and
medicine, besides dealing with curing, caring and alleviating pain, are also
concerned with ideas and views on the world, relationships, redemption
and transcendence, in other words: with doctrines of faith.

Furthermore, in the case of health and medicine, the articulation of
the communality of experiences of suffering is an urgent task. This is not
only the case because dealing with illness and disease requires transparent communication between doctor, nurses and patients, or because health
and medicine have a cultural impact. The influence of politics and policies of hospitals and nursing homes on medical caring and curing and
their responses to medical consumerism is also important for furthering
cultural and communal awareness in the medical sciences.[21] Nowadays, an

increasing number of medical faculties appoint professors of public health. Medical anthropologists have recently been developing an ethnography of experience, articulating that suffering is a shared and interpersonal experience.[22] Theologians and other scholars in the field of religion are well equipped to take part in this debate. Through the recognition of patterns of meaning in medical practice, they could offer their expertise on the historical and socio-cultural meaning or, perhaps better, religious views on the meaninglessness of pain and suffering, and of sickness and health.

Entering the debate on the meaning of pain and suffering, and of health and medical care, is perhaps the most important contribution of theology to an interdisciplinary conversation about medicine. Apart from sharing concerns about individualism, therapeuticism, instrumentalism and consumerism, theology and religious studies have their specific tasks in this conversation, if only to articulate the givenness of life and the politics of belonging to the people of God. But the specificity of the theological conversation with medicine does not have to limit itself to a specific narrative, if 'narrative' is defined as the concrete history and identity of scripture and tradition.[23] It could also add to the conversation a certain sensibility for that which Rowan Williams has described as 'what brings to speech that absence which makes possible the shifting space of prayer and witness that is Christian life.'[24]

Responding to that sensibility and confronted with the instrumentalism of both theological and medical reasoning and research into the effects of spirituality, an incarnational theology could speak the unspeakable, and be the voice of the sick and the sufferers. Not through the resignation to either the positivism of science by following the same patterns of approach and achievement, or the fatalism of a misunderstood concept of spirituality without resistance, but through the search for an understanding of suffering as a shared – i.e. historical, social and cultural – experience and through interpersonal compassionate presence. That way, medical practice could be recognized as one of these public spaces both recognizing suffering and compassionate care, in which traces of the divine can be encountered: places where theology emerges.

## Theological rationality and publicness

Peter Ochs argued that 'scholars of religious studies *or* theology practice a kind of "colonialism writ small" when they remove their subject matter from its lived, societal contexts and re-situate it in conceptual worlds of their own devising'.[25] Using the example of medicine, we have tried to relate religious faith and doctrines to the world in which they emerge by tracing them in supposedly secularized contexts. In this way we have countered the modern tendency to see religion as a separate sphere of human behaviour, or as a distinctive way of experiencing reality that depends on the decision to attribute religious meaning to it. This overtly theological approach is often criticized as 'colonialism writ large', as subjecting modern reality to the categories of a religious tradition, which has become foreign to it since secularization. However, views on the relation of religion to modern secularization and rationalization are strongly debated and rightly so.

To clarify this, we return to Max Weber, because we seem to be living in the world he predicted at the beginning of the twentieth century.[26] Our culture is thoroughly rationalized. There is no encompassing worldview, religious or otherwise, giving meaning and coherence to reality and human life as a part of it, nor do people feel a need for such a worldview. They see and evaluate their lives in terms of ends they want to achieve and the means available to get to these ends. This is what Weber calls 'rationalisation'. This rationalization of our lives in terms of means and ends has brought us a historically unique level of prosperity, has given us a life expectancy previously unknown and has brought cultural goods formerly reserved for the elite within the reach of many. At the same time, however, contemporary societies are characterized by a high level of dissatisfaction and frustration. In the midst of rationality and prosperity, people experience a fundamental lack and long for a life that is good in a way that cannot be captured in terms of using rational means to achieve a reachable end. In a rationalized culture, this makes it very difficult for them to articulate and discuss what this good life is, and one could argue that this is the major crisis of the contemporary Western culture. In Max Weber's analysis, modern society thus becomes an 'iron cage' that calls forth the will to escape, but from which such an escape is impossible.

We would like to argue that this accounts for the present religious situation. On the one hand – and contrary to some influential recent opinions – there is a continuing secularization, understood as both the growing insignificance of traditional religious beliefs and their institutional expressions for society and the increasing irrelevance for individuals. On the other hand, there is a 'return' or 'resurgence' of the religious in unexpected forms and ways, and a social, existential and intellectual turn to religion and religious traditions in the human search for guidance, identity and understanding. This is the modern condition in general. People in modernity are in a continuous process of losing their religious ways of experiencing the world as their world by dealing with it and inhabiting it, but at the same time develop new ways to deal with the ever recurring, ever new question how to respond to life as it is given, how to understand this givenness and how make this given life as a good life. In other words, modernity is both secular and religious, both secularizing and religionizing. This means that, counter to Weber's own expectations, theological topics remain current in modern, rationalized societies and even tend become more urgent. Questions about where we are going, who we are and how we can deal with the trials and tribulations in our personal and collective histories gather a new momentum in societies that become ever more rationalized structures in which individuals are on their own in finding a way of life that satisfies both their needs and their longings.[27]

The problem is that although theological questions remain relevant in modernity, or even become relevant anew, they cannot be decided in the same way as disputes on scientific insights are decided. To Weber, this means that the rational thing to do is to negotiate a compromise between groups committed to different value systems, worldviews, metaphysical or religious convictions, etc., because their truth is not decidable.[28] Against Weber, Jürgen Habermas has argued in a number of publications following 11 September 2001, that for a democratic society to remain vital there is the need to truly discuss the fundamental orientations of its citizens. In Habermas' view, modern democratic societies depend on the commitment of their people to find the best way forward by arguing about all the possible views and options. For Habermas this implies the necessity of bringing into the public discussion religious convictions on how to live and what a good life entails.[29]

Contrary to Weber's view, which has become dominant in modernity, religious convictions are not arbitrary, unsubstantiated and authoritarian truth claims. Religious traditions present views on what is at stake in the reality we live in, applying a rationality, which differs from the instrumental rationalization in de Weberian sense. Studying religions as value systems, as changing and developing ways in which people give meaning to their existence, as clusters of formulas and rituals that help to cope with suffering and trauma, is necessary and important, but fundamentally does not do them justice. To do justice to religions, they should be presented as what they claim to be: traditions of justifiable forms of understanding the world and human existence, in relation to and in discussion with other forms of understanding in our current situation – be they theoretical, or practical, or both as is the case in the practice of medicine. In other words, religious studies is not only the future of theology, theology is also the future of religious studies.

## Theology as the future of religious studies

The unique relevance of religion to people in the contemporary situation relates to its ability to help them order and understand reality in ways that go beyond the iron cage-rationalization that characterizes life in contemporary society. The intellectual relevance of religion in the contemporary situation relates to its ability to argue for these alternative ways to view reality and our collective and individual relation to it. The existential relevance of religion relates to the fact that it shows that reality demands commitment and choice, and thus explains why people cannot but engage themselves in their situation and act upon the fact that their lot is cast with that of other people.

In this situation, what is of major importance is not only to describe religion or religious behaviour, although that is needed, and not only to understand it in terms of predetermined forms of what counts as rationality in our culture, although that can be helpful. What is especially needed is to test the relevance, the pertinence and both the analytical and critical-transforming power of the particular religious rationality. This rationality is summarized by the classical adagio to approach everything *sub ratione Dei*, which is the definition of theology. How to develop this rationality publicly is suggested in the declaration *Dignitatis Humanae*, drawn up and accepted at the Second Vatican Council (1962–1965). This document is generally seen as a belated attempt to reconcile the tradition of modern liberal thought in terms of human rights with roman-catholic doctrine. The authors of the document acknowledge that they are responding to developments outside the church. Round about the time of the Second Vatican Council the conviction took root within the Catholic Church that it should 'read the signs of the times in the light of the Gospel' in order to carry out its task. Despite the fact that *Dignitatis humanae* could have paid more attention to why it had taken until 1965 before the Catholic Church saw fit to declare that 'the human person has a right to religious freedom', it is mistaken to suggest that it took until *Dignitatis humanae* for the Catholic Church to finally arrive at the same conclusion the rest of the world had reached long ago, thanks to liberalism.

The document offers initiatives for a specifically theological vision on the discussion between different religious ideas about what can ultimately be called true and good. In its reflections on religious freedom, *Dignitatis Humanae* expressly avoids the liberal reasoning that religion is a personal choice which needs to be free because it is part of private life. In this document, the right to religious freedom is based upon the religious duty to seek the truth and obey it:

> It is in accordance with their dignity as persons – that is, beings endowed with reason and free will and therefore privileged to bear personal responsibility – that all men should be at once impelled by nature and also bound by a moral obligation to seek the truth, especially religious truth. They are also bound to adhere to the truth, once it is known, and to order their whole lives in accord with the demands of truth. However, men cannot discharge these obligations in a manner in keeping with their own nature unless they enjoy immunity from external coercion as well as psychological freedom. (no. 2)[30]

By deriving the right to do so from the duty to seek the truth in the way it does, *Dignitatis humanae* presents the space for religious freedom as being religious itself. The liberal concept of religious freedom considers it to be the result of the right to be protected in one's private life. *Dignitatis humanae* on the other hand, emphasizes that the right to religious freedom cannot be limited to our private lives. What is at stake in the document is the importance of a free and open discussion about what should be believed. Reason, free will and direction to community should be given their rightful place as integral parts of human nature. As the document puts it: 'truth . . . is to be sought after in a manner proper to the dignity of the human person and his social nature'. This means that the

> inquiry is to be free, carried on with the aid of teaching or instruction, communication and dialogue, in the course of which men explain to one another the truth they have discovered, or think they have discovered, in order thus to assist one another in the quest for truth. (no. 3)

That is why religious communities 'should not be prohibited from freely undertaking to show the special value of their doctrine in what concerns the organization of society and the inspiration of the whole of human activity' (nr. 4). Followers of religions should be free to show how they are working for good community life and what their interpretation of it entails. They should be free to take part in the public discussion on the way society is structured, so that people really can 'assist one another in the quest for truth'.

*Dignitatis humanae* suggests that in the end it is the free search for the truth that deserves to be protected, exactly in name of the religious truth that is being sought (nr. 7). The human tendency to seek the truth is a demonstration of the human orientation towards God. In their freedom to act in accordance with this tendency, humans are honoured as seekers, and in acting in accordance with this freedom, God is honoured as the One that is sought and who will manifest Himself as the Truth. For those who take the theological perspective on reality *sub ratione dei*, the different forms of human life present themselves as attempts to achieve the good life. Religious symbols, activities and convictions are expressions of the longing, the hope and the firm belief that this is indeed about the true and good life which will fulfil human existence. That is why merely studying religion will not suffice. Inevitably, we need to ask whether what they claim, either in theory or in practice, can truly be maintained, and in what sense. We need to confront the various religions with each other in our attempts to answer this question. This is both a theological question and a theological confrontation, which explains why theology is the future of religious studies.

It should be established that this form of theology does not presuppose the truth of any single religious conviction. This truth is sought. It does however presuppose the ultimately religious conviction that people exist both individually and collectively so that they 'might feel after God and find him', because 'He is not far from each one of us' (Acts 17, 27). The necessity to 'feel after God' means that any religious input is worth exploring and explaining for the sake of the discussion on origin, range and purpose of the good life. The assertion that God is not far from each one of us means that the search for a truly good life is not in vain.

## Conclusion

We have been trying to articulate theology's role in the world. First, we have described the current situation of theology in the Netherlands and pointed at the problems that occur when theology is all too strictly divided from religious studies. To remedy these, we have proposed an incarnational theology, which sees the world in which it is itself involved and in which people have tried and continue trying to survive and realize a good life *sub ratione dei*. We have illustrated this theological proposal with an example from a research project on the interface of theology and the medical sciences. We have explained what it means to find and rediscover theology *in* medicine.

Theology is well equipped to locate religious views and relations with religious traditions in medical practices and in the views and behaviour of all parties involved in it. This is, we argued, the condition and background of what is often called the 'return' or 're-emergence' of religion. The lasting presence of religious questions and concerns in communal practices like medicine can explain the ongoing relationship of secularization and religionization in modernity in general. From this, we have drawn the conclusion that a confrontation of the diverse religious and theological views on contemporary reality is of vital importance to further the development of our culture. And we have shown that this discussion is ultimately to be seen as in itself a religious practice of seeking the truth and dedication to it.

This way, we have developed possible ways of viewing the practice of theology not as a kind of 'colonialism writ small'. Its subject matter is not at all removed from its lived, societal contexts, as Peter Ochs has suggested. On the contrary, the subject matter of theology is precisely located in the lived and societal contexts of communal practices in the world. We are convinced that in this way we do not only enhance theology's cultural relevance, but also help Christian theology to trace its incarnational authenticity.

# Notes

Prof. Dr Erik Borgman is Full Professor of Systematic Theology at the University of Tilburg, the Netherlands. Dr Stephan van Erp is Senior Researcher and Lecturer Systematic Theology at Radboud University Nijmegen, the Netherlands.

[1] P. Ochs, Revised: Comparative Religious Traditions, *Journal of the American Academy of Religion*, 74, 2006, 483–494, 484.

[2] What we present in this article, is work in progress. The 'theology in the world' we are trying to develop, akin but not identical to what Oliver Davies has proposed under this term, is heavenly under construction. Some characteristics of it are presented to Dutch-speaking world by Erik Borgman, printed in a substantially extended form as '. . . *want de plaats waarop je staat is heilige grond*': God als onderzoeksprogramma. Amsterdam: Boom, 2008 ['. . . for the place on which you are standing is holy ground': God as a Research Programme].

[3] M. E. Brinkman, N. F. M. Schreurs, H. M. Vroom and C. J. Wethmar (eds), *Theology between Church, University, and Society*. Assen: Van Gorcum, 2003.

[4] Especially in the Dutch journal *Tijdschrift voor Theologie*, which published a special issue on the relationship between theology and religious studies and has since then dominated and accommodated the debate in the Netherlands. E. Borgman, J. A. van der Ven (eds), Religie en haar wetenschappen, special issue of *Tijdschrift voor Theologie*, 45, 2005, 2 [Religion and its Disciplines/Sciences].

[5] Cf. H. J. Adriaanse, H. A. Krop and L. Leertouwer, *Het verschijnsel theologie: Over de wetenschappelijke status van de theologie*. Amsterdam: Boom, 1987 [The

Phenomenon of Theology: On the Academic/Scientific Status of Theology]; H. J. Adriaanse (ed.), *Tweestromenland: Over wijsgerige en belijdende theologie.* Leuven: Peeters, 2001. [Mesopotamia/Land of Between Two Streams: On Philosophical and Confessional Theology].

6   For the necessity of 'methodological agnosticism' as distinctive mark of religious studies, see D. Wiebe, *The Politics of Religious Studies: The Continuing Conflict with Theology in the Academy.* London: St Martin' Press, 1999.

7   Cf. R. Williams, *Reading, Criticism, Performance,* in *The Nature of New Testament Theology,* ed. C. Rowland and C. Tuckett, Oxford: Blackwell, 2006, xiii–xix. Cf. *The Written Gospel,* ed. M. Bockmuehl and D. A. Hagner, Cambridge: Cambridge University Press, 2005.

8   Important critics of making such radical distinctions are: G. Flood, *Beyond Phenomenology: Rethinking the Study of Religion.* London: Cassell, 1999; T. Fitzgerald, *The Ideology of Religious Studies.* Oxford: Oxford University Press, 2000; R. T. McCutcheon (ed.), *The Insider/Outsider Problem in the Study of Religion: A Reader.* London: Sage, 1999; R. T. McCutcheon, *The Discipline of Religion: Structure, Meaning, Rhetoric.* London: 2003; G. D'Costa, *Theology in the Public Square: Church, Academy, and Nation.* Oxford: Blackwell, 2005.

9   Others may not share this view of the current state of Catholic theology in the Netherlands. We do need to see the problem in its local context, however. Many discussions on the relation between church, science and culture are necessarily also dependent on regional culture and society, the scholars involved and the communication with local bishops. The influence of this local culture may be limited on the meta-disciplinary and methodological discussions, which have abounded so far. It does however have a very real influence on the different ways in which these discussions are used when faculties are rearranged, despite the fact that the current developments in the Netherlands are often justified from a rather more global context. In what follows, we will show that this use depends upon a certain concept of theological sub-disciplines, rather than on a well-balanced methodological decision.

10  Cf. David Tracy's distinction between 'proclamation' and 'conversation' in D. Tracy, *The Analogical Imagination: Christian Theology and the Culture of Pluralism.* London: Crossroad, 1981. See also S. van Erp, *The Art of Theology: Hans Urs von Balthasar's Theological Aesthetics and the Foundations of Faith.* Leuven: Peeters, 2004, esp. 11–40.

11  Cf. J. Webster, 'Theological Theology', in J. Webster, *Confessing God: Essays in Christian Dogmatics II.* London/New York: T&T Clark, 2005, 11–32.

12  O. Davies, 'Violence in Bloomsbury: A Theological Challenge', *International Journal of Systematic Theology,* 8, 2006, 252–265, 253. Cf. O. Davies, P. Janz, C. Sedmak, *Transformation Theology: A New Paradigm of Christian Living.* London/New York: T&T Clark, 2007.

13  D. Tracy, *The Analogical Imagination.* 57.

14  G. D'Costa, *Theology in the Public Square: Church, Academy and Nation.* Oxford: Blackwell, 2005, 1–37.

15  www.pubmed.gov last accessed 28/08/2008.

16  For similar query experiments, see H. G. Koenig et al., *Handbook of Religion and Health,* 6, 513–590.

[17]  For an example of instrumentalism, see J. Levin, *God, Faith, and Health: Exploring the Spirituality-Healing Connection*. New York: Wiley, 2001. For a criticism of instrumentalism, see E. Biser, 'Kann Glaube heilen? Zur Frage nach Sinn und Wesen einer therapeutischen Theologie', in B. Fuchs and N. Kobler (eds), *Hilft der Glaube? Heilung auf dem Schnittpunkt zwischen Theologie und Medizin*. Münster: Lit-Verlag, 2002.

[18]  S. Hauerwas, Suffering *Presence: Theological Reflections on Medicine, the Mentally Handicapped, and the Church*. Notre Dame: Notre Dame University Press, 1986, 70.

[19]  See M. Weber, 'Die Wirtschaftsethik der Weltreligionen (1915–19)', in M. Weber, *Gesammelte Aufsätze zur Religionssoziologie*. Tübingen: J. C. B. Mohr, 1988, 207–573, here especially 241–252.

[20]  Cf. E. J. Cassell, *The Nature of Suffering and the Goals of Medicine*. Oxford: Oxford University Press, 2004 (1991).

[21]  Cf. M. Little, *Humane Medicine*. Cambridge: Cambridge University Press, 1995.

[22]  A case that recently has been made by medical anthropologists: A. Kleinman and J. Kleinman, 'Suffering and its professional transformation: Toward an ethnography of experience', *Culture, Medicine & Psychiatry*, 15, 1991, 275–302.

[23]  Cf. J. J. Shuman and K. G. Meador, *Heal Thyself: Spirituality, Medicine, and the Distortion of Christianity*. Oxford: Oxford University Press, 2003.

[24]  R. Williams, 'God', in *Fields of Faith: Theology and Religious Studies in the Twenty-first Century*, ed. D. Ford, B. Quash and J. M. Soskice, Cambridge: Cambridge University Press, 2005, 75–89, 81.

[25]  Ochs, Comparative Religious Traditions, 483.

[26]  M. Weber, 'Die protestantische Ethik und der Geist des Kapitalismus (1904–05)', in M. Weber, *Gesammelte Aufsätze zur Religionssoziologie*, l.c., 17–206, here 203–206.

[27]  It is impossible to argue this thesis sufficiently in the context of this chapter. See however E. Borgman, *Metamorfosen: Over religie en moderne cultuur*. Kampen: Klement, 2006; E. Borgman '. . . want de plaats waarop je staat is heilige grond': *God als onderzoeksprogramma*. Amsterdam: Boom, 2008.

[28]  Zie M. Weber, 'Wissenschaft als Beruf (1919)', in *Gesammelte Aufsätze zur Wissenschaftslehre*. Tübingen: J. C. B. Mohr, 1988, 582–613, here 603.

[29]  Cf. J. Habermas, 'Glauben und Wissen', in *Jürgen Habermas, Glauben und Wissen: Friedespreis des Deutschen Buchhandels 2001*. Frankfurt am Main: Suhrkamp, 2001, 9–31; J. Habermas, 'Religion in der Öffentlichkeit: Kognitivie Voraussetzungen für den "öffentlichen Vernunftgebrauch" religiöser und sekularen Bürger', in J. Habermas, *Zwischen Naturalismus und Religion: Philosophische Aufsätze*. Frankfurt am Main: Suhrkamp, 2005, 119–154; J. Habermas, 'Vorpolitische Grundlagen des demokratischen Rechtsstaates?', in J. Habermas/Joseph Ratzinger, *Dialektik der Säkulairsierung*. Freiburg/Basel/Wien: Herder, 2005, 15–37. Cf. A. Harrington, 'Habermas's Theological Turn?', *Journal for the Theory of Social Behaviour*, 31, 2007, 45–61.

[30]  The translation of the document is the translation on the official website of the Vatican: http://www.vatican.va/archive/hist_councils/ii_vatican_council/documents/vat-ii_decl_19651207_dignitatis-humanae_en.html last accessed 28/08/2008.

Chapter 5

# The Irony of Religious Studies
## A Pro-theological Argument from the Swedish Experience

Mattias Martinson

Is the continuous quarrel between theology and religious studies really grounded in a true clash between scientific ideals? Or could it rather be construed as a misguided fight, hiding the fact that theology and religious studies share essential problems, which emanate from their *common* Christian heritage?

By questioning one or two established ideas about theology, the purpose of this article is to make a case for the continuing – not to say intensified – relevance of theology in an academic setting.[1] More precisely, I want to argue for the importance of a committed critical form of theological reflection at the core of *any* serious notion of religious studies. However, this defence of theology has to be performed without lapsing into a narrow defence of Christianity as a sheltered and timeless objective of theology. My perspective may therefore be characterized as *post-Christian*, given that such a position, among other things, indicates a profound awareness of the limitations of Christian academic theology in the context of contemporary religious plurality.[2]

To some extent, I agree with the rising number of scholars who criticize theology for being an outdated form of academic reflection – all too biased by Christian prejudices and therefore a dead end for any future model of serious scholarship. Yet, since I suspect that this rage against theology in many cases reveals its own insensitivity to contemporary cultural challenges, the agreement is only partial.

In my opinion, the way ahead is to be found (1) in the recognition of religion as a *living* and *changing* cultural phenomenon, which religious studies must face in a very flexible mode, due to continuous changes over time and differences between social and cultural contexts; and (2) in the understanding of theological reflection as a generally significant (although not the only) way to approach such a changing notion of religion and religious phenomena; and (3) in our capacity to proceed from these two insights without relapsing into an abstract, non-contextual notion of theology, that is, without relapsing into the standard identification between theological reflection and reflection on Christian faith, that is, an outmoded identification founded on the fact that Christianity once was the only significant living religion of the West.

I will therefore make a serious attempt to locate the discussion in my contemporary Swedish cultural, religious and intellectual context.

## Theology and faith

But let me start at a more general level. In his book *The Irony of Theology and the Nature of Religious Thought* (1991) the Canadian scholar Donald Wiebe claims that theology – especially modern and postmodern theology – is a thoroughly ambiguous, aporetic and, ultimately, deeply ironic intellectual undertaking. He develops a 'dialectical' interpretation of theology, locating its essence within the context of faith, that is, the practice of religion.

At the same time, however, Wiebe argues that theology (at least as a public academic undertaking in contemporary society) must be characterized as a deeply rationalistic project, dissolving the integrity of the religious content of its sources. He maintains that modern academic theology in one way or another is bound to explain away the very essence of its own religious significance. This happens through the constant theological adaptation of Christian ideas to the present state of secular reason. Through its strivings towards a rational account of Christian faith, Wiebe suggests that academic theology becomes fundamentally 'destructive of Christian (mythic) faith'.[3]

This course of 'dysfunctional' involvement in religious faith constitutes what Wiebe understands as 'the irony of theology'. Momentarily, theologians act as if they stood firmly on the side of scientific reason, but throughout their work they succumb to a displacement which jeopardizes theology's identity as a secular academic endeavour (through its basically religious intent) as well as undermines its *raison d'être* (through failing as religion).[4] As such, it cannot be upheld as a reasonable form of religious studies. (Religious studies, on the other hand, is an undertaking that Wiebe more recently has characterized as the attempt 'to understand and explain the [religious] activity rather than to be involved in it'.[5])

A lot more could be said about Wiebe's perspective on these issues.[6] As an academic theologian myself, I question some aspects of his proposal, but I would still like to underscore the importance of his dialectical argument. Theologians must always be aware of the immense problems within their own discourse, which emanate from cultural and religious changes, in particular within postmodernity. Wiebe is on the right track when he detects a contradiction within theology, especially when it is based on a static notion of Christian ideas, or implicit theories about the immutable essence of Christianity. Consequently, the motivation for my headline, 'The Irony of Religious Studies', is not to proclaim theology as unproblematic, compared to religious studies. Rather, I would like to extend Wiebe's dialectical understanding of the field, and use it in a way that gradually, as it were, can be turned against the very notion of religious studies that Wiebe and others defend.

## Religious studies and ideology

To accomplish this, one may turn to post-colonial scholarship. Especially important is Talal Asad's painstaking attempts to deconstruct the notion of the secular.[7] Another highly interesting scholar in this connection is the American-Japanese historian Tomoko Masuzawa, and especially her book *The Invention of World Religions*.[8]

Masuzawa convincingly shows how the fundamental concepts in the objectivist-scientific discourse on religion developed more or less directly out of Christian and deeply political-theological interests, stemming from the colonial era.[9] Her main focus is the ambiguous notion 'world religion'. In relation to that concept, she detects a dubious ideological impact on the totality of our contemporary understanding of religious phenomena. Masuzawa argues that the basic scholarly inclination for classification and characterization of 'other' religions – that is non-Christian belief-systems – was entwined with (although not necessarily consciously related to) a series of Eurocentric, racist, colonial and in the last instance Christian strategies, which still are deposited or sedimented in our contemporary theories and concepts.[10]

It is against this background one can envision a certain 'irony of religious studies', as Wiebe and others describe the field. They reject theology from a position within the disciplinary structure of the old theological faculty. But according to post-colonial thought, that structure will inevitably reflect an awkward Christian logic and a particular *theological* motivation, which religious studies fail to scrutinize or even comprehend in terms of their own theoretical models.

The fact is that religions, apart from Christianity, cannot be approached in their own terms, but only though a set of 'neutral' concepts, whose neutrality are moulded on a basically *Christian* understanding of religion. Being more or less unintentionally supportive of such an ideological framework, one may therefore criticize religious studies for being supportive of a concept of religion that *undermines religion's position as a culturally significant phenomenon.* So defended, it becomes difficult to see how religious studies could ever function as a progressive intellectual force in a time when religion once again – although now in the form of an immense religious plurality – has become a new and very tangible cultural factor.

Needless to say, these suggestions are not enough for any defence of traditional theology as a progressive force within religious studies. If religion has returned as an important cultural factor, the natural question to ask is *how* it has returned and *in what sense* that return can be related to the discussion about theology and religious studies? According to my view, any successful contemporary defence of a theological aspect of religious studies must be carefully contextualized and related to the religious situation in society as a whole; otherwise one runs the risk of returning with an abstract idea about the immutability of traditional Christian theology as a driving force of theology as such (which would be alien to my view).

The next step, therefore, is to apply the outline to my own Swedish context. I will proceed, first, by giving a brief sketch of the historical debate about theology,[11] and secondly, by suggesting a critical interpretation of the contemporary field of Swedish theology and religious studies.

## Philosophical critique of Swedish theology

Compared with several other Western settings, Sweden has a predominantly homogeneous population in terms of ethnicity, cultural background and religion. Furthermore, it is a small nation with few full-fledged universities. Lutheran Christianity has dominated the academic theological scene. Until quite recently there were only two theological research institutions: the theological faculties at the universities of Lund and Uppsala. Thus, even though these and other relevant institutions gradually have been deconfessionalized, most of the significant debates on principles of religious studies have tended towards the scientific status of the theological faculty as a whole and the status of *Religionswissenschaft* in general.[12] This is not least due to the fact that the most significant criticism has been issued from the outside, especially from atheist philosophers.

In the early 1950s the Swedish philosopher Ingemar Hedenius started a highly influential 'debate' about Christian theology and its supposed intellectual bankruptcy.[13] He wrote a series of essays in one of the major national newspapers. These outright attacks on various Swedish theologians were collected in several books and gained immense popularity. In a relatively short time the broad layer of the secular Swedish public – from the cultural elite to ordinary school teachers – had turned against academic theology, but also against religion as such.[14] From the 1950s and on through the following decades Swedish society and culture faced many strong public forms of atheism. This is a fact which often has been accompanied by the understanding of Sweden as a country among the most secular in the world.

Hedenius' basic idea was that the academic theology and research on religion of his time reflected a dubious institutional tie between church and academia. More fundamentally, however, he insisted that it revealed a disturbing intellectual dependence on what he understood as a morally and intellectually corrupt system of belief, namely Christianity. In that respect, Hedenius' criticism of theology was grounded in a highly normative critique of Christianity and Christian belief. His most far reaching idea concerning the whole field of research and education in religion was to claim that the theological faculties should be closed down, while the departments of theology should be included in the art faculties and thereafter put on probation by the department of philosophy. This arrangement was to prevail until the day when the corrupt theological practice had faded away and a new generation of genuinely critical scholars of religion had formed.[15]

This totalitarian argument seems odd to our post-modern setting, and his program was certainly not realized in Sweden. However, Hedenius' informal impact on the intellectual life changed the self-understanding of theology for a long time. One of the earliest strategies from the side of dogmatic theology (at least in Uppsala) was to flee into mere methodological descriptivism, in order to keep up the remainder of its academic reputation.[16] Hedenius himself had suggested history of ideas as a core discipline in the new department of religious studies.

A more constructive development – closely related to Hedenius critique – was the introduction of a program for empirical studies of life- and world-views, drawn up by young Uppsala-theologians in the late 1960s (some of them students of Hedenius and in agreement with important aspects of his critique). In Uppsala this new program replaced dogmatics in 1975, under the headline 'Studies in Faiths and Ideologies'. In many ways this new field was a success. It established a new agenda for constructive reflection on religious problems, as well on popular beliefs (even atheistic 'beliefs') in secular culture. The basic aim was to make various forms of faith available for genuinely theological forms of reflection. One can perhaps say that it formed a defence for the cultural significance religion and belief as such, in a time of prevailing indifference to religious and existential perspectives.

On the one hand, the overall tendency is quite clear: 'theology' was preserved only as a kind of external philosophical criticism of religion and related beliefs. Neither Christianity, nor any other established religion could be approached as a serious intellectual option in and of itself. In that respect secularism had triumphed over Christian consciousness, as a way of approaching religious problems.

On the other hand, one may approach Hedenius and his influence somewhat differently. As a secular philosopher he actually dared to engage with religion in a highly normative way. One could even argue that Hedenius was doing his own 'theology'. The outcome was of course strictly negative (from the perspective of Christianity and traditional understanding of religion). But he approached Christianity seriously, as a believing secularist. Not as an 'immunized' object, unworthy of intellectual critique (on that point he actually differs from many contemporary protagonists of disengaged religious studies like Wiebe). The result of Hedenius' thought on these matters can, thus, at least experimentally, be characterized as a kind of secularism formed by reference to Christianity, a determinate negation of traditional theology. In turn, his mode of thought can be described as a distinctively 'Christian' form of secularism.[17]

According to this view, the problem in Swedish theology during the last four or five decades of the last century cannot be isolated to the influence of Hedenius and other harsh critics. It should rather be seen as an all too distrustful *reaction* against such criticism, founded on a more or less unconscious acceptance of certain aspects of the 'Christian' secularism related to Hedenius. Given this interpretation, the new initiatives in Uppsala were not enough to counter Hedenius' narrow understanding of religion, and the result became a further 'de-theolgization' of *Religionswissenschaft*. In the contexts where Christian theology still flourished, a tangible distance was established between theology and religious studies.

## Division of labour: ideology in Swedish theology and religious studies

The present situation in Swedish theology still reflects this development. The very structure of Swedish departments of theology and religious studies displays a very segregated social and religious reality, based, as it were, in an implied form of 'Christian secularism'.[18]

First, one dominant group of scholars consists of mainly ethnic Swedes and Christian believers, with a basic focus on Christian faith. They readily call themselves theologians. Postmodern arguments, not to mention a more relativistic situation in the humanities at large, have helped them to rebuild something of a traditional theological identity, beyond the influence of Hedenius and other critics. These scholars can be found in various special fields, not the least in exegetical studies. The highest concentration, however, is found in the philosophical and systematic disciplines where the very methods and perspectives are explicitly derived from the broad tradition of Christian dogmatics and fundamental theology (On the whole, I count myself among them.).

Secondly, there is a large group of ethnic Swedish scholars, mainly Christian or secularized, who focus on distinctively non-Christian religions or faiths, by means of more or less descriptive – historical, philological, sociological, anthropological, etc. – methods, which are related both to the broad tradition of *Religionswissenschaft*, dating back to the second half of the nineteenth century, and to the more recent tradition of Cultural Studies. Many individuals in this group have an understanding similar to Donald Wiebe's, although many postmodern and post-colonial influences contribute to a somewhat more complex picture.

Besides the fact that a lot of interdisciplinary work is going on around different areas of interest, the very *structure* of the field as a whole reflects a fundamental *methodological division of labour,* which in its turn implies that field as a whole – not only systematic theologians – assigns Christianity an exclusive position. *Through the very structure of the academic field, therefore, Christianity is promoted as an integral part of 'our' culture, while the 'other' religions are approached as if they lack all cultural importance and therefore the necessary intellectual content to be worthy of theological reflection.* In opposition to Wiebe, thus, who argued that theology virtually ruins religion, one is tempted to claim that the Swedish situation is indicative of an academic competence on religion which does not treat all religious people with equal seriousness.

I suspect the division of labour between so called theologians and so called scholars of religion situation effectively blocks the development of new theological competences that could bridge traditional disciplinary borders and move us in the direction of a more pluralistic academic study of religion. A neat conclusion, therefore, is that representatives from both sides (theology and religious studies) will have to work, not against each other, but *against this division of labour,* against the structure and the kind of unwarranted Christian normality that it expresses – otherwise one can say, ironically as it were, that a secret *theological* agreement threatens to blur our critical view.

If one looks closer, this problem is not only acute in relation to non-Christian religions. The face of Christianity is changing rapidly. Quite recently, scholars like Lamin Sanneh and Philip Jenkins have made it clear that a critical study of a contemporary global Christianity cannot proceed as if Christianity is still the well known religion of the West, the home ground of western theologians and the domestic religion of traditional European countries.[19] Coupled with the fact that non-Christian religions are rapidly becoming parts of the established religious life of post-Christian Western nations like Sweden, the plurality of Christianity must lead to the conclusion that we need a field that provides us with a 'post-secular' theological competence in the critical self-reflection on various faith traditions. Such a competence can only be developed if the present division of labour is done away with.

Inspired by scholars like Masuzawa, one can argue that a renewal of critical studies of religions along these lines would force us to develop a thorough historical understanding of religious life, as a changing cultural rationale of theology and religious studies. The result would be a more nuanced understanding of theology, as *the mode of religious studies which tentatively approaches religion as an option for critical reflection on a whole range of philosophical, cultural and social problems.*

## Islam as a test case

Notwithstanding the relative homogeneity of the religious life of Sweden, like many other countries we are today facing the rapid growth of Islam and Islamic cultural influence in our society. Our universities have not been slow to react with new chairs in Islamic studies. Virtually every significant place of religious education has some form of program of Islamic studies.

However, the initial picture of the sharp division of the field along strict lines of methodology is still at work. With some exceptions, the typical Swedish scholar on Islam is an ethnically and culturally Swedish Christian or non-believer. And perhaps even more important, Islamic studies harbours scholars who are among the most explicit in their critique of theology. Swedish scholars of Islam and Muslim thought are thus prone to reject any form philosophically informed argumentation within the framework of Muslim belief as a part of Islamic studies.

Although many would perhaps deny it, the field is not fundamentally involved in Islam as a living religion with a potential impact on the scholar's own life world. I have actually come across the idea that Islamic studies can accept Christian theology, as long as that does not imply that Islamic studies should involve theological reflection. The irrationality of such a position is more than obvious, but even scholars who argue that theology *always* is an illegitimate undertaking in the academy (as does Wiebe) run into problems when they face the new social situation and the reality of the theological faculty. What happens, for instance, when believing Muslims want to study Islam at a high level at Swedish university? The situation today is more or less that students are forced to associate themselves either with:

(1) A type of competence (tied up with an enclosed ideology) reacting with more or less instinctive fear and disgust against the very idea of being involved in a more constructive interpretation of Islam, or,
(2) A type of competence (tied up with an enclosed ideology) well-suited for constructive and philosophical reflection on Christian belief, but more or less incompetent when it comes to the field of Islam.

In the present order, then, a Muslim student has enormous difficulties to avoid either being discouraged from entering religious studies at all, or drawn into a highly aporetic discourse, in which the conflicting parties express a basic (unconscious) agreement, namely: that Christianity is still to be treated as a special case, surrounded with special rights that cannot be questioned within the scientific context.

## Towards a new theological consciousness

The irony of religious studies, sketched in relation to Wiebe, can now be expressed more distinctively in relation to the Swedish situation: to keep up with the secular-scientific spirit a significant part of contemporary scholars on religion – very often Christian by confession – have distanced their own professional research from Christianity and thus accepted the traditional idea that Christianity should be left over to a competing group of scholars, whose scientific status they fundamentally question. Taken together, all this is nothing less than a praxis based on an unwarranted theological statement, giving in to the fact that Christianity for long has been a special case, treated as more than just a religion among others.

In light of all this, it is probably not too far fetched to claim that Swedish theology and religious studies runs the acute risk of losing touch with the present religious situation in Sweden, characterized by increasing religious plurality. The theoretical debate appears to be stuck in the problems that arouse in the shift from a Christian to a secular culture. It becomes more or less self-evident that such a background makes it virtually impossible to think of a dogmatic – constructive and systematic theological study – of Islam. There are no existing institutional structures, no qualified competence, no social roles, and hardly any examples to support such an undertaking. Of course, this does not say anything about the quality or appropriateness of a dogmatic or systematic theological undertaking as such, it just under-scores that such an undertaking is generally not a real possibility in relation to non-Christian religions, no matter how culturally important they have become in the very context where religious studies is practiced.

The fact that many of the European societies today can be construed as post-Christian societies has often been considered synonymous with an interpretation of the same societies in terms of secularization. If we take that route, no one should be surprised to find that we have moved from a situation where academic theology had its *raison d'être* in the Church, to a situation where religious studies has its *raison d'être* in the religiously indif-ferent spirit of the secular state.[20]

But there is something wrong with that picture. Today, it becomes more and more obvious that the movement from a Christian to a post-Christian situation is much more complicated. It is somewhat peculiar that the idea of a 'post-secular' situation becomes relevant almost at the same time as the notion of the 'post-Christian' situation. As my sketch has indicated, secularism has very often been a product of a basically Christian senti-ment, or at least not of a reflection on the significance of other religions. If this is right, it explains why the post-Christian study of religion cannot be constructed wholly in terms of traditional visions of neutrality and scien-tific objectivity. To be able to include the religious reality that constitutes the pluralistic post-Christian society of our days, we must rather approach religion as a constantly shifting expression of a divergent cultural praxis. In Sweden this means, more than anything, that Islamic studies should be integrated in a more self-consciously *theological* discourse. Or if we look upon the problem from the opposite direction: *Islam* has been among the most significant forces in promoting a *Swedish* shift from Christian-secular to a post-Christian cultural situation.

Religious studies in Sweden must rethink its task in relation to this reality, and give up Wiebe's type of objectification of religion: religion is not *a priori* the wholly other of a sound academic logic. Like traditional theology, especially dogmatics and Christian ethics, religious studies must take its subject matter seriously enough to allow for the appropriate critical engagement with theological aspects of any belief – but especially with religions producing the scholar's own context. Only as such can it function as a serious public response to religious problems and possibilities in a post-Christian setting. Something similar, although not at all identical, might as well be needed in other Western contexts.

As long as proponents of religious studies are prepared to deny the basic aspects of this argument, my suspicion is that theology will continue to function not only as Christian theology in a strict sense, which in itself is questionable, but will also silently disclose the flawed spirit of a Christian secularism at odds with the religious reality of our time.

## Notes

[1] In this article, 'theology' designates 'the form of modern academic scholarship on lived religion, taking place in Christian societies, at public universities but in historic relation to dominant Christian churches; a discourse with an explicit or implicit understanding of itself as closely related to a critical-constructive – and to some extent normative – religious discourse, which is nevertheless often realized in a relatively autonomous and non-confessional fashion'.

[2] The notion 'post-Christian' has several connotations in contemporary debate. One interesting, although largely undeveloped notion can be found in Hampson (1996). My own perspective is more of a dialectical and historical–philosophical kind, where the prefix 'post' both preserves and displaces the notion of Christianity in terms of its cultural content. I have developed this at length in Martinson (2007) (written in Swedish). N.B. My aim is not to discredit Christian theology as such, just to widen the possible scope of academic theology as a genuinely theological discourse.

[3] Wiebe (1991), p. 45.

[4] Ibid. p. 7.

[5] Wiebe (1999), p. ix.

[6] Wiebe has gone through a significant development, from being very positive to theology in the 1970s, to a very critical attitude nowadays. Aspects of this interesting journey are documented in Wiebe (1994).

[7] Asad (2003).

[8] Masuzawa (2005).

[9] Among other things, Masuzawa pays attention to the forgotten nineteenth-century tradition of 'comparative theology' and its links to religious studies, Masuzawa (2005), pp. 71ff.

[10] See for instance the genealogical accounts of the notions of Buddhism and Islam in Masuzawa (2005), chapters 4–6.

[11] For a more developed view of Swedish systematic theology in the twentieth century, see Rasmusson (2007).

[12] The German notion *Religionswissenschaft* represents exactly the same idea as the Swedish, 'religionsvetenskap', that is, the research and education going on at a theological faculty as a whole (i.e. both theology and religious studies). It could be translated 'science of religion', but since 'science' has slightly different connotations than the German/Swedish 'Wissenschaft/vetenskap', I prefer to use that term as a contextually more appropriate alternative to the expression 'theology and religious studies'.

[13] As Rasmussen shows, Hedenius is not the first significant Swedish philosopher to issue an atheistic critique of theology and religious studies. Back in the 1920s, important Swedish theologians, as Anders Nygren, had already developed a rigorous scientific prolegomenon to dogmatics. See Rasmusson (2007), pp. 132–135.

[14] For an interesting account on this debate and the climate in Swedish theology (although unfortunately written in Swedish), see Lundborg (2002).

[15] Hedenius (1964), pp. 298, 314–316.

[16] Cf. Jeffner (1987), p. 37.

[17] This becomes evident in Hedenius book on the doctrine of hell, see Hedenius (1972). For the notion 'determinate negation', see for example, Adorno (1993), pp. 80–87.

[18] I have stated my position in a somewhat programmatic article (in Swedish), see Martinson (2004).

[19] See for example, Jenkins (2001) and Sanneh (2003).

[20] A scholar like John Milbank would most certainly agree with my idea that there are two competing structures of belief at work, the Christian and the secular. The basic difference between his radical orthodox position and my sketch, however, lies in my idea of a common cultural task of theology: theology is not to be construed primarily in terms of one distinctive faith tradition (as if the basic aim of theology is to develop the essential truths or characteristics of that faith), but as an adequate critical response to the religious situation in a given context. The radical orthodox theologian Graham Ward has developed a somewhat different perspective on theology and culture, which perhaps has more potential affinities with my approach than Milbank's. See Ward (2005).

# Bibliography

Adorno, Theodor W. (1993), *Hegel: Three Studies*, trans. Shierry Weber Nicholsen. Cambridge Mass.: MIT Press.

Asad, Talal (2003), *Formations of the Secular. Christianity, Islam, Modernity*. Stanford: Stanford University Press.

Hampson, Daphne (1996), *After Christianity*. Valley Forge: Trinity Press International.

Hedenius, Ingemar (1964), *Tro och livsåskådning*. Stockholm: Bonniers.

—(1972), *Helvetesläran*. Stockholm: Bonniers.

Jeffner, Anders (1987), *Theology and Integration: Four Essays in Philosophical Theology.* Stockholm: Almquist & Wiksell International 1987.

Jenkins, Philip (2001), *The Next Christendom: The Coming of Global Christianity.* Oxford: Oxford University Press.

Lundborg, Johan (2002), *När ateismen erövrade Sverige: Ingemar Hedenius och debatten kring tro och vetande.* Nora: Nya Doxa.

Martinson, Mattias (2004), 'Nio teser om kritisk religionsvetenskap i dagens Sverige', *Swedish Theological Quarterly*, 80, 146–159.

—(2007), *Postkristen teologi: Experiment och tydningsförsök.* Gothenburg: Glänta Produktion.

Masuzawa, Tomoko (2005), *The Invention of World Religions: Or, How European Universalism Survived in the Language of Pluralism.* Chicago: The University of Chicago Press.

Rasmusson, Arne (2007), 'A Century of Swedish Theology', *Lutheran Quarterly*, 21, 125–162.

Sanneh, Lamin (2003), *Whose Religion is Christianity? The Gospel beyond the West.* Grand Rapids: Eerdmans.

Ward, Graham (2005), *Cultural Transformation and Religious Practice.* Cambridge: Cambridge University Press.

Wiebe, Donald (1991), *The Irony of Theology and the Nature of Religious Thought.* Montreal: McGill-Queens University Press.

—(1994), *Beyond Legitimation: Essays on the Problem of Religious Knowledge.* New York: St Martins Press.

—(1999), *The Politics of Religious Studies: The Continuing Conflict with Theology in the Academy.* Houndmills and London: Macmillan.

Chapter 6

# The Inevitability of Normativity in the Study of Religion
## Theology in Religious Studies

### Thomas A. Lewis

Discussion of the relation between theology and religious studies is largely about policing boundaries – deciding whether or not theology belongs inside the academic study of religion. In the United States at least, this debate is the yield of a long history of religious studies' attempts to establish itself as a legitimate discipline within a secular, or at least non-confessional, university. While excellent recent work on the history of the discipline has raised these debates to new levels, recent iterations still echo earlier charges that work in the discipline is too often theology – particularly Protestant theology – in disguise.[1]

In much of this debate, a crucial background assumption – sometimes stated but often not – is that whereas theologians make normative claims, religious studies scholars should refrain from doing so.[2] Rather, scholars in religious studies should distinguish themselves from theologians precisely by striving for some type of distance, neutrality or objectivity in relation to their subject matter. The object of study should be clearly distinguished from the study itself. The account of this relationship might be formulated in a variety of ways, some more modern, some with a postmodern aspect.[3] To take one example, at times those who do normative work are contrasted with historians, who are presumably investigating an object with a degree of openness to the data and determination to abstain from judging that is seen as lacking in the normative thinker.

Yet it is also noteworthy that a number of other disciplines, whose legitimacy in the university is in no way suspect, regularly make explicitly normative claims. Philosophy and political science are perhaps two of the most obvious. Explicitly normative claims associated with religion provoke greater suspicion than normative claims in other areas. This inequality of suspicion, I want to suggest, reflects a pervasive assumption that religion cannot be argued about – that it is, in essence, reason's other. In this view of religion, normative claims related to religion cannot be argued about but are fundamentally matters of 'faith'. This I take to be the most problematic theological presupposition that continues to haunt discussions of religion – a presupposition shared by many of religion's critics as well as its supporters.

Thus, the drive to exclude theology from religious studies too often rests on two closely related, highly problematic presuppositions: first, of those writing on religion, only the theologians make normative claims, and, second, normative claims related to religion are fundamentally a matter of faith, where faith is juxtaposed with reason. While the latter claim is undoubtedly valid for some normative religious claims, it is not for all. As we think about how to construct the discipline of religious studies, it is essential that we not build this presupposition into its foundations. We should not exclude such views, but neither should they be fundamental to the conception of the discipline.

In an effort to unmask these presuppositions and advance the debate about the borders of the discipline of religious studies, I want to argue that we should focus on the issue of normativity and the justification of normative claims rather than on theology and religious studies *per se*. Framing the debate in terms of theology and religious studies is ultimately neither intellectually defensible nor heuristically productive. The term 'theology' covers too much that is too diverse in crucial respects; it occludes by eliding differences. Shifting the frame should help to dissolve a number of pseudo-arguments and illuminate the substantive intellectual issues.

Focusing on the issue of normativity, I want to begin with a rather simple claim: Normative claims are inevitable in the study of religion (as in most if not all disciplines). What is important is not to try somehow to exclude normative claims but rather to be willing to offer justification for the norms that we invoke. Participants in the academic study of religion must be willing to bring the norms themselves into debate and subject them to critical inquiry. The shift of attention I propose, then, is ultimately to the justification offered for the authority of particular norms. The result is a conception of religious studies that allows a significant space for theology. The only move or claim that justifies someone's exclusion from the discipline is an appeal to any authority as unquestionable or as not needing justification.[4]

In speaking of normativity, I have in mind claims – whether made explicit or merely presupposed – regarding the way we ought to act or think. In describing ethical claims as 'normative', Christine Korsgaard writes, 'They make *claims* on us; they command, oblige, recommend, or guide. Or at least, when we invoke them, we make claims on one another. . . . Concepts like knowledge, beauty, and meaning, as well as virtue and justice, all have a normative dimension, for they tell us what to think, what to like, what to say, what to do, and what to be.'[5] This encompassing conception of normativity, in itself, leaves a great deal open regarding the different ways in which norms are understood to be grounded.[6]

For the present purposes, a few relevant examples will be more helpful than further theorizing of the concept of normativity. (I am actually more concerned with the commonality between these types of claims than with the concept of normativity itself.) The most obvious examples of normative claims are those we associate with the language of 'should' or 'ought'. Kant's categorical imperative, 'act only in accordance with that maxim through which you can at the same time will that it become a universal law', provides a classic example.[7] Much scholarship in ethics – whether philosophical or religious – falls into this category, as in arguments about the morality of the abortion, the war in Iraq, or social justice.

Although such claims might be explicitly religious, they need not be. The philosopher Martha Nussbaum argues that all human beings face certain common problems: 'the distribution of limited resources', 'bodily appetites and their pleasures', and so forth.[8] Based on what she understands to be universal human experiences that can be empirically observed, she makes arguments about the best responses to these problems. Her responses to these problems generate normative claims about how human beings should live. Significantly, though she is explicitly normative, her being so does not raise questions about whether she belongs in a secular university.

Though these types of claims are explicitly normative, we also make normative claims when we describe a practice with language such as 'cruel', 'oppressive' or 'liberating'. Each of these words makes strong claims about value, about whether a practice is appropriate or inappropriate.

Slightly more subtly, we are also making normative claims when we interpret a particular religious practice as an expression of a universal human need – for community or solidarity, for instance. Such theories implicitly make the satisfaction of such needs normative for human beings. Value is attributed to the practice by virtue of its satisfaction of this need.

Take, for example, the work of the historian of religion, Robert Orsi. Orsi has been deeply concerned with how religion should be studied academically and with the ongoing influence of Protestant theology on the field. Even he, however, makes important normative claims. One example comes from his recent book *Between Heaven and Earth*. The background for this passage is his research for his earlier book, *Thank You, St. Jude*, on devotion to the patron saint of hopeless causes. One of the women he interviewed had asked him whether he had ever prayed to St Jude. At a later point, he did not exactly pray to St Jude but he did something that he viewed as comparable: 'Instead of actually praying to Saint Jude I tried to find some analogue to this act in my own emotional and behavioral repertoire.'[9] As a result of this experience and its impact on him, he writes, 'what I learned as I tried to take Clara's challenge seriously is that we were alike nonetheless in our need, vulnerability, and risk.'[10] Here, Orsi is claiming a 'common humanity', characterized by need and vulnerability, and discussing the value of a variety of responses to this human predicament.

More generally, any time we claim – explicitly or implicitly – that human behaviour can be explained in a particular way – as the pursuit of economic interests or cultural capital, for instance – we are making controversial claims about the nature of human existence with important consequences for how we should live. These claims too, then, are normative.

Finally, we make normative claims whenever we try to identify 'what is really going on here'. To describe an experience as delusional or as transcendent, for instance, is to make a claim about the nature of reality. And such claims are normative in the relevant sense: they have strong consequences for how we should act.[11]

The latter kinds of normativity highlight that we are not only making normative claims when we declare, 'This is good', 'This is orthodox', or 'This is an abomination'. The various claims described above presuppose (and sometimes make explicit) strong claims about the nature of human existence – and/or reality more generally – and have important consequences for how we should live. I focus on these kinds of claims, because they strike me as precisely the type that are seen by some to constitute grounds for excluding theology from the academic study of religion. Too often, we distinguish those who are explicitly doing normative work – ethicists, theologians and philosophers of religion, for instance – from those who are doing more descriptive work – such as many historians. Instead, I believe we should read this as a shorthand: All are making normative judgements. It's just that the first category are *more likely* to be reflecting explicitly on the justification for their normative claims.

The work of Martha Nussbaum and Robert Orsi, for instance, is not intrinsically more normative than the work of many theologians whose work might be considered suspect or inappropriate in religious studies. They are examples of normative claims that seem clearly to belong within secular academia, but they are not necessarily radically different from the work of a theologian analyzing Augustine's account of original sin as a distinctly Christian formulation of a universal human condition of finitude and a response of pride.

Yet many are much more comfortable with Nussbaum and Orsi than the Augustinian, an observation that returns us to the second of the presuppositions I identified above. We might begin by asking, why do explicitly religious thinkers making normative claims raise so much more suspicion about their place in the modern, pluralistic university than a philosopher such as Nussbaum? Although I can only sketch my response to this question here, I believe that much of the reason normative claims that are explicitly 'religious' raise this suspicion while others do not is that much of our academic as well as other public discourse is shaped by a conception of religion as 'reason's other'. Many of our discussions take for granted that religion is not something about which one can argue rationally. It is fundamentally about a 'faith' that one either has or does not. With everything resting on that, all subsequent argument is futile or trivial. Without a doubt, religion has often functioned in this way, and this arational strand has deep elements in Christianity. But this conception received a significant boost in the wake of Enlightenment challenges to religion. Facing these challenges, one of the most prominent Protestant responses was a division of territory – a kind of non-competition agreement. Religion would dominate – but be confined to – a realm that reason could not reach. Schleiermacher is a crucial figure in this tradition, though it seems to flow more from an oversimplification of his views than from his own vision. This tradition arguably lies behind much of the discourse of religion as *sui generis*.[12]

Though few would defend this conception of religion in the simple form I have sketched it here, it nonetheless seems to have a surprising influence – at least in the United States. It is used to justify excluding theologians from the university as well as to defend religious claims from rational criticism. It is the hidden, shared presupposition in many disagreements between religions critics and its caretakers, to borrow Russell McCutcheon's language.[13] I suspect it also operates in the work of a number of contemporary continental philosophers whose call for a return to religion appears motivated in part by their views on the limits of reason. If reason fails, turn elsewhere – i.e., to religion. And it is both powerful and dangerous in our public political discussions. As stated above, this is one of the most significant ways in which discussions of religion continue to be shaped by an unacknowledged but specific Protestant theological vision. (In my own scholarship on Hegel, I interpret him as offering a more adequate account of religion and its relation to reason and politics, a strategy of responding to the Enlightenment without simply dividing responsibilities between religion and reason.)

To argue that this conception of religion should not be foundational to the discipline, it is important to demonstrate the ways in which that conception is inadequate. The focus on norms and their justification illustrates this inadequacy well. If we frame the discussion in terms of normativity, the crucial issue becomes whether someone is willing to offer an argument or justification for a norm – and thus what counts as offering an argument. In thinking about the discipline of religious studies as a whole, we need to conceive of this process broadly enough to encompass a wide range of justificatory strategies. That doesn't mean I have to agree with them all, but I don't want to exclude people from the field just because I do not agree with the arguments they offer in favour of their position. Rather than developing examples at length, in the present context it is more important to emphasize the breadth of possibilities. It is precisely the breadth of approaches to theology that challenges many of the easy dismissals of theology from the university.

One set of strategies includes various forms of epistemological foundationalism. Though different, appeals to purportedly universal human experience – and here we might even be able to define this broadly enough to encompass Otto's account of the *mysterium tremendum* – also enter the realm of debate.[14] We can argue, for all kinds of reasons, against the universality of this experience, and it is this space for argument that is essential.

Even Schleiermacher, who is such a central figure in the tradition of Protestant theology that seems to motivate many of the critics of theology in the academy, can be understood in these terms. There is certainly much to argue about in his *Speeches on Religion*, and the *Glaubenslehre* makes extensive arguments for the normative authority of a particular community.[15] Though it is not a universal community, it is by no means individual. More importantly, the claims regarding why the consciousness of a particular community should be authoritative do not themselves presuppose faith of any sort. Rather, they take place in a sphere of argument in which religious and non-religious people can participate. The point can be made more polemically by saying that Schleiermacher – or at least parts of Schleiermacher – belong in the academy not because he is right but rather because we can show he is wrong regardless of whether we are Christians or not. And he can argue back – about the nature of feeling and intuition, the limits of reason, and so forth – in terms that all members of the academy can and should take seriously.

More generally, the diversity of justificatory strategies prompted by the perceived failure of foundationalist epistemology suggests how wide the range of justifications might be. I think here of arguments that seek to justify the normative status of a religious tradition for a particular linguistic community (such as the work of George Lindbeck) or that argue for the importance of traditions of enquiry (such as Alasdair MacIntyre's).[16] Lindbeck and MacIntyre represent two different models of making arguments for their normative claims that neither appeal to self-evident foundations of which so many are suspicious nor simply take for granted the authority of any particular claim or canon. Though some might view MacIntyre as making blind appeals to tradition, to the contrary, he makes important and sophisticated arguments.[17] And though he is often critical of the modern university, academia has seen fit to recognize him with important positions, and many scholars have been deeply influenced by his work; broadly speaking, we largely recognize him as belonging. It is this willingness to argue and to eschew any self-evident foundations, in my mind, that places their work within the category of religious studies.

Tyler Roberts has indicated the ways in which Hent deVries, Eric Santner, and Charles Winquist develop theological positions that fall outside the narrow vision of theology 'simply as a foundationalist, mystifying "authorizing practice"'.[18] While some would raise questions regarding the extent to which their claims can be meaningfully argued about, these and other negative theologies are significant in the way that they eschew claims of certainty or final authority.

In another intellectual tradition, the neo-pragmatist Jeffrey Stout has sought to bring our attention to the diversity of argumentative strategies that we use in our everyday discourse on public matters, including religion, in pluralistic societies. Rejecting the idea that once we come to the topic of religion, all argument stops – i.e., that religion is a conversation stopper – Stout stresses the important role of immanent criticism, in which we start with our the other person's own viewpoint and argue that in some respect it contradicts itself and/or should lead to another conclusion than the person thinks.[19] Championing the pervasiveness and power of immanent criticism over against John Rawls's conception of public reason, Stout writes,

> Immanent criticism is both one of the most widely used forms of reasoning in what I would call public political discourse and one of the most effective ways of showing respect for fellow citizens who hold differing points of view. Any speaker is free to request reasons from any other. If I have access to the right forum, I can tell the entire community what

reasons move me to accept a given conclusion, thus showing my fellow citizens respect as requesters of my reasons. But to explain to them why *they* might have reason to agree with me, given their different collateral premises, I might well have to proceed piecemeal, addressing one individual (or one type of perspective) at a time.[20]

The non-confessional university is a public forum in just this sense, and immanent criticism will be one important way in which we argue with others in this context. Perhaps more importantly, it is a context in which '[a]ny speaker is free to request reasons from any other'. That sentence expresses well a basic feature of this setting: no claim is beyond questioning.

Discussing these examples so briefly, I imagine that you will find some of them unconvincing. There is certainly room for argument, for instance, about whether Otto, Lindbeck or deVries, offer arguments that seek to appeal to a broader community of scholars. But that is the point: there is room for argument. And the arguments can be made without appealing to transcendent authority and without presupposing 'faith'.[21]

In defining so broadly what it means to offer justification for our normative claims, I seek to define religious studies inclusively. I would err on the side of inclusiveness with regard to the kinds of arguments that might be offered. We might not agree with the arguments, but as we try to conceive of the field as a whole, we should be slow to rule arguments simply out of bounds.

It can thus appear that I'm saying something along the lines of 'why can't we all just get along?' That is, up to this point, my proposal has likely appeared highly inclusive and irenic in character. But there is a rub as well. The vision of the study of religion that I am proposing does require everyone to be willing to debate – and in doing so to submit to critique and criticism – their normative claims. No claim and no canon can stand as unquestionable or as free of the need for justification of its authoritative status. To cordon off a set of texts or body of doctrines as simply 'givens', whose normative status requires no justification or cannot be argued about, is to remove oneself from this discussion. So does attaching authority to holders of a particular office simply by virtue of their holding that office. Similarly, appeals to anything like private revelation or unique experiences do not allow much basis for conversation if this is the only justification someone is willing to offer.[22] Of course, many believers from many religions make these kinds of moves. I am not saying that they should not. But by making claims of this sort, an individual removes him – or herself from the realm of academic discourse. They are not basing their claims on grounds that are in any sense verifiable or even subject to constructive debate by a larger community. (How much – or how many – this excludes, I am not entirely sure. I would be interested to hear your comments on that matter.)

This conception provides an extensive – though not unlimited – space for theology within religious studies. In allowing for some types of theology while excluding others, I seek to capture some of the grounds that make many wary of theology's role in religious studies, without excluding theology altogether. Yet I think the more important contribution lies in framing matters differently. Focusing on normativity and the willingness to offer justification for normative claims redirects the debate towards the substantive issues at stake and away from some of the dead ends that leave us wondering exactly how far the debate has come since the 1960s and 1970s.[23]

Finally, with an eye towards broader issues, let me close with a reason that I think it is important to provide this space for theology within religious studies. Theology's exclusion from religious studies is often premised on an assumption that religion is fundamentally non-rational. Whether understood as an irrational superstition, as based in feeling and intuition, and/or as an irreducibly personal experience, religion understood in this manner becomes something about which reasoned exchange is virtually impossible. In accepting this picture and excluding theology altogether from the university, adamant secularists unwittingly join forces with anti-intellectual adherents of religious traditions in supporting the idea that we cannot engage religious ideas constructively. One of the greatest costs of allocating religion such a small role in public and secular education in the United States is that it results in broad swaths of the population – including many educated elites – who never question that faith is some primordial given about which it is impossible to reason. The public discourse about religion that results is remarkably uninformed and uncritical. Ultimately, then, one of the most important reasons for including these theological elements in the study of religion in the secular university is that it educates people to think more critically about religious claims.

## Notes

[1] Where earlier chapters were concerned with obviously theological work being done in religious studies, recent work has highlighted the more subtle endurance of Protestant presuppositions even in supposedly more pluralistic conceptions of the study of religion. For a small sampling, see Jonathan Z. Smith,

*Drudgery Divine: On the Comparison of Early Christianities and the Religions of Late Antiquity*. London: University of London, 1990; Daniel Dubuisson, *The Western Construction of Religion: Myths, Knowledge, and Ideology*, trans. William Sayers. Baltimore: Johns Hopkins University Press, 2003; Tomoko Masuzawa, *The Invention of World Religions, or, How European Universalism Was Preserved in the Language of Pluralism*. Chicago: University of Chicago Press, 2005; and Russell T. McCutcheon, *Critics Not Caretakers: Redescribing the Public Study of Religion*. Albany: State University of New York Press, 2001.

² I draw my observation about the prevalence of this point largely from infor-
mal conversations. Russell McCutcheon provides an example when he contrasts
the approach he advocates with that of 'normative critics'; 'Religion, Ire, and
Dangerous Things', *Journal of the American Academy of Religion*, 72, 1 (2004), 177.
For an outstanding critique of McCutcheon, see Tyler Roberts, 'Exposure and
Explanation: On the New Protectionism in the Study of Religion', *Journal of the
American Academy of Religion*, 72, 1 (2004), 143–72.

³ McCutcheon exemplifies this appeal to postmodernism as well, though Roberts
has pointed out the way in which 'despite a "postmodernist" veneer, he holds
an essentially modernist view of the conceptual hierarchy by which the study of
religion is related to theology' (Roberts, 'Exposure and Explanation', 158).

⁴ Before going further, let me stress that my concern here is with the boundaries
of religious studies, not the particular approaches I find most convincing. There
are of course many approaches with which I disagree but that I do not want to
exclude from the discipline.

⁵ Christine Korsgaard, *The Sources of Normativity*. Cambridge: Cambridge University
Press, 1996, 8–9.

⁶ Given my present purposes, I am less concerned with the precise borders of
the concept of 'normativity' than with illustrating the commonality between
the different types of normative claims that I discuss below. I realize that by
defining 'normative' so broadly in this paragraph, I seem to include all forms
of epistemic normativity, thereby opening the way to the idea that virtually all
statements are normative. My arguments , however, do not require such a broad
claim – merely the acceptance of the normativity of the kinds of claims I discuss
below. Many of these issues could also be approached in terms of the ongoing
debate over the fact value distinction.

⁷ Immanuel Kant, *Groundwork of the Metaphysics of Morals*, in *Practical Philosophy*,
ed. Mary J. Gregor and Allen W. Wood and trans. Mary J. Gregor. Cambridge:
Cambridge University Press, 1999, 73.

⁸ Martha C. Nussbaum, 'Non-Relative Virtues: An Aristotelian Approach', in *The
Quality of Life*, ed. Martha C. Nussbaum and Amartya Sen. Oxford: Clarendon
Press, 1993, 246. Although Martha Nussbaum holds an appointment at the
University of Chicago Law School, the Philosophy Department, and the Divinity
School, I identify her principally as a philosopher.

⁹ Robert A. Orsi, *Between Heaven and Earth: The Religious Worlds People Make and the
Scholars Who Study Them*. Princeton: Princeton University Press, 2005, 172.

¹⁰ Orsi, *Between Heaven and Earth*, 173.

¹¹ There is the question whether a certain conception of discourse as nothing
more than a language game can abstain from making the kinds of normative

claims that I have in mind here. While that might be possible, were we to limit academic discourse to language conceived in this way, we would have to exclude most of what currently happens in the academy – particularly in the natural and social sciences – from the university.

[12] For an excellent discussion of related matters in terms of the 'sacred/profane' dichotomy, see Robert Orsi, 'Everyday Miracles: The Study of Lived Religion', in *Lived Religion in America: Toward a History of Practice*, ed. David D. Hall. Princeton: Princeton University Press, 1997, 3–21, especially 5–7.

[13] Russell T. McCutcheon, *Critics Not Caretakers: Redescribing the Public Study of Religion*. Albany: State University of New York Press, 2001.

[14] Rudolf Otto, *The Idea of the Holy: An Inquiry into the Non-rational Factor in the Idea of the Divine and its Relation to the Rational*, trans. John W. Harvey. London and Oxford: Oxford University Press, 1950.

[15] See Friedrich Schleiermacher, *On Religion: Speeches to its Cultured Despisers*, trans. Richard Crouter. Cambridge: Cambridge University Press, 1988 and Friedrich Schleiermacher, *The Christian Faith*, ed. H. R. Mackintosh and J. S. Stewart. London and New York: T & T Clark, 1999, §§ 1–31.

[16] George A. Lindbeck, *The Nature of Doctrine: Religion and Theology in a Postliberal Age*. Philadelphia: Westminster Press, 1984; Alasdair MacIntyre, *Whose Justice? Which Rationality?* Notre Dame, IN: University of Notre Dame Press, 1988; and Alasdair MacIntyre, *Three Rival Versions of Moral Enquiry: Encyclopaedia, Genealogy, and Tradition*. Notre Dame, IN: University of Notre Dame Press, 1990.

[17] I have developed my views on MacIntyre in Thomas A. Lewis, 'On the Limits of Narrative: Communities in Pluralistic Society', *Journal of Religion*, 86, 1 (2006), 55–80 and 'Heterogeneous Community: Beyond New Traditionalism', *Critical Studies*, 28 (2006), 55–72.

[18] Roberts, 'Exposure and Explanation', 162.

[19] Stout's work is particularly relevant because one of his significant targets is the claim – made but subsequently disavowed by another neo-pragmatist, Richard Rorty – that religion is a conversation stopper. See Richard Rorty, 'Religion as a Conversation-stopper', in *Philosophy and Social Hope*. London: Penguin Books, 1999, 168–174. Rorty has revised his position in 'Religion in the Public Square: A Reconsideration', *Journal of Religious Ethics* 31, 1 (2003), 141–149.

[20] Jeffrey Stout, *Democracy and Tradition*. Princeton: Princeton University Press, 2004, 73.

[21] To say that a scholar must be willing to provide reasons for any particular claim or position, however, does not entail that she must do so in every piece of writing. Just as an economist might make use of game theory without providing an extensive justification of its validity in every piece of writing, so scholars of religion may produce works that take certain claims for granted within that context. Doing so only becomes problematic when the scholar declares those presuppositions illegitimate objects of enquiry. Part of the academic enterprise is that, when pressed, a scholar should be able to offer such a defence. We do not need to write a philosophical treatise every time we use the word 'cruel', but we need to be willing to accept the concept of 'cruelty' as a legitimate issue for enquiry. It is likely the case that scholars of religion encounter claims that a particular authority or experience is beyond question more frequently than

scholars in many other disciplines, but I suspect that the same dynamic is common to other fields as well.

22  Here I do want to allow space for appeals to purportedly universal experiences, such as those emphasized by Martha Nussbaum.

23  At the same time, it leaves space for diverse approaches within religious studies. Too often our discussions of what is proper in the study of religion sound as if there should be one way of doing religious studies. Against such presuppositions, I think the strength of the discipline derives in large part from the plurality of types of investigations we conduct and questions we ask.

Chapter 7

# Towards a Socio-cultural, Non-theological Definition of Religion

James L. Cox

## Introduction

This chapter contends that the academic study of religions is undertaken not to achieve any number of worthy or noble ends, such as fostering world peace, encouraging inter-religious dialogue, elevating dispossessed peoples to positions of power or to substantiate philosophical or theological arguments. Rather, its aim is to provide a framework for identifying those human activities which can be called 'religion', and to make assertions about such activities that can be tested empirically. For this reason, a proper understanding of the relationship between the academic study of religions and theology depends on the way religion is defined. In this chapter, the author proposes a two-pronged definition. One part focuses on the beliefs and experiences which identifiable communities postulate about non-falsifiable alternate realities and the other, following the French sociologist Danièle Hervieu-Léger, examines religion as the authoritative transmission of tradition. The chapter concludes that by defining religion in these ways, notions of theological essentialism are uprooted from their longstanding association with the study of religions, thereby firmly situating religious studies among the social sciences.

I have chosen to present a religious studies perspective on the topic by proposing what I am calling a socio-cultural, non-essentialist definition of religion. I regard a definition as an appropriate starting place, because, in my view, much confusion has been generated by the so-called 'object' of the study of religions, which in turn has led to further confusion about methods appropriate to religious studies. By clarifying the meaning of religion, I hope to decouple the category from its longstanding association with theology. I will approach this topic in three sections: (1) I will make clear the pragmatic and empirical assumptions that support my definition; (2) I then define religion in two parts, one which defines its substantive content and the other, which employs a sociological model; (3) I will conclude by discussing the implications of my proposed definition.

## A pragmatic approach to defining religion

In his introduction to the volume *The Pragmatics of Defining Religion*, which he co-edited with J. G. Platvoet, the Dutch scholar of religion Arie Molendijk argues that 'we cannot do without stipulative definitions, in order to demarcate the subject in a particular context' (1999: 3). A stipulative definition for Molendijk is a pragmatic one, developed 'for the sake of a specific undertaking' (9). In the context of defining religion, therefore, we are not looking for a 'true' definition, but for an appropriate and useful definition that at the same time corresponds to actual usage. This does not mean that our definition must conform to language used by religious practitioners, but it must be capable of furthering academic clarity while remaining recognizable to wider, non-academic audiences, including those who fit into the definition proposed. The value of pragmatic definitions depends entirely on their utility in promoting the practical applications for which they are intended.

If we follow this largely utilitarian interpretation, in the context of this chapter, my aim is not to achieve any number of worthy or noble ends, such as fostering world peace, encouraging inter-religious dialogue, elevating dispossessed peoples to positions of power or of substantiating philosophical or theological arguments. My aim is to provide a framework for identifying those human activities, which can be called 'religion', and for making assertions about these activities that can be tested empirically. Following the thinking of Karl Popper (1959 [1935]), for a theory to be fully scientific, it must be falsifiable. If whatever idea being considered cannot be falsified, it operates outside the bounds of scientific investigation, and belongs to another, non-empirical realm – such as the metaphysical, theological or spiritual. If something cannot be verified, this does not make it unscientific. Many theories cannot be verified, at least according to known evidence, but in principle, they could be falsified. Popper famously used the example of an inductive method to test the proposition: 'All swans are white'. Obviously, this proposition cannot be verified finally, unless every swan everywhere could be accounted for and confirmed as white (1959: 27, 101).[1] Such a proposition, however, can be falsified, and indeed has been, by a species of black swans native to Australia. The proposition, 'All swans are white', in this sense is not verifiable, but fits fully into the category of a scientifically testable statement, since it can be falsified. This, of course, reflects what has been called a 'naïve' use of the inductive method, using the principle of falsifiability, but Popper preferred to apply the concept to theoretical considerations by contending that theories which cannot be falsified must be placed outside the process of scientific consideration (Smart 1999: 265; Kippenberg 2003: 159). I do not intend here to go into detailed discussions in the philosophy of science, in which Popper plays an important historical role, but, following the pragmatic approach of Molendijk, I am suggesting that for purposes of a scientific definition of religion, the principle of non-falsifiability performs a utilitarian function in circumscribing a scientific approach to the study of religions.

My own definition of religion concentrates in the first instance on the key phrase: an identifiable community's beliefs about and experiences of postulated non-falsifiable alternate realities. The principal elements in this formulation include an identifiable community or socially recognizable group, what that community believes and claims to have experienced about and in response to what it collectively postulates to be realities that are clearly distinguishable from ordinary beliefs about the world and everyday experiences in it. I regard this way of referring to religion as one side of a two-pronged definition. The other, based on the work of the French sociologist, Danièle Hervieu-Léger, situates religious communities in historical, social and cultural contexts by insisting that religion transmits an authoritative tradition, or what Hervieu-Léger calls 'a chain of memory' (1999: 89). This two-sided approach, at once focusing on what adherents themselves postulate, while at the same time emphasizing patterns of community authority, provides a definition of religion freed from theological associations.

## Part one of the definition: focus on the community's beliefs and experiences

The first part of my definition of religion restricts the study of religion to 'identifiable communities', which means that religion is always, in the words of Jeppe Jensen (2003: 117) a 'social fact'. Theories about religion, of course, as Jensen (2003: 118–21) argues further, are also social facts, which means that scholars of religion must always conduct their research in a self-critical, reflexive and transparent manner. Nonetheless, when we speak about religion, we are describing and interpreting that which is observable and testable as part of identifiable social systems. The scholar of religion cannot study individual experiences as religion, unless the experiences are somehow embedded in shared social constructs that are codified, symbol-ized and institutionalized in communities. In the case of individuals who testify to intense experiences of an extramundane reality, these can be treated as religion only if the individual incorporates the experiences into the life of an already existing identifiable community, or, as in the case of many charismatic leaders or prophets, forges the experience into a new religious movement comprising a definite group. Individual experiences are interesting to psychologists or to those who wish to classify types of experiences, but on my definition, without the community element, they cannot be included within the category 'religion'. The term identifiable refers to the requirement that a scholar place limits around communities under study, using sometimes historical methods, at other times defining them geographically, or in other contexts restricting them according to social or cultural criteria. In the end, we must be able to locate, delimit and contextualize the groups about which we are speaking.

The identifiable community often entails far more within it than 'reli-gion', but in its religious dimension, it possesses certain characteristics. Its primary focus points towards what members of the community postulate collectively as an alternate reality or realities. The term 'postulate' favours the view of the outside researcher, since it attributes to the alleged source of a community's beliefs and experiences the status of a theory, or even an opinion, which is not subject to the rules of empirical investigation. Communities themselves engage in acts of believing, expressed symbol-ically in language, usually in rituals, texts or stories, which in turn prod-uce experiences that the outsider presumes are similar, since they result from shared symbolic systems. Religious communities thus believe in and experience what, from the perspective of the scholar of religions, adherents merely postulate about alternate realities. Adherents themselves do more than postulate; they testify, bear witness, declare, affirm. For the scholar, the objects towards which these declarations of faith point remain entirely non-falsifiable and thus the declarations themselves cannot be credited scientifically with any higher status than that of postulations.

The identifiable communities postulate about something quite specific, what I call alternate realities. I am using this term quite deliberately, and not as it is often employed in everyday language as meaning 'alternative', such as might be implied in the phrase, 'alternate sources of oil'. Alternate, when used adjectivally, as I am employing it, literally has the meaning of switching between, or going from one to another, as in turns. The 'alter-nate' reality refers to another type of belief and experience from what we normally believe and experience in the world. Scholars writing from within the cognitive science of religion frequently refer to this as 'counter-intuitive'. For example, the Finnish scholar Ilkka Pyysiäinen argues that intuitive knowledge is universal since 'the material environment surrounding us is *to some* extent everywhere the same' and thus our way of thinking is also '*to some* extent similar' (2003: 19) (emphasis his). Intuitive knowledge is necessary for humans to survive in the natural environment. We know intuitively, for instance, that in the physical world we cannot 'go through' material objects, but in counter-intuitive ways of thinking, 'the boundaries of these domains are violated' (2003: 20). Counter-intuitively, people can pass through physical objects; they can leave their bodies as spirits or even rise from the dead or be re-incarnated. Pyysiäinen concludes that 'super-human agents' are 'counter-intuitive agents in the sense that in their case we are dealing with agents that typically lack some basic biological and physical properties, such as growth, aging or the need for food' (2003: 21).

I mean something similar, but not identical, to counter-intuitive when I use the term 'alternate realities'. When religious communities speak about their alternate realities, they refer to something like a spirit, a god, a power or force that, although clearly occurring in this world and within consciousness, refers to something quite identifiably different from ordinary experience and consciousness. When members of a group participate in a religious ritual, for example, they know that they are relating to what they postulate to be an entity or entities that operate in a time and space clearly differentiated from the time and space they experience normally outside the ritual context. In one sense, they switch their focus from the ordinary to the non-ordinary, or to an alternate reality. This is not best thought of as an *alternative* reality, as in another, contrasting reality, as implied in the term 'counter-intuitive', but as alternate in the sense that for believers the ordinary enters into and experiences the non-ordinary, moving in turns from the one and back to the other. The term 'realities' applies to the beliefs and practices shared by most communities, by referring to a multi-dimensional non-ordinary world. It can also refer to the fact that religious communities often experience what is alternate in different ways, and thus may switch between not just one alternate reality but numerous realities.

The scholar of religion, of course, cannot study the experiences themselves, nor the postulated alternate realities, but can only describe the observable social facts surrounding what communities do or say in response to that which they claim to be real. This is because beliefs about and experiences of postulated alternate realities are entirely non-falsifiable. Naturally, the fact of believing certain things or not believing them can be falsified, just as it is possible to falsify whether or not individuals in the community claim to have undergone extraordinary experiences. Analyses can proceed about the connections between belief and experience, and the ways these are expressed in mythic, ritual, legal, artistic or other symbolic ways. It is also possible to outline what types of experiences are most likely to be associated with particular belief systems. Yet, neither the objects of belief nor the alleged extramundane character of the experiences can be studied scientifically. This means that academic work is concerned with what communities postulate rather than the object or objects about which their postulations are made. This also suggests that when communities perform certain actions, affirm particular beliefs, organize social relations, endow particular individuals with positions of importance or engage in types of ritual behaviour, all in relation to their postulated non-falsifiable alternate realities, the scholar of religion describes these as accurately as possible and interprets them according to his or her declared theoretical positions. In this way, the process of scientific investigation proceeds based on empirical observations, which produce falsifiable conclusions in a fully transparent manner.

## Religion as the authoritative transmission of authority

In several recent publications, I have sought to interpret a theory of religion as advanced by the French sociologist, Danièle Hervieu-Léger, by applying it to various contexts, including contemporary shamanistic revivals and the religious dimensions of land claims in Alaska and Zimbabwe (See Cox 2003: 69–87; Cox 2004: 259–64; Cox 2006: 239–43). My initial interest in Hervieu-Léger's model of religion was generated by her attempt to remove 'sacredness' from a definition of religion by insisting that religion must be understood as a social expression through its institutions and the authority they maintain over the communities which relate to them. In this way, I hoped to overcome the problem identified by Timothy Fitzgerald who argues that the category 'religion' must be dropped as a legitimate field in the social sciences since, as he has observed correctly in the cases of many writers, it hides within it a theological assumption that defines religion always in relation to a transcendental referent (2000: 17–18). In Hervieu-Léger's analysis I discovered a way to separate the 'sacred' from religion, while still retaining the category as a distinct field of study irreducible to theology. In the end, I wanted to drive a wedge between Fitzgerald's dilemma which forces the study of religion either into theology or into a field Fitzgerald regards as more amenable to scientific approaches he calls 'cultural studies' (2000: 227–34).

It is important to understand at the outset that Hervieu-Léger's concern is to discuss religion in the context of sociological theories of secularization, particularly in light of an idea maintained by scholars well into the 1960s that religion had entered into the last phases of an inevitable decline as society had come increasingly under the sway of scientific rationalism (Hervieu-Léger 1993: 129). The reduction of church membership and affiliation to religious institutions in Western Europe was seen as a clear sign of the eroding influence of religion in modern society. By the 1980s, this interpretation was shown to have suffered from underlying anti-religious presuppositions and as having been quite limited in scope with relevance only to particular established religious institutions operating within Western Europe and North America (Hervieu-Léger 2001: 114–116). Towards the end of the twentieth century, secularization theories seemed to have been proved wrong by contemporary events, such as the revival of religion in the West through charismatic Christianity and the upsurge in New Religious Movements, which on a global scale had parallels in the rapid intensification of religious activity and growth throughout Africa and South America (Lambert 1999: 303–332). Hervieu-Léger's discussion of religion in terms of various themes, such as the originating place of emotion in religion, the boundaries of religion vis à vis widely perceived 'secular' collective activities and the place of tradition in religion must all be understood as part of the ongoing secularization debate. This debate does not define my main concern in this book, but the insights Hervieu-Léger offers about the boundaries between the religious and the non-religious add strength to my wider aim of developing a socially embedded, non-theological definition of religion.

One of Hervieu-Léger's most explicit attempts to define religion is found in her contribution to the Platvoet and Molendijk volume in an article entitled 'Religion as Memory', in which she analyses what she calls the 'diverse surreptitious manifestations of religion in all profane and reputedly non-religious zones of human activity' (1999: 76). The diffusion of religion out of clearly demarcated institutional settings into nebulous, almost ubiquitous, contexts in contemporary Western society makes distinguishing the religious from the non-religious not only more difficult than in previous generations, but one that demands careful academic scrutiny. The modern context raises for Hervieu-Léger fundamental questions which scholars are forced to address when investigating the nature of religion in modernity. On the one hand, she asks, are scholars limited to studying the 'discrete' but clearly identifiable religious influences traditional or 'historic' religions like Christianity, Islam and Judaism exert outside their own institutional spheres? Or are they permitted to study the broad, but loosely defined, effects of religion over wide areas of social life, including political, economic, artistic and scientific interests? To answer these questions, Hervieu-Léger asserts, we must return to the question of defining religion (1999: 76).

Hervieu-Léger argues that recent efforts to address the problem of identifying the boundaries of religion in modernity have become entangled in the old debate between substantive and functional definitions of religion, the former defining religion in terms of supernatural entities and hence in a restricted way, and the latter defining religion according to its function, such as providing meaning, and thus operating in an overly broad way. Substantive definitions render improper all scholarly efforts to comment on expressions of 'sacredness' in modern society, as evidenced, for example, in the ecstatic fervour expressed by fans at football matches. Functional definitions, on the other hand, stretch the limits so widely that religion can include almost anything that relates to questions of meaning in the world (1999: 78). Substantive definitions tend to restrict the study of religions to 'the historical religions' and thus 'condemn sociological thought to being the paradoxical guardian of the "authentic religion" which these historical religions intend to incarnate' (1999: 83). Functional definitions 'turn out to be incapable of mastering the unlimited expansion of the phenomena they try to account for' (1999: 83). It thus becomes clear on Hervieu-Léger's analysis why those who define religion substantively have stressed the decline of religion in the modern world, while those who maintain functional positions emphasize the dispersal of religious symbols in diverse ways through many avenues, previously considered secular, that reflect the atomization of life within contemporary Western culture.

Hervieu-Léger contends that the problem cannot be resolved by siding either with a substantive or functional approach to defining religion, but by turning the focus of defining religion towards a sociological perspective. She asserts that the concern of sociology is not 'knowing, once and for all, what religion is in itself' but of understanding 'the dynamic transformations that are occurring within society that affect religion. From this point of view, religion is not defined 'ontologically', but practically as a tool 'to aid the researcher in his attempt to think socio-religious change, as well as to think the modern mutation of the religious' (1999: 84). This implies that religion cannot be defined as a fixed entity, the parameters of which are demarcated clearly for all time. Nor can religion be defined in terms of the changing beliefs that come to characterize religious transformations. Rather, for Hervieu-Léger, religion must be understood precisely by analysing '*the mutating structures of believing*' (1999: 84) (emphasis hers). The term belief is central to Hervieu-Léger's position, which she prefers to cast in terms of action, as 'acts of believing', not dissimilar to my concept of 'postulating'. She explains: ' "To believe" is belief in motion; it incorporates "the practices, languages, gestures and spontaneous automatisms in which these beliefs are themselves inscribed" ' (1999: 84). Again, in a way similar to the way I explained earlier, Hervieu-Léger notes that 'the actual act of believing . . . escapes experimental demonstration' but 'one can affirm its existence from the point of view of those who believe' (1999: 85).

The act of believing outlines a relationship between the one who believes and the object of belief, whereby 'both individuals and groups submit themselves (consciously or unconsciously) to an exteriorly imposed order' (1999: 85). The act of believing in the modern world, of course, is quite different from believing in a pre-scientific era, but, Hervieu-Léger insists that humans still crave 'security', which remains 'at the heart of the quest for intelligibility' (1999: 85). For individuals, this is expressed in the face of death; for society, it results from the effort to avoid the threat of anomy, or a descent into disorder, chaos and lawlessness (1999: 86). These concerns with individual death and social disorder do not represent leftovers from a previous era; rather, they arise 'out of modernity itself' (1999: 86). Paradoxically, as modernity dissolves the old systems of certainty about the world and substitutes its own ways of maintaining order, 'it develops . . . the social and psychological factors of incertitude' (1999: 86). This makes the scholar's task a complex one, where 'the modern act of believing' is analysed in terms of structures or modes of response to incertitude, since in modernity, a new situation has emerged: 'In the mobile, "fluid" universe . . . all symbols are interchangeable, combinable and transposable into the other' (1999: 86). To define 'religion' in such a context requires the scholar to analyse not a fixed object, or reified thing, but to think of religion as 'a process, as motion' (1999: 87). This means that the content of religion can no longer be thought of as restricted to a certain way of believing, either excluding or including political, social and economic factors, as required both by substantive and functional definitions. 'Religious' believing is not delimited by content, but must be understood in 'an ideal-typical manner' as 'a particular modality of the organization and function of the act of believing' (1999: 87).

If we follow Hervieu-Léger's train of thought to this point, we will see that the question confronting scholars is not, for example, could a modern

spectator sport like football be considered a 'religion', any more than it asks
if modern expressions of Christianity, Judaism or Islam can be regarded
as religious. The important issue for a socially embedded interpretation
of religion depends on the question of legitimization. How is the act of
believing legitimized? And here Hervieu-Léger reaches her own definition
of religion as a mode or structure of the act of believing: 'There is no
religion without the explicit, semi-explicit, or entirely implicit invocation
of *the authority of a tradition*; an invocation which serves as support for the
act of believing' (emphasis hers) (1999: 88). What makes something religious depends on whether or not the forms of believing invoke or 'justify
themselves, first and foremost, upon the claim of their inscription within a
*heritage of belief*' (emphasis hers) (1999: 87–88). The ensuing continuity of
belief defines for any religious group who is included within or excluded
from 'a spiritual community assembling past, present and future believers'.
In this way, religion functions as a mode of 'social integration' and, at the
same time, distinguishes insiders from outsiders by differentiating 'those
who are not of the same heritage' (1999: 88). These considerations lead
to Hervieu-Léger's 'definition' of religion 'as an ideological, practical and
symbolic framework which constitutes, maintains, develops and controls
the consciousness (individual or collective) of membership to a particular
heritage of belief' (1999: 88). Hence, religious groups define themselves
'objectively and subjectively as *a chain of memory*, the continuity of which
transcends history' (1999: 89) (emphasis hers). By relating to a chain of
memory, religious communities collectively share in acts of remembrance
of the past which give 'meaning to the present' and contain the future
(1999: 89).

## Distinguishing the religious from the non-religious

In order to clarify how this definition helps us distinguish what is religion
from what is not, Hervieu-Léger considers the question of sport as religion.
We will be aware, of course, in the case of football, that huge crowds gather
regularly to support a team. These supporters are united by common symbols acting as emblems of the team; they recite chants in unison, as in a ritual; they share beliefs about the superiority of their team, if not by winning,
in an ethical sense, by asserting that their team somehow 'ought' to win.
On Hervieu-Léger's criteria, therefore, football supporters express beliefs
about their team, they carry a memory of great achievements of the past
and they often tell the authorized version of the history of the team in order

to inspire greater loyalty in the present. Yet, Hervieu-Léger refuses to accept that football supporters constitute a religion, although she admits that they may experience moments of euphoria or despair that coincide with many accounts of religious experience. The main point of differentiation is found in the fact that 'high-level competitive sport . . . functions *in the moment*, in the immediacy of the gathering in a kind of corporate emotional awareness' (2000: 103) (emphasis hers). In this sense, football matches correspond to the 'instantaneous production of collective meaning' which characterizes the atomized, individualized and subjective 'systems of meaning' operating within contemporary Western society. In a football match, for example, 'of their own accord' supporters 'fulfil the expectations they arouse' (2000: 103). This means, for Hervieu-Léger, that such sporting events mirror the difference in modern society between 'sacredness', which indeed is a collective experience of a force transcending the individual that provides meaning, as in devotion to the team, its history and shared symbols, but it is not religion, which must have as its defining characteristic 'a ritualized remembering of a core lineage, in relation to which present experience constructs meaning' (2000: 103–104). The inevitable conclusion from this analysis is that sporting events, like mass rock concerts and political demonstrations 'offer in small pieces . . . access to an experience of the sacred (an immediate, emotional realization of meaning) which *en masse* no longer functions in the religious mode' (2000: 104).

I regard the value of Hervieu-Léger's distinction at this point to result from her attempt to separate 'sacredness', understood as immediate gratification, individualized emotional meaning, subjective states and atomized spirituality, from religion, which always and everywhere follows from the transmission of an authoritatively binding tradition over the lives of individuals who identify themselves collectively in a group. This means that, in Western society, the process of atomization or intense individuality erodes the power of authoritative traditions and thus explains why such traditions have lost their hold over individuals, but, at the same time, it helps us separate religion as a social phenomenon from theological assumptions. If there is a transcendental referent in Hervieu-Léger's thinking, it is precisely the historical transmission of tradition, interpreted and re-interpreted by communities, as binding on the group. This is far different from defining religion in terms of divinities, spiritual entities or a supernatural realm. The 'pick and choose' approach towards individual self-fulfilment in modern Western society, whereby traditions are divested of their authority and overtaken by matters of taste suited to the particular needs or interests of individuals, distinguishes experiences of the 'sacred' from religion. Even in great sporting events, the immediate gratification of the individual is evident and is lost in the emotional satisfaction or despair conveyed in the transience of a result on any given day.

If we push this analysis very far, we will soon discover that Hervieu-Léger is open to the criticism that her distinction between the religious and the non-religious points to a difference of degree rather than of substance. The transmitted authority must in some sense be overwhelming and not moderate; the emotional effect must be lasting and not transient; the power over life must be total and not split between many competing interests; the allegiance of the individual must reside in the group and not depend on personal needs. When such intense commitments fade and other interests become more consuming, we see individuals seeking experiences of 'sacredness', which confer existential meaning, but, for Hervieu-Léger, this cannot be religion, since these experiences lack the overwhelming authoritative power of a tradition that has been transmitted, according to the community's myths, from ancient times. If the dividing line between religion and experiences of sacredness is simply one of degree, the arguments about the constitutive factors within religion are not resolved. Indeed, to continue with the example of sport, the Scottish football clubs, Glasgow Celtic and Glasgow Rangers, with their historic roots in sectarian allegiances, may engender something much stronger than transient emotional fulfilment for their respective supporters when one team triumphs over the other (Giulianotti and Robertson 2006: 171–198; Giulianotti and Gerrard 2001: 23–42). This explains why I find unconvincing Hervieu-Léger's submission that 'there is every justification for treating the celebration of the Olympic Games as a religion in the full meaning of the term' (2000: 104). There seems only a relative difference between the Olympic Games, which in Hervieu-Léger's words, 'convey meaning and legitimacy to the rites and celebrations' (2000: 104) and football matches, where supporters may well trace their team's traditions to collective struggles for independence and identity. The Hervieu-Léger definition, in my view, although extremely useful for embedding religion in socio-cultural contexts, cannot stand on its own, and requires the first part of my two-sided definition to indicate unambiguously what we mean by the academic category 'religion'.

## A delimited socio-cultural definition of religion

By incorporating my earlier discussion of religion as outlined in the Platvoet and Molendijk volume into the one developed by Danièle Hervieu-Léger, I am thus able to create a definition which I contend is empirical, socio-cultural, non-theological and non-essentialist. It is embedded in a sociological perspective, but avoids Hervieu-Léger's lack of clarity when distinguishing the religious from the non-religious on sociological grounds alone. I thus offer the following definition as one that promises to break new ground in the way we conceive and study religion:

> *Religion refers to identifiable communities that base their beliefs and experiences of postulated non-falsifiable realities on a tradition that is transmitted authoritatively from generation to generation.*

The emphasis in my own earlier definition of religion on an identifiable community is fully consistent with Hervieu-Léger's assertion that there is no religion without the transmission of an authoritative tradition amongst social groups. The problem Hervieu-Léger encounters when trying to separate the religious from the non-religious is overcome by inserting into her account a limitation that contends that communities are acting religiously only in so far as the traditions they are transmitting derive their authority from postulated non-falsifiable alternate realities. On this definition, no degree of emotional attachment is necessary before experiences within identifiable communities can be regarded as religious. The components of religion are entirely objective and include an identifiable community, its beliefs about and experiences of postulated non-falsifiable alternate realities, and its traditions that are derived from and centred around an authority that is passed on from generation to generation.

On this account, football is not religion, simply because its referent is neither non-falsifiable nor an alternate reality, even if its traditions are transmitted with such a hold over the supporters that they adhere to the team's authority and undergo intense emotional experiences as a result. On the other hand, Marxism might be regarded as a religion, since, not only do adherents follow an authority that is transmitted, but the reality envisaged is alternate, in the sense that it is eschatological and involves a non-falsifiable claim that history will achieve an inevitable utopian conclusion. If Marxism is included within this two-pronged definition of religion, but sport is not, it is clear that a religion is not a religion unless the identifiable community postulates beliefs about and experiences of a non-falsifiable alternate reality. Equally, a group does not qualify as a religion if it does not transmit its tradition authoritatively. Many recent movements, including self-help groups, associations founded by neo-shamanistic practitioners and contemporary Western paganism, fit better into Hervieu-Léger's model as individualistic responses to the crumbling of a collective memory than they do as bona fide new religions.

**Implications of the definition**

The definition I have proposed challenges theologically inspired definitions of religion, the essentialist assumptions of which lie buried within
most approaches to teaching world religions in schools and universities,
where the great traditions are presented as discrete, self-contained systems
that have appeared in history from a common or universal ahistorical core.
It could be argued that the definition I have created falls into the same
trap as other substantive definitions by limiting religion to a belief in gods
or supernatural entities, which although understood differently in various cultural contexts, reflects the same essential focus. This could even be
extended to the charge that my definition veils theological assumptions,
since it is restricted in one part by insisting that religions focus on alternate
realities.

I have sought to avoid this by stressing in my definition the importance
of 'identifiable communities', which tends to localize the discussion and at
the same time insists on arriving at conclusions derived from specific historical research and ethnographic descriptions. The term 'discrete' in this
sense applies to the identifiable communities, and only within a very limited
frame of reference, can this be extended to similar communities that share
elements of a common heritage. This, however, is not the major argument
that could be put against my definition. It is clear that I have employed a
modified version of a substantive definition of religion by insisting that
religions everywhere must refer to non-falsifiable alternate realities. This
sounds very similar to those who argue that for a religion to be defined as
a religion, it must direct its primary attention towards supernatural entities
or divinities. I have tried to show that I am not restricting the definition
to supernatural entities, but to experiences in time and space that clearly
are distinguished by adherents from their ordinary experiences in time
and space. These can include ritual contexts or reverence paid to special
objects or landmarks, but something other than the ordinary is associated
with the attention paid by devotees within such times and to such places.
Without such a focus, I am arguing we do not have religion, but something
else that is quite identifiable in other terms, such as a political order, an
economic system, a psychological reaction or a social construct. Religion,
of course, is interwoven into each of these elements, and only artificially
extracted from them for scholarly analyses. This is not a practice restricted
to religious studies, but occurs in all academic disciplines. The political
scientist examines how decisions are legitimated; the economist studies
means of exchange and market forces that affect them; the psychologist
analyses individual reactions to external stimuli; the sociologist outlines

structures that influence community behaviour. The scholar of religion describes and interprets how communities relate to non-falsifiable alternate realities. The focus in the study of religion, as I have already argued, is not on the alternate realities, which cannot be studied, but on the communities that do the postulating, and thus follows an entirely empirical methodology.

This is essentialist only in the sense that every academic discipline must define what it means by its field of study. It is not essentialist in a theological way. This is because the study of religion concentrates precisely on what identifiable communities postulate about non-falsifiable alternate realities, not on what the scholar postulates about them. As a student of religion, I do not define the focus towards which people direct their attention when they act religiously; I simply define what I mean by actions that I regard as religious. That identifiable communities organize many of their activities around what they postulate to be alternate realities is incontrovertible. They tell stories about them, perform rituals to them, communicate directly with them, appeal to them in times of crisis or at moments of significance in the life of the community. The communities act in these ways according to their own declarations about their non-falsifiable alternate realties. In other words, they do the postulating; the scholar describes, classifies and interprets, but does not postulate about non-falsifiable alternate realities unless the scholar is a theologian. The scientist of religion remains focused entirely on empirical facts and on observable behaviours.

Another objection to my revised definition could employ the charge that it favours the historical religions, precisely because it emphasizes authoritative tradition and its cross-generational transmission. This might even seem to be restricting the study of religions to institutions, and thus placing out of bounds the new forms of spirituality that are becoming extremely popular in Western society. In this sense, somewhat by the back door, the world religions would gain precedence over loosely organized movements in the academic study of religions. Although my definition restricts itself to identifiable communities, this does not refer exclusively to the historic or world religions. This definition, for example, can be utilized quite pragmatically in the study of indigenous societies. By insisting that religion must be defined in relation to authoritative traditions, I am suggesting that the identity of religious communities is constrained by their association with the traditions they have inherited and by the authority these exert over them. In other words, religion is not about individual tastes, preferences, choices or needs unless these are connected directly into a community that legitimates its authority by reference to a tradition that constitutes its heritage. This does not exclude religions outside those conventionally designated as the world's historical religions, such as Indigenous Religions, but it excludes transient, popular, individualistic movements.

If my socio-cultural, non-essentialist definition of religion is accepted, we will be led to conclude inevitably that the academic study of religions is not theology; yet, it is not strictly anthropology, sociology, psychology, economics or politics. As a scholar of religion, my aim is to describe, fairly represent and interpret what identifiable communities say, do and believe as a direct result of postulating alternate realities. My descriptions are accountable to the data; my representations need to include the communities I am representing and my interpretations need to be grounded in my own acknowledged and transparent personal constructs. This approach is scientific, because it is a study of a human activity, which is entirely testable, and indeed capable of falsification. Religious studies on this analysis includes theology as a part of its arena of study. Theologians, at least on one definition, are practitioners. They study, analyse and interpret, generally from within one tradition, the meaning of what that tradition maintains is a revelatory act. Scholars of religion regard theologies as ways some communities reflect, often systematically and analytically, on their own non-falsifiable alternate realities. In other words, theologies, like ritual, morality, myth, scripture, community, law and art, form part of the data on which religious studies carries out its work. This is not to assert a position of superiority, but merely to define quite different and distinctive roles for religious studies and theology. It is for this reason that if my definition of religion is employed, religious studies will obtain a fully separate role in the academy from theology or at least be seen as existing alongside theology in university departments only as an accident of history, and not as complicit with an oftentimes unstated ideological commitment to a transcendental referent.

## Notes

This chapter is derived from a section of chapter 4 of the author's book, *From Primitive to Indigenous: The Academic Study of Indigenous Religions*, published in 2007 by Ashgate.

[1] Popper observes: 'No matter how many instances of white swans we may have observed, this does not justify the conclusion that all swans are white' (emphasis his) (1959: 27).

# Bibliography

Bruce, Steve (2002), *God is Dead. Secularization in the West.* Oxford: Blackwell Publishing.

Chryssides, George D. (1999), *Exploring New Religions.* London: Cassell.

Cox, James L. (1998). 'Religious Typologies and the Postmodern Critique', *Method and Theory in the Study of Religion*, 10, 244–262.

—(1999), 'Intuiting Religion: A Case for Preliminary Definitions', in J. G. Platvoet and A. L. Molendijk (eds), *The Pragmatics of Defining Religion: Contexts, Concepts and Contests.* Leiden: Brill, 267–284.

—(2003), 'Contemporary Shamanism in Global Contexts: "Religious" Appeals to an Archaic Tradition?', *Studies in World Christianity: The Edinburgh Review of Theology and Religion*, 9 (1): 69–87.

—(2004), 'Afterword. Separating Religion from the "Sacred": Methodological Agnosticism and the Future of Religious Studies', in S. Sutcliffe (ed.), *Religion: Empirical Studies.* Aldershot: Ashgate, 259–264.

—(2006), *A Guide to the Study of Religion: Key Figures, Formative Influences and Subsequent Debates.* London and New York: Continuum.

—(2007), *From Primitive to Indigenous: The Academic Study of Indigenous Religions.* Aldershot and Burlington: Ashgate.

Fitzgerald, Timothy (2000), *The Ideology of Religious Studies.* New York and Oxford: Oxford University Press.

Giulianotti, Richard and Gerrard, Michael (2001), 'Cruel Britannia? Glasgow Rangers, Scotland and "Hot" Football Rivalries', in G. Armstrong and R. Giulianotti (eds), *Fear and Loathing in World Football.* Oxford: Berg, 23–42.

Giulianotti, Richard and Robertson, Roland (2006), 'Glocalization, Globalization and Migration: The Case of Scottish Football Supporters in North America', *International Sociology*, 21 (3), 171–198.

Hervieu-Léger, Danièle (1993), 'Present-day Emotional Renewals. The End of Secularization or the End of Religion?', in W. H. Swatos, Jr. (ed.). *A Future for Religion? New Paradigms for Social Analysis.* Newbury Park, California, London and New Delhi: Sage Publications, 129–148.

—(1999), 'Religion as Memory: Reference to Tradition and the Constitution of a Heritage of Belief in Modern Societies', in J. G. Platvoet and A. L. Molendijk (eds), *The Pragmatics of Defining Religion: Contexts, Concepts and Contests.* Leiden: Brill, 73–92.

—(2000), *Religion as a Chain of Memory* (translated by Simon Lee). Cambridge: Polity Press.

—(2001), 'The Twofold Limit of the Notion of Secularization', in L. Woodhead (ed.), *Peter Berger and the Study of Religion.* London and New York: Routledge, 112–125.

Jakobsen, Marete Demant (1999), *Shamanism. Traditional and Contemporary Approaches to the Mastery of Spirits and Healing.* Oxford and New York: Berghahn Books.

Jensen, Jeppe Sinding (2003), 'Social Facts, Metaphysics and Rationality in the Study of Religion as a Human Science', in J. S. Jensen and L. H. Martin (eds), *Rationality and the Science of Religion.* London and New York: Routledge, 117–135.

Kippenberg, Hans G. (2003), 'Rationality in Studying Historical Religions', in J. S. Jensen and L. H. Martin (eds), *Rationality and the Science of Religion*. London and New York: Routledge, 157–166.

Lambert, Yves (1999), 'Religion in Modernity as a New Axial Age: Secularization or New Religious Forms?', *Sociology of Religion*, 60 (3): 303–332.

Leeuw, van der, Gerardus (1938), *Religion in Essence and Manifestation. A Study in Phenomenology* (translated by J. E. Turner). London: George Allen and Unwin.

Molendijk, Arie L. (1999), 'In Defence of Pragmatism', in J. G. Platvoet and A. L. Molendijk (eds), *The Pragmatics of Defining Religion: Contexts, Concepts and Contests*. Leiden: Brill, 3–19.

Morris, Brian (1987), *Anthropological Studies of Religion: An Introduction*. Cambridge: Cambridge University Press.

Otto, Rudolf (1926), *The Idea of the Holy: An Inquiry into the Non Rational Factor in the Idea of the Divine* (translated by John W. Harvey). London: Humphrey Milford and Oxford University Press.

Partridge, Christopher (ed.) (2004), *New Religions: A Guide. New Religious Movements, Sects and Alternative Spiritualities*. New York: Oxford University Press.

Popper, Karl L. (1959 [1935]), *The Logic of Scientific Discovery*. New York: Basic Books.

Pyysiäinen, Ilkka (2003), *How Religion Works: Towards a New Cognitive Science of Religion*. Leiden: Brill.

Smart, Ninian (1999), *World Philosophies*. London and New York: Routledge.

Sutcliffe, Steven and Bowman Marion (eds) (2000), *Beyond New Age: Exploring Alternative Spirituality*. Edinburgh: Edinburgh University Press.

Tiele, C. P. (1973 [1897]), 'Extracts from *Elements of the Science of Religion*' in J. Waardenburg, *Classical Approaches to the Study of Religion: Aims, Methods and Theories of Research. I. Introduction and Anthology*. The Hague and Paris: Mouton, 96–104.

Trigg, Roger (2003), 'Rationality, Social Science and Religion', in J. S. Jensen and L. H. Martin (eds), *Rationality and the Science of Religion*. London and New York: Routledge, 99–116.

Chapter 8

# A Spatial Analysis of the Relationship between Theology and Religious Studies
## Knowledge-power Strategies and Metaphors of Containment and Separation

Kim Knott

*Scholarly labor is a disciplined exaggeration in the direction of knowledge; taxonomy is a valuable tool in achieving that distortion.*

Smith (2004a: 175)

Jonathan Z. Smith was referring here to the classification of 'religion' and its sub-sets but his comment is no less apt for the ways in which we study such things.[1] Whether we class what we do as theology, religious studies, comparative religion, science of religion, divinity or the study of religions, why we chose that designation, and how we live by it, arguably constitutes a strategy of 'disciplined exaggeration in the direction of knowledge'. How we as scholars designate what we do and who we do it with reveals a good deal about our standpoint, perspective and values. The designation is more than a clue to such things, however; it becomes a heading around which knowledge is produced, and a key to the methods we use, to the focus of our attention, the scholarly traditions to which we adhere, and the way we relate to other bodies of knowledge or disciplines.

This is a study of how those who devote their scholarly lives to understanding, analysing, discussing and interpreting 'religion' and everything associated with it name and order who they are and what they do. I know that voicing it in this way, around the concept of 'religion', already begins to locate what I will say both historically, in terms of modernity, and personally, in terms of my own scholarly background, but we all have to start somewhere.[2] My particular approach is socio-spatial. I will use the tools that I have developed in recent years to locate 'religion' in ostensibly 'secular' spaces (Knott 2005a, 2005b) in order to examine this question of

'Theology *and* Religious Studies or Theology *v.* Religious Studies?'. This is appropriate because, as a contested issue (Theology *v.* Religious Studies) that involves professional communities and the institutional and discursive spaces in which they work, it is amenable to a socio-spatial analysis.

## Disciplines, space and language

Groups, classes or fractions of classes cannot constitute themselves, or recognise one another, as 'subjects' unless they generate (or produce) a space. Ideas, representations or values which do not succeed in making their mark on space, and thus generating (or producing) an appropriate morphology will lose all pith and become mere signs, resolve themselves into abstract descriptions, or mutate into fantasies.

(Lefebvre 1991: 416–417)

The debate about the relationship between theology and religious studies, as well as being 'disciplined exaggeration in the direction of knowledge', also concerns the struggle to create and authorize autonomous spaces – whether physical, mental or social.[3] However, neither the process of disciplinary classification nor the socio-spatial struggle around it can be achieved in a vacuum, or without others to contend with. As separate disciplinary fields, both theology and religious studies require other bodies of knowledge in relation to which they can define themselves, as well as other communities of scholars to debate and engage with.

In what follows I will examine the spatial language present in discourse about the disciplines of theology and religious studies. Already in this chapter I have made use of the language of struggle and space. Some terms, like 'discipline' and 'knowledge', indicate the subject matter but, at the same time, are also suggestive of order and power (Foucault 1970; Gordon 1980). This is further reinforced by references to 'trial, 'debate', 'strategy' and 'contestation', not surprising given what Lefebvre writes about the need to generate and authorize discursive and social space.[4] Socio-spatial terminology has already been in evidence, whether with reference to 'bodies', 'communities', 'standpoint', 'location', 'direction', even 'classification' and 'designation'. The use of such terminology is not accidental; it is fundamental to how we place others in relation to ourselves.

The embodied realist agenda of George Lakoff and Mark Johnson (1999; Johnson 1987) helps to clarify this. Lakoff and Johnson link our human embodiment with the metaphors we use and our attempts at categorization by means of the cognitive unconscious: In asking philosophical questions 'we use a reason shaped by the body, a cognitive unconscious to which we have no direct access, and metaphorical thought of which we are largely unaware' (1999: 7). Categorization, they suggest, is not merely an intellectual matter (19). We categorize as we do 'because we have the brains and bodies we have and because we interact in the world the way we do' (18), on the basis of up/down, front/back, left/right, in and out. Others are 'outside' my body, but those who are closest to us are 'inside' the social body, the family, clan or tribe. Beyond this social body is a territory inhabited by 'others', 'outsiders' with their own unknown identities and orders (Anttonen 1996). Between inside and outside there is a boundary. The operation of this 'container schema', to use Lakoff and Johnson's term, will become evident later in the chapter. Their principal point, however, is that 'our bodies define a set of fundamental spatial orientations that we use not only in orienting ourselves but in perceiving the relationship of one object to another' (1999: 35). So, in looking at the spatial language that theologians and scholars of religion use to talk about what they do, and to distinguish themselves from others, I start from the body and its unconscious processes of conceptualization and categorization.

What do I hope to achieve in looking at the language we use – as 'bedfellows' in the study of religion – to describe our discipline or field and its relationship to others? As Bourdieu wrote in *Homo Academicus* (1988: xi),

> The sociologist who chooses to study his own world in its nearest and most familiar aspects should not, as the ethnologist would, domesticate the exotic, but, if I may venture the expression, exoticize the domestic, through a break with his initial relation of intimacy with modes of life and thought which remain opaque to him because they are too familiar.

I shall trouble the familiar waters of what we say about theology and religious studies, the everyday terms we use, in order to examine how we imagine and relate to one another within and beyond our disciplinary territory.

## What scholars say about theology and religious studies: a socio-spatial analysis

Let me move now to the data themselves, and my approach to them. As part of their scholarship, theologians and academics in religious studies have commented on the nature, form and mission of their disciplines, whether by way of introduction to students or in methodological discussions with peers. What some of them have said provides the data for this analysis; their concepts and models thus become 'folk' or *emic* categories for this meta-analysis. As a scholar of religion myself, I cannot claim much objectivity or distance from these categories or their creators. However, I shall adopt the operational stance of a meta-outsider, not because I wish to endorse the possibility of a 'position from nowhere' (Nagel, in Hufford 1999: 296), but rather to make the temporary and strategic move from 'inside' (the religious studies camp) to 'outside' both theology and religious studies camps in order to assess the two parties and their discursive interrelationship.

Necessarily, given the considerable body of material on the nature of theology and religious studies and their interrelationship, I have had to be selective, using relevant documents from professional bodies and a major introductory textbook on the study of religion. I shall begin with the mission statements of two academic associations to which many British scholars in theology and/or religious studies are connected: the Society for the Study of Theology (SST) and the International Association for the History of Religions (IAHR), to which the British Association for the Study of Religions (BASR) is linked.

> SST exists . . . to promote excellence in the study of Christian Theology by facilitating and shaping theological thought, conversation and community. In particular, the Society's object is to identify and discuss important themes, questions and dialogues which call for theological engagement; and to explore the nature of and foster theological integrity, responsibility and vocation in academy, church and other areas of public life.[5]

> The IAHR seeks to promote the activities of all scholars and affiliates that contribute to the historical, social, and comparative study of religion. As such, the IAHR is the preeminent international forum for the critical, analytical and cross-cultural study of religion, past and present. The IAHR is not a forum for confessional, apologetical, or other similar concerns.[6]

Clearly, these statements reveal very different intentions. The SST statement does not explain the meaning of theology but presupposes an understanding of it. What is clear though is the connection in pursuing a theological agenda between different kinds of institutions, including the academy and the church. The IAHR statement provides more detail on its methodological remit (historical, social, comparative, critical, analytical, cross-cultural). It also says what it is not. Theology as such is not overtly excluded, but confession and apology are. Interestingly, SST fosters 'community', IAHR the 'forum', the former conveying a sense of what the group holds in common, the latter suggesting a meeting for the exchange of views between certain agreed kinds of participants. These two organizations present themselves in very different ways; there is clearly no intention of overlap; the boundary between them appears clear (Fig. 1). Of the two, IAHR expresses the greater anxiety about the boundary and what it excludes.

This is less the case with the British Association for the Study of Religions, the British wing of the IAHR, which limits its statement of purpose to 'the academic study of religions' (as do many other national affiliates of IAHR).[7] It is not impossible to envisage the academic theological study of religions falling within such a definition (Fig. 2), and, indeed there are some scholars who have membership of both BASR and SST and who attend the annual conferences of both.

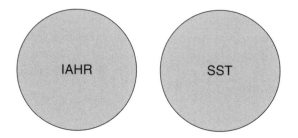

**FIGURE 1** The remit of IAHR and SST and the boundary between them

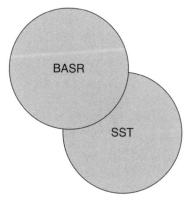

**FIGURE 2** The remit of BASR in relation to SST

The porous boundary between religious studies and theology in the British situation is further evidenced in what is called the 'national benchmark statement', one of many statements commissioned by the Quality Assurance Agency for Higher Education (QAA) in order 'to describe the nature and characteristics of programmes in a specific subject' and 'set out expectations about standards of degrees'.[8] The benchmark statement for BA honours degrees treats theology and religious studies as a single subject, referred to as 'TRS'. It provides a historical narrative of the emergence of its various distinctive branches which suggests that TRS is a 'flag of convenience' (Pye in Wiebe 2005: 120) for the full collection of different methodological approaches, noting that, in the British situation, 'as a result of this history, TRS is marked by diversity but also elements of convergence' (see Fig. 3).[9]

Notwithstanding this view, as Sutcliffe points out (2004; xxi), the effect of operating with the inclusive term 'TRS' is that religious studies 'is made to function as an institutional subset of, or at best a "junior" partner to, a theology "master" taxon'.

Having examined the spatial configuration of some aspects of the professional and institutional relationship between theology and religious studies in Britain, I turn now to a recently published collection of essays that currently informs the way in which students approach and think about our disciplines: *The Routledge Companion to the Study of Religion* (2005). As editor, John Hinnells writes as follows:

> This book looks at the many perspectives from which religions may be viewed . . . Contrary to popular imagination there are many disciplines or approaches involved in the study of religions; each is discussed here in a separate chapter. The obvious routes are theology and religious studies, though there is much debate about the relationship between the two. In America there are indications of a *growing difference*, whereas in

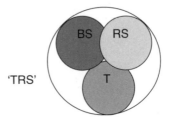

'TRS'

**FIGURE 3**    QAA national benchmark statement: theology, religious studies and biblical studies within 'TRS'

Britain the two appear to be *coming closer together* as can be seen in their respective chapters. (2005: 1)[10]

In light of the difference between America and Britain to which Hinnells refers, it is hardly surprising that this British scholar should choose to include both theology and religious studies alongside one another in a book about the study of religion.[11] However, it is instructive to note the order, as well as the classification, of the disciplines described in the book. Clearly, 'religion' is the book's focus, as the book title and the titles of the various chapters show, with the *modus operandi* being different academic perspectives on 'religion' (Fig. 4).

Introductory, historical and theoretical chapters are provided to situate the reader. Then comes the chapter on theology, followed by philosophy, then religious studies. Is the role of the philosophy chapter to keep theology and religious studies apart, like a referee? Is it historically placed in a narrative about the development of disciplines, or as appropriately located in a continuum from theology (at the one end) to the social sciences (at the other) with philosophy and then religious studies situated in between?[12] We do not know what was in the mind of the editor when he chose this structure. Nevertheless, it is clear that theology precedes religious studies. Some scholars, such as Tim Fitzgerald (2000) and Russell McCutcheon (1997), might well see this as an expression of the place still attributed in the academic study of religion – wittingly or unwittingly – to an 'ecumenical liberal

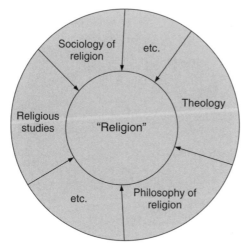

**FIGURE 4** Academic perspectives on religion in *The Routledge Companion to the Study of Religion*

theological' agenda (Fitzgerald 2000: 7). Further, it is evident, as Figure 4 shows, that, in using a container metaphor or model for the study of religion, theology is included within some greater whole that also includes philosophy of religion, sociology of religion, psychology of religion and so on, as part of a poly-methodic field focused on 'religion'. The foregrounding of the category 'religion', the idea that such an object (with its institutions, beliefs, practices, etc.) can provide the focus for disciplinary endeavour is, of course, a modern one that goes hand in hand with the emergence of notions of 'non-religion', or 'secularity', with its own beliefs and practices. This 'ideologically loaded distinction' (Fitzgerald 2000: 15) provides the context for the disciplinary formation of religious studies and the concept at its heart. 'Religion', or so it appears, takes the place of 'God' as we move from the focus of the theological enterprise to its religious studies counterpart.[13]

I turn now to the two essays in *The Routledge Companion to the Study of Religion*, by David Ford (2005: 61–79) and Donald Wiebe (2005: 98–124), about theology and religious studies respectively. Both provide typologies which organize distinct approaches within the two disciplines. I treat them in the order they are presented in the volume and focus on the authors' use of spatial terminology, metaphors, typologies and their attention to relations in and between the disciplines.

David Ford begins his essay by stating that 'theology at its broadest is thinking about questions raised by, about and between the religions' (61) (Fig. 5).

This broad approach, like that of Hinnells in relation to 'the study of religion', is inclusive, potentially incorporating territory that religious studies

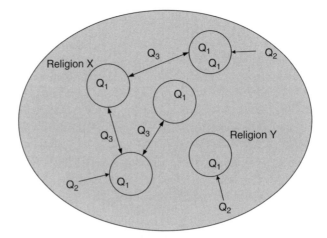

**FIGURE 5**  Ford on theology as questions raised by, about, between religions

scholars would see as part of their domain (i.e. 'questions *about* religions'). Is what we see here an attempt to include 'outsider' perspectives within theology, a discipline normally associated with 'insider' voices?

Ford goes on to discuss the history of academic Christian theology and its differentiation into different branches. He maps the field, providing evidence of the discipline's 'corporate intelligence', its 'second-order tradition', that which is transmitted from generation to generation of scholars and materializes in research practice (Capps 1995; Anttonen 2004). As he does in his book, *Theology: A Very Short Introduction* (1999), he refers in particular to academic theology as it is practised in the modern university,[14] distinguishing geographically and institutionally between the German pattern, of confessional theology (2005: 65), the North American separation of theology and religious studies, confined respectively within the seminary or divinity school and the university department (65), and the British pattern, which he refers to as the 'embrace':

> In Britain university theology has become largely state-funded, and has developed from being exclusively Christian and Anglican to *embracing*, first, other Christian traditions, and then, in the later twentieth century, other religions. Departments in British universities are called variously theology, religious studies, theology and religious studies, and divinity. Whatever the name, most now *embrace* both theology and religious studies. (66)

The British case is interesting because the suggestion here is that the institutional space afforded to religious studies has developed from within that previously allotted to Christian theology.[15] While Ford says in his final sentence that departments embrace theology and religious studies, his first states that it is theology that is doing the embracing. This corporal and social metaphor has the potential to be read and experienced as expansive and welcoming on the one hand, but as colonizing and oppressive on the other. However, not all theologians would approve of such a gesture, nor would all religious studies scholars eschew it.

Ford then goes on to advance reasons for why scholars representing the two disciplines have felt the need either to distinguish them from one another or to bring them closer. He posits his preferred approach, integration, which I will come to shortly, before articulating five types of Christian theology. Based on Hans Frei's types, these revolve around 'the way in which past is related to the present and the future' (Ford 1999: 28). Irrespective of whether or not this is the case, I would suggest that these types can also be organized according to their insider/outsider status in relation to Christian faith and tradition (see Fig. 6).

Here is what Ford says about the types in *Theology: A Very Short Introduction*:

> At one extreme (Type 1) theology is assessed from the *outside* according to whether or not it agreed with some modern framework or agenda. At the other extreme (Type 5) theology is a repetition of some past expression of Christian faith and so is completely *internal* to it . . . Type 2 tries to do justice to what is distinctive in Christianity while choosing one modern framework through which to show its relevance. Type 3 *does without any overall integration* and engages in continual *correlation* between Christian faith and various questions, philosophies, symbols, disciplines, and worldviews. Type 4 gives priority to Christian self-description and is best summed up as 'faith seeking understanding'. But any sophisticated thinker is likely, like Karl Rahner, to *transcend* any one type. (1999: 28–29)

Types 1 and 5 are at the extremes as theological positions wholly outside or inside Christian faith; types 2, 3, and 4,[16] and exemplified by the approaches of Bultmann, Tillich and Barth respectively, are progressively closer to the inside, with 4 giving 'priority to Christian self-description'. The most sophisticated approach is one that 'transcends' the continuum – beyond the limits of the territory and the limitations of the typology.

Clearly this is a model of Christian theology, so how, if at all, does religious studies relate to it? I would suggest that it has much in common with Type 1, because, as Ford says,

> Religious studies has usually wanted *to bracket out* . . . any conception of God being involved in the knowing that goes on in the field; and its pursuit of questions of meaning, truth, beauty and practice has tended to be *limited* to the methods of its constituent disciplines. (2005: 67)

In general, according to Ford, '[religious studies] treats Christian theology from the *outside*, coming to it with a mind . . . already made up and simply

**FIGURE 6** Ford's five types of Christian theology arranged on an insider/outsider continuum

using it within its own framework where it fits' (1999: 21). But he evidently wishes not to foreclose so summarily on the relationship between theology and religious studies. His own hope is for 'integration' which he sees as a distinct possibility, at least within the British system. He begins by noting the symbiotic nature of their relationship.

> Theology is not in competition with religious studies but needs it. If theology is to be rigorous in pursuit of its questions of meaning, truth, beauty and practice then it needs to draw on work in other disciplines. This will not just be a matter of using their results when they are congenial, but rather of *entering into them from the inside* and engaging both critically and constructively with their methods and results . . . [Furthermore] religious studies need not be in competition with theology. Certain definitions of the field *exclude* certain definitions of theology . . . but other definitions of religious studies *open it towards integration* with theology. A key issue is how far questions intrinsic to the field may be pursued, and whether some answers to those questions are to be ruled out in advance. For example, is the question of truth regarding the reality of God as identified by a particular religious tradition to be pursued and then answered in line with that tradition? If so, then the way is *opened* for critical and constructive theology *within* a religious studies milieu. If not, what reasons can be offered for *cutting off* enquiry and *disallowing* certain answers? (2005: 68–69)

I have quoted from Ford at length here to show some familiar terms at work – 'outside', 'open', 'exclude', 'field' – but also to present a new image, of 'cutting'. The idea that some forms of religious studies 'cut off' enquiry and 'disallow' answers gives the impression of a strong version of the discipline of religious studies which has certain limits and a boundary which it polices, one that is neither congenial to Ford's notion of integration between the two nor open to the inclusion of theology within its own boundary. How, if at all, does this conception of religious studies, or indeed a more inclusive one, map on to the types presented in the same volume by the religious studies scholar, Donald Wiebe?

Wiebe's approach is rather different, being an analysis of how a number of scholars have depicted religious studies in introductory books on the subject.[17] We are able to see, just from his selection – though he does not comment on it himself – just how many use spatial terminology. Key ways in which it is employed are, to juxtapose theology and religious studies ('differentiate', 'distinct from', 'exclude'), to show their differing relationship to 'religion' ('instruction *in* religion', 'teach *about* religion'), and to reflect the oft-cited poly-methodological nature of religious studies ('including', 'community of disciplines gathered around', 'field'). Although such discussions help to separate religious studies as a new enterprise emerging in the twentieth century academy from theological studies of religion, none begin to reveal the internal struggles within the new discipline. Not that Wiebe himself wishes to hide them, but many of those he quotes from contribute to obscuring such struggles and to the continued ambiguity of the very term 'religious studies' (2005: 123). His quotation from the American scholars Myscofski and Pilgrim is revealing:

> Religious studies, however defined or wherever located, remains suspect in the eyes of many within the rest of the academy and continually finds itself *marginalized* or otherwise *obscured* due to the fact and/or perception of *blurred boundaries* between studying religion and being religious, or between education about and education in religion. (Myscofski and Pilgrim in Wiebe 2005: 110)

A soft edge borders religious studies as it touches both theology and religious education, and as it merges from scholarship into religiosity. This 'problem' within religious studies with regard to its boundaries with theology and religious education, and implicitly its nature, motivation and objectives as a discipline, is reflected in Wiebe's own analysis and typology. First, he notes that the term 'religious studies' has been used in two distinctive ways,

(A)  for 'whatever study of religion and religions is undertaken in any post-secondary institution of education, whether religious or secular, and regardless of the methodology adopted' (115), and

(B)  'as a designation for a particular kind of approach to the study of religion with a particular aim, methodology, or style that distinguishes it from the type of study of religion antedating it.' (115)

These two meanings suggest rather different spatial, and indeed temporal, representations. In (A), religious studies is inclusive of theological and educational perspectives (Fig. 7).[18] In (B), it is exclusive: religious studies as a discipline is substantively distinguished from theology, its principal antecedent (Fig. 8).

Following this, Wiebe identifies four different types of study under the designation of 'religious studies', all of which have spatial implications (Fig. 9). He

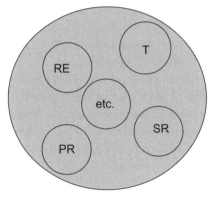

**FIGURE 7** Religious studies (A): Any study of religion/s undertaken in tertiary institutions of education, regardless of the methodology adopted (Wiebe)

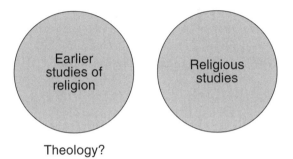

**FIGURE 8** Religious studies (B): An approach to the study of religion that distinguishes it from the type of study of religion antedating it (Wiebe)

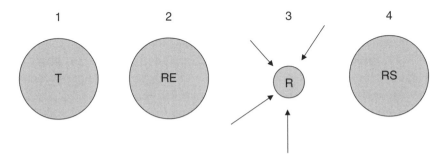

**FIGURE 9** Wiebe's four types of religious studies: 1. RS as theology; 2. RS as religious education; 3. RS as empirical and scientific studies of religion; 4. RS as an autonomous scientific discipline

refs to his first type as 'theology under new management' (116), religious studies as humanistic studies, including the study of questions of meaning and truth. Type 2 is tertiary religious education, in which the aim is to provide an experiential understanding of religion. The third type of religious studies, while being scientific in approach, does not constitute a distinct discipline. It is the empirical study of religions carried out by a wide array of other disciplines, including history, sociology, psychology and anthropology. Finally, type 4 is 'a scientific discipline on a par with other scientific disciplines' (120), and unified by the application of theory.

Wiebe does not offer his own view, though his other work suggests he leans towards type 4 while recognizing that, given the lack of unanimity on the subject and the demise of theory in the post-war period, religious studies has neither been capable of nor even fully committed to transforming itself into an autonomous discipline on a par with others (Wiebe 2000, 2006; for further discussion, see also McCutcheon 2003; Anttonen 2004; Griffiths 2006). Wiebe's own typology, like Ford's, may be represented as a continuum, in this case with a conflation between religious studies and theology at one end (Type 1), a radical disciplinary separation of the two at the other (Type 4) and two intermediary positions.

## Disciplinary communities:
## their insides, outsides and boundaries

In looking briefly at what several professional bodies and scholars have said about 'theology' and 'religious studies' and at how they have typologized the various approaches to these disciplines, it has become clear that a variety of views are held about their interrelationship. One discipline can be portrayed as wholly containing the other; they can be seen as distinctive and separate disciplines with different objects, goals and motivations; they can be envisaged as largely separate but partially overlapping; they can both be contained within a larger meta-discipline ('TRS' or 'the study of religions'); one can be distinguished from the approach that pre-dated it; one can 'embrace' the other: or the embrace can be mutual.

I turn now to the language of boundary and insider/outsider[19] and their socio-spatial implications in the work of these and other commentators as it is here that we find issues relating to power and social exclusion at work.

Each tribe has a name and a territory, settles its own affairs, goes to war with the others, has a distinct language or at least a distinct dialect and a variety of ways of demonstrating its apartness from others. (F. G. Bailey from 1977, in Becher 1989: 1)

It is with this quotation, the substance of which is at the heart of my perspective on the theology and religious studies question, that Tony Becher begins his book on *Academic Tribes and Territories: Intellectual Enquiry and the Cultures of Disciplines*. He goes on to illustrate and discuss Bailey's account of what makes a tribe in relation to the development of disciplines. Becher's references to tribe and territory are useful in helping us to think about theology and religious studies: 'The tribes of academe, one might argue, define their own identities and defend their own *patches of intellectual ground* by employing a variety of devices geared to the *exclusion of illegal immigrants*.' (1989: 24) He refers explicitly to the socio-spatial manifestation of the boundary devices employed by disciplinary communities, as well as to their constitution and the way in which they define themselves in relation to others, sometimes keeping inappropriate outsiders at bay. He also refers to those things which hold an academic tribe or community together or bind it, that integrate it, that can be transmitted to new members, and can be practised. He goes on to note that disciplines have folk myths, founding figures, cultural capital, and tacit knowledge. These are all aspects which pertain to the 'inside' of disciplines and can be learnt and practised by 'insiders', but which also assist in separating them from 'outsiders', from other disciplinary communities, their beliefs and practices, and the knowledge associated with them.

As Becher states, not all disciplinary communities are alike. Some are 'convergent and tightly knit in terms of their fundamental ideologies, their common values, their shared judgements of quality, their awareness of belonging to a unique tradition' (1989: 37), and, as such, they are likely to have 'well-defined external boundaries' (37) to protect themselves from outsiders. Other groupings are 'divergent and loosely knit'; they lack 'a clear sense of mutual cohesion and identity' (37), are less likely to police their boundaries, and more likely to overlap with other disciplinary groupings. In presenting a range of types of theology and religious studies respectively, Ford and Wiebe suggested that their disciplines could be defined and practised in various ways, some more convergent, tightly knit and resistant to outsiders; others less so. Closed boundaries were a feature of two of Ford's types (5 and possibly 4, see Fig. 6 above), and Wiebe's type 4 (Fig. 9 above) certainly aspired to autonomous disciplinary status (while not yet achieving it), convergent upon theories of religion. The other types represented more loosely bounded and divergent approaches to the study of religion.

However, given its history and presentation in introductory books, I would suggest that, as a whole, theology is the more 'convergent' of the two disciplines. It is the more focused, having been understood 'as systematic analysis of the nature, purposes and activity of God' (McGrath 2001: 138). Many works, including Ford's *Theology: A Very Short Introduction*, still begin with God. Most of those who write about the nature of theology as a discipline refer to Anselm on 'faith seeking understanding' (Migliore 1991; Ford 1999; McGrath 2001; Gunton et al. 2001; Gunton 2002), to the inseparability of faith and inquiry (Migliore 1991), to faith and reason (Gunton et al. 2001), or belief and analysis (McGrath 2001). They refer to its 'architecture': biblical studies, systematic theology, historical theology, pastoral theology, philosophical theology, spirituality or mystical theology. Yes, some of these branches, and the scholars who work within them, are more or less open to other disciplines, whether religious studies, another humanities subject, or a social science, but they are in general agreement about these core issues, these integrating factors.

This is certainly not the pattern with religious studies. Even if we leave aside Wiebe's first two types (theology under new management and religious studies as tertiary RE, see Fig. 9) and concentrate on the social scientific modes of the discipline, it appears to be divergent. We would find it difficult to identify common theories, methodology, practices, norms and structures upon which the majority of scholars could agree. And it is for this very reason that, as Wiebe notes, no formally autonomous discipline of religious studies has yet emerged. The concepts 'religion' and 'religions' are central, of course, if much contested, but otherwise the discipline is notable for its plurality of methods and theories, the majority of which have been developed 'outside' the new enterprise of religious studies, in other disciplines. Indeed, some of the very approaches and theories that have been most notably associated with the 'inside' of religious studies have been the most hotly contested, such as phenomenology and the work of Otto, Wach, Eliade and Smart. Religious studies as a discipline does not have an agreed 'corporate intelligence' (Anttonen 2004: 105) or well developed body of theory (Wiebe 2005: 121). It is no doubt for these reasons that the term 'field' is often preferred to 'discipline', there being relatively open boundaries, a diversity of methodologies present, and little by way of an agreed core or focus. 'Who, if anyone, *cannot* be invited to table: who, if anyone, is to be excluded?' asks Steven Sutcliffe (2004: xviii–xix). He goes on to suggest that the chief motivating factor continues to be the relationship with theology. Is theology the uninvited guest? Religious studies, he suggests, 'has often operated with a monolithic representation of

"Christian theology", as a sharply differentiated, taboo *"other"*, *standing over against* a purified "Religious Studies" ' (2004: xx).

While theology has been presented in this way by some religious studies scholars, others have been more inviting. June O'Connor (1997), for example, has referred to academic theology as 'truthclaimology', and seen it as 'a *component* of religious studies' (84), with both disciplines employing critical reasoning in pursuit of knowledge and understanding about religion. Gavin Flood, in search of a way out of the phenomenological impasse in religious studies, has noted the connection between contemporary academic theology and religious studies. They are both 'kinds of writing *about* religion, *with convergence and divergence,* and both arise from the practice of rational method' (1999: 19), he suggests. They constitute different types of discourse, with theology being 'an internalized discourse' about something 'of which it is itself a part' whereas religious studies is 'a language about religion', an externalized discourse (20–22).

## Spatial language and the relationship of theology and religious studies: a conclusion

In analysing the language of their relationship, I have only taken the first step in a spatial analysis of theology and religious studies. Not only would a full analysis require a more systematic consideration of these disciplines as discursive spaces, it would demand consideration of their physical and social presence and production too. Such attention to the socio-spatial properties of the disciplines would provide us with further opportunities to examine their genealogies, to look more closely at the power issues informing their relationship, and to take seriously their simultaneous spatial location (in and beyond the West). Only after such an analytical process could we really be said to have used the full potential of a spatial approach.

But what has this initial analysis offered? It has brought to our attention the spatial language at work in discourse by and about the disciplines of theology and religious studies. The territory of the study of 'religion' and of 'God' is contested; it is marked by continuous struggle. There are competing conceptions of the disciplinary interrelationship and these can be represented spatially, as the diagrams have shown. One commonly used knowledge-power strategy is that of containment. When expressed as the 'embrace' of one discipline by another, there is a suggestion of mutuality and expansiveness which may be welcomed by some but experienced as an expression of dominance by others.

Furthermore, we have seen that the 'insides' of the two disciplines are differently conceived in terms of the objects of their study, beliefs and practices, academic and methodological traditions, mission and purpose. Theology is arguably the more convergent of the two; religious studies the more loosely bounded and divergent. There are differing views about the nature of the boundary between the two, about who and what can be accommodated on either side of it and who and what must be excluded, and about the scholarly possibilities generated by the maintenance and/or dissolution of the boundary.

All the views about theology and religious studies presented here – and many others on this subject that have not been considered – contribute to the reproduction of a dynamic knowledge-power field in which disciplinary struggle occurs for many reasons. From time to time the various parties are locked in battle over methodological or standpoint issues, or because they disagree about the object of study, but at other times they agree to join forces against external threats. I would suggest that, much like the cultural order in which their relationship has been forged – the Western symbolic and epistemological order in its modern form and with its religious and secular facets – theology and religious studies are discursively as well as historically intertwined and mutually imbricated. They are like twins, ever bound to one another though sometimes striving to be free and to experience themselves as separate and distinctive. As such, they cannot help but struggle with one another. Across the boundary between them, they are attracted and repelled. When the boundary is approached and sometimes transgressed the 'other' must be engaged, whether in discussion, fight, embrace, or in an act of consumption.

In this 'disciplined exaggeration in the direction of knowledge' I have demonstrated how the tribes and territories of the disciplines of theology and religious studies, and their discourse of containment and separation, can be analysed spatially in order to reveal some of the competing perspectives on their interrelationship and the knowledge-power strategies that inform them.

## Notes

1 When I use the plural pronoun 'we' I am referring to the 'community' of scholars of religion – if so it can be called – including those in both theology and religious studies.

2 As a scholar in the tradition of religious studies I have focused on the category 'religion' (rather than 'God'), see below. In this article I have attended to the way

in which scholars of both religious studies and theology construct their disciplines; for a more in-depth examination of the use of spatial language by scholars of the former type, see Knott (2007).

3   In this article I focus primarily on the 'mental', and to some extent 'social', spaces rather than the 'physical' ones. Further analyses could also be conducted of university departments of theology, religious studies (physical and social space), and of professional subject associations and their conferences (largely social, but also physical and mental spaces).

4   As Lakoff and Johnson pointed out in the 1980 book, *Metaphors We Live By* (1980: 4–5), the metaphor 'argument is war' is a common one in English parlance (cf. Thorne 2006).

5   From article 4 of the constitution of the Society for the Study of Theology, http://www.theologysociety.org.uk last accessed 28/08/2008.

6   From 'What is the IAHR?' http://www.iahr.dk/iahr.htm last accessed 28/08/2008, the website of the International Association for the History of Religions.

7   From the British Association for the Study of Religions homepage, http://basr.open.ac.uk/index.html last accessed 28/08/2008. IAHR changed its mission statement in 2005 from a shorter and more general statement to the present one.

8   QAA national benchmark statements, see http://www.qaa.ac.uk/academicinfrastructure/benchmark/default.asp and, for theology and religious studies, http://www.qaa.ac.uk/academicinfrastructure/benchmark/honours/theology.asp last accessed 28/08/2008.

9   From 'Introduction: Theology and Religious Studies in HE', http://www.qaa.ac.uk/academicinfrastructure/benchmark/honours/theology.asp last accessed 28/08/2008.

10  My italics. I shall use italics in the quotations that follow to indicate socio-spatial concepts and metaphors.

11  This is further supported by the fact that the North American Association for the Study of Religion (NAASR) was formed in 1985 'to encourage the historical, comparative, structural, theoretical and cognitive approaches to the study of religion among North American scholars', and, as such, has a more specific methodological focus than BASR. By implication, it excludes the theological study of religion. See http://www.as.ua.edu/naasr/about.html last accessed 28/08/2008.

12  There is no chapter on the history of religion as a perspective.

13  See Smith on the concept of 'religion' and its role in establishing a disciplinary horizon: 'There can be no disciplined study of religion without such a horizon' (Smith 2004b: 194); but see Griffiths (2006) for a discussion of the (in)adequacy of 'religion' as a disciplinary object for 'not-theology'.

14  Other theologians also deal with the institutional location of theology: seminary, university or society (McGrath 2001, Migliore, 1991).

15  With a few exceptions, e.g. Lancaster University, the University of Stirling, the Open University and the School of Oriental and African Studies at the University of London.

16  These are similar to the Praxis approach, Correlation method and Christocentric theology types presented by David Tracy (Migliore 1991: 14).

[17] Donald Wiebe has written extensively about the nature of religious studies as a discipline and its position within the university (e.g. Wiebe 1998, 2000).

[18] 'Religious studies', incorporating theology (T), religious education (RE), sociology of religion (SR), philosophy of religion (PR), etc.

[19] The terms 'insider' and 'outsider' have also been used to refer to standpoint issues within the study of religions (e.g. McCutcheon 1999; Arweck and Stringer 2002; Knott 2005c).

# Bibliography

Anttonen, V. (1996), 'Rethinking the Sacred: The Notions of "Human Body" and "Territory" in Conceptualizing Religion', in T. A. Idinopulos and E. A. Yonan (eds), *The Sacred and its Scholars: Comparative Religious Methodologies for the Study of Primary Religious Data*. Leiden: E. J. Brill, 36–64.

—(2004), 'Pathways to Knowledge in Comparative Religion: Clearing Ground for New Conceptual Resources', in T. Light and B. C. Wilson (eds), *Religion as a Human Capacity: A Festscrift in Honor of E. Thomas Lawson*. Leiden and Boston: E. J. Brill, pp. 105–120.

Arweck, E. and Stringer, M. (eds) (2002), *Theorizing Faith: The Insider/Outsider Problem in the Study of Ritual*. Birmingham: University of Birmingham Press.

Becher, T. (1989), *Academic Tribes and Territories: Intellectual Enquiry and the Culture of Disciplines*. Milton Keynes: The Society for Research into Higher Education and the Open University.

Bourdieu, P. (1988), *Homo Academicus*. Cambridge: Polity Press.

British Association for the Study of Religions, http://basr.open.ac.uk/index.html last accessed 23/10/2006.

Capps, W. (1995), *Religious Studies: The Making of a Discipline*. Minneapolis: Fortress Press.

Fitzgerald, T. (2000), *The Ideology of Religious Studies*. New York and Oxford: Oxford University Press.

Flood, G. (1999), *Beyond Phenomenology: Rethinking the Study of Religion*. London and New York: Cassell.

Ford, D. (1999), *Theology: A Very Short Introduction*. Oxford: Oxford University Press.

—(2005), 'Theology', in J. Hinnells (ed.), *The Routledge Companion to the Study of Religion*. London and New York: Routledge, pp. 61–79.

Foucault, M. (1970), *The Order of Things: an Archaeology of the Human Sciences* (first published 1966). London: Tavistock.

Gordon, C. (1980), *Power/Knowledge: Selected Interviews and Other Writings, 1972–77, by Michel Foucault*. Hemel Hempstead: Harvester Press.

Griffiths, P. J. (2006), 'On the Future of the Study of Religion in the Academy', *Journal of the American Academy of Religion*, 74 (1), 66–74.

Gunton, C. E. (2002), *The Christian Faith: An Introduction to Christian Doctrine*. Oxford: Blackwell.

Gunton, C. E., Holmes, S. R. and Rae, M. A. (eds) (2001), *The Practice of Theology: A Reader*. London: SCM Press.

Hinnells, J. (ed.) (2005), *The Routledge Companion to the Study of Religion*. London and New York: Routledge.

Hufford, D. J. (1999), 'The Scholarly Voice and the Personal Voice: Reflexivity in Belief Studies', in R. T. McCutcheon (ed.), *The Insider/Outsider Problem in the Study of Religion: A Reader*. London and New York: Cassell, pp. 294–310.

International Association for the History of Religions, http://www.iahr.dk/iahr. htm last accessed 2/07/2006.

Johnson, M. (1987), *The Body in the Mind: The Bodily Basis of Meaning, Imagination and Reason*. Chicago and London: Chicago University Press.

Knott, K. (2005a), *The Location of Religion: a Spatial Analysis*. London and Oakville, CT: Equinox.

—(2005b), 'Spatial Theory and Method for the Study of Religion', *Temenos: Nordic Journal of Comparative Religion*, 41 (2), 153–184.

—(2005c), 'Insider/Outsider Perspectives in the Study of Religions', in J. Hinnells (ed.), *The Routledge Companion to the Study of Religion*. London and New York: Routledge, pp. 243–258.

—(2007), 'Religious Studies and its Relationship with Theology: A Spatial Analysis', *Temenos: Nordic Journal of Comparative Religion*, 43:2.

Lakoff, G. and Johnson, M. (1980), *Metaphors We Live By*. Chicago and London: Chicago University Press.

—(1999), *Philosophy in the Flesh: The Embodied Mind and its Challenge to Western Thought*. New York: Basic Books.

Lefebvre, H. (1991), *The Production of Space* (first published 1974). Oxford and Cambridge, MA: Blackwell.

McCutcheon, R. T. (1997), *Manufacturing Religion: The Discourse of Sui Generis Religion and the Politics of Nostalgia*. New York and Oxford: Oxford University Press.

—(2003), *The Discipline of Religion: Structure, Meaning, Rhetoric*. New York and London: Routledge.

McCutcheon, R. T. (ed.) (1999), *The Insider/Outsider Problem in the Study of Religion: A Reader*. London and New York: Cassell.

McGrath, A. E. (2001), *Christian Theology: An Introduction*. Third edition. Oxford: Blackwell.

Migliore, D. L. (1991), *Faith Seeking Understanding: An Introduction to Christian Theology*. Grand Rapids: Eerdmans.

North American Association for the Study of Religion, http://www.as.ua.edu/ naasr/about.html last accessed 23/10/2006.

O'Connor, J. (1997), 'Taking the Bull by the Tail: Responses to the *Lingua Franca* Article', *Council of Societies for the Study of Religion Bulletin*, 26 (4), 78–85.

Quality Assurance Agency for Higher Education, benchmark statements, http://www.qaa.ac.uk/academicinfrastructure/benchmark/default.asp last accessed 23/10/2006.

Smith, J. Z. (2004a), 'A Matter of Class: Taxonomies of Religion', in J. Z. Smith, *Relating Religion: Essays in the Study of Religion*. Chicago and London: Chicago University Press, pp. 160–178.

—(2004b), 'Religion, Religions, Religious', in J. Z. Smith, *Relating Religion: Essays in the Study of Religion*. Chicago and London: Chicago University Press, pp. 179–196.

Society for the Study of Theology, http://www.huss.ex.ac.uk/theology/sst/ last accessed 2/07/2006.

Sutcliffe, S. (2004), 'Introduction: Qualitative Empirical Methodologies: An Inductive Argument', in S. Sutcliffe (ed.), *Religion: Empirical Studies*. Aldershot: Ashgate, xvii–xliii.

Thorne, S. (2006), *The Language of War*. London and New York: Routledge.

Wiebe, D. (1998), *The Politics of Religious Studies: The Continuing Conflict with Theology in the University*. New York: St Martin's Press.

—(2000), 'Why the Academic Study of Religion? Motive and Method in the Study of Religion', in T. Jensen and M. Rothstein (eds), *Secular Theories on Religion: Current Perspectives*. Copenhagen: Museum Tusculanum Press, pp. 261–279.

—(2005), 'Religious studies', in J. Hinnells (ed.), *The Routledge Companion to the Study of Religion*. London and New York: Routledge, pp. 98–124.

—(2006), 'An eternal return all over again: The religious conversation endures', *Journal of the American Academy of Religion*, 74(3), 674–696.

Chapter 9

# 'A Coat of Many Colours'
## Interweaving Strands in Theology and Religious Studies

Ursula King

## Introduction

I have a continuing interest in the debate concerning the relationship between Theology and Religious Studies because of my own academic training in both areas (or 'fields' or 'disciplines', or whatever one may wish to call them) and as the former chair of a Department of Theology *and* Religious Studies, and because of my current title of Professor Emerita of Theology and Religious Studies which carries these two designations in tandem. Thus I have had plenty of opportunity to reflect on these issues, and some of my thoughts on these matters have on various occasions been put into print.

Not long ago I touched on these issues in an interview for *Discourse: Learning and Teaching in Philosophical and Religious Studies* conducted by Darlene Bird. I briefly quote from this before I reflect on some arguments in greater detail. When asked, 'How do you manage to bridge the gap, if there is a gap, in your teaching of both theology and religious studies?', I replied: 'I don't think there is a real gap. I see it more as different ends of the spectrum, because I look at the study of religions in a very comprehensive and inclusive way, and I don't like sharp disciplinary boundaries. I think more in terms of cross-fertilization, and many of the skills that the traditional theology courses require, the linguistic skills, hermeneutic skills, historical or social scientific study of church communities and so on, are actually skills that belong to the wider study of religion. It's different if you teach for the nurturing of a faith, rather than academic theology; then of course you take a position which is very strongly informed dogmatically, but I don't think that the right place to do this is at university. I feel that non-dogmatic, open-ended teaching about any subject should follow a dialogical and exploratory model.'[1] It is these informal comments that I wish to unpack further and explain more clearly my views on theology *and* religious studies rather than theology *versus* religious studies.

## Doubting discourse

From a contemporary postmodern perspective many traditional categories used in the academy have become thoroughly destabilized and are continuously being reinterpreted. Questions about clearly recognizable academic 'fields', 'disciplines', firm 'boundaries' and 'disciplinary identities' have been sharply called into question, and so has the entire production of separate 'bodies of knowledge'. Thus we can observe paradigmatic changes in many fields, but also fractured identities and new subjectivities which are emerging among different bodies of scholars, whether they belong to theology, religious studies, to both areas, or to other so-called 'disciplines'. Many of the aspects pertaining to these conceptual, linguistic, institutional and pragmatic shifts that are being debated leave me uncomfortable in their often highly abstract rhetoric, their distanced, unengaged attitude, their antagonistic stance that tries to score points over perceived opponents struggling to maintain a strict intellectual boundary maintenance in order to exercise power and control.

To understand ourselves and our areas of teaching and research, it seems helpful to stand back and examine the origin and manner of our discourse, the location and context of our speaking, and the positioning we consciously or unconsciously adopt in our institutions and among our colleagues. What does it mean to become religiously and theologically literate in a critically nuanced manner in a postindustrial and postmodern society? How can we teach people to relate creatively to the richness of religious traditions and the vast scholarship about them, so that the richly varied inheritance of faiths (in the plural) is respected and drawn upon as the irreplaceable cultural resource they represent?

Some debates about theology and religious studies are couched in static and essentialist discourses that seem to reflect a real fortress mentality where the surrounding walls of a clearly demarcated territory are represented as high and solid, almost impenetrable. Such a mentality may provide a strong sense of certainty and secure identity to those occupying the inside territory, but it is not particularly helpful for dealing with the multitude of people living in lands beyond, for relating to alternative worldviews or for understanding different religions as organic forms of life. Other metaphors may prove more helpful here. If religions are viewed dynamically and organically, it may be more appropriate to approach them in the spirit of a journey where scholarship remains an exploration that is ever open-ended, continuing and unfinished. Or we could liken the study of religions to the weaving together of many-coloured threads of diverse provenance to create an attractive coat of many colours. Interweaving the many rich and separate strands of theology and religious studies would thus be a very different undertaking from the task of a master-builder erecting an architectonic edifice with a clearly planned design and precise measurements. Thus a great deal of one's own attitude towards the multiple academic perspectives and possibilities of theology and religious studies depends on one's approach to life as well as the predominant politics of knowledge.

## Interweaving multiple strands

We have to be aware of the limits of language and of conceptual thought, however exciting and intoxicating concepts and language may be at times; we need to be suspicious of our tendency to box in and pigeonhole manageable bits of information and knowledge. Questions of academic boundaries may be important because of our need to 'manage' intellectual, human, financial and political resources, but from a perspective of critical self-reflexivity we have to be aware that we are carving up the immeasurable richness and density of the world in order to cope with it, control and possess it, so that we can claim it as our own.

Like others in this volume, I question the binary, oppositional thinking often expressed as theology *versus* religious studies. I am less interested in sharp 'boundaries' that often mask claims to territorial possession, power hierarchies and ego affirmation, than in expanding universes of thought and experience. Thus we need to doubt and examine our current discourse in order to untie the bondage that locks us into over-familiar, highly fashionable concepts, theories and images.

I find it helpful to reflect on Pierre Hadot's comment about classical philosophy that 'ways of life have been reduced to forms of discourse', a dictum that can equally be applied to our treatment of religion.[2] Perhaps we need to rediscover the sense of adventure in religion by seeing beyond our current disciplinary horizons and discovering new lands. The much vaunted 'interdisciplinarity' is not enough; instead, a truly 'transdisciplinary' approach is needed by using organic metaphors of process and emergence that interact with certain scientific and ecological perspectives and leave room for further development, growth and transformation as well as cross-fertilization of different views and disciplines. Writing about the science of religion, the Israeli Scholar Shaul Shaked speaks of 'interlocking circles of tradition' and notes that in studying religion, 'we have to take it apart' and '[t]he study of religious phenomena . . . has an effect similar to that of dissecting a living organism. What one gains in understanding, one loses in terms of its vitality and truth.'[3] This recognition can provide a healthy corrective to the danger of intellectual arrogance which, I fear, can at times be detected in *both* theology *and* religious studies.

It will be clear by now that I advocate a strong connective, at times even integrating, relationship between theology and religious studies. For a creative and enquiring mind, theology – and that means Christian theology for most of us – is still one of the most challenging subjects to study, a subject which requires personal commitment and engages one's heart as well as one's mind, since it still revolves around some of the great questions of life and existence. I think that a thorough textual, historical and systematic philosophical training in theology continues to give students a solid foundation for creative thinking, provided theological disciplines are not taught in a narrow sectarian manner, but in a dynamic way that engages with the burning issues of our time. But some of this could also be said about the study of religions that has developed in Europe for almost the last 200 years by emancipating itself from the dogmatic tutelage of theology. This process of separation and search for a distinct identity has produced a wealth of new historical, phenomenological, methodological and comparative knowledge which deserves its rightful place. But it should not become narrowly ideological and dogmatic by refusing to even consider theological questions which also belong to the wider area of the study of religions.

In any case, we are now experiencing new processes of social, political and intellectual developments where these historically carved out identities have to be renegotiated and reconceived. We are right in the middle of this painful process, and that is why we are so confused and struggling so much. But a more open-ended, exploratory and dialogical way of studying religions in a most comprehensive and inclusive sense cannot fight shy of certain theological questions either. It seems to me that the whole enquiry into religion in contemporary society – formally crystallized in teaching and research activities that are conventionally and conveniently labelled as 'theology *and* religious studies' – is faced with a number of similar challenges which are destabilizing while repositioning their hitherto separately held location and significance. I will briefly explore four of the most important challenges here which, although distinct, are interdependent and impacting on each other.[4]

## The challenge of the global

This volume with its debate about the relationship between theology and religious studies is to a great extent located within the educational spaces of British higher education which, for all practical purposes, affect us most. Yet it must also be positioned within a much larger global context which impacts on staff and students as well as on course contents and programmes, although this is not always made sufficiently explicit. Even when travelling just around Europe, I am often aware of the somewhat different resonances and connotations that the words 'theology' and 'religious studies' carry in different language zones, and that they can relate to quite different institutional practices and powers.

To quote an example from the most recent number of *Discourse*, the trenchantly critical article 'New Lines of Flight? Negotiating Religions and Cultures in Gendered Educational Spaces'[5] by John l'Anson and Alison Jasper on defining the problematics of knowledge practices in religious studies does not reflect on its own specific location which, in my view, seems still rooted in too limited a perspective where the questions and critiques raised are mostly shaped by Eurocentric and English-dominated debates rather than global ones.

The word 'global', though often mentioned in other contexts, is not always critically analysed and reflected upon in its determining significance. It is all too often repeated as a fashionable idea of renaming what was previously described as the 'world', as in 'world literature', 'world history' or even 'world religion'. In other words, it simply refers to the geographical spread and diffusion around the world. Thus I recently came across Hans Schwarz's study *Theology in a Global Context: The Last Two Hundred Years*[6], praised as the best available overview. Yet the author does not reflect on the concept of the 'global' at all and deals largely with Protestant theology in Germany, England and the United States of America with an additional chapter on Catholic and Orthodox Christianity entitled 'Theology is More Than Protestant' (!) and another one on 'Emerging New Voices'. I consider this hardly a *global* history of theology. Similar examples can be found elsewhere.

Discussions about globality stem largely from the 1980s and are mostly found in works on economics and ecology. The sociologist Roland Roberson defines globalization as 'the process by which the world becomes a single place' and also as 'the consciousness of the globe as such'.[7] The process of globalization and the consciousness of its occurrence, in spite of the postmodern scepticism of the universalizing vision of 'grand narratives', has profound implications for individual groups, national societies and different institutions, including our universities and teaching programmes. It is accompanied by a greater recognition of and respect for marked historical, cultural, ethnic, racial and religious differences. The global challenge in the study of different theologies and religions expresses itself in a number of ways, which I cannot examine in detail here, but to characterize it briefly, it can mean first that these studies are now diffused worldwide and involve the study of *all* religions, not just those of a particular part of the globe. Second, it indicates the necessity to take seriously the insights of scholarship from *all parts of the globe*, so that the study of religions and theologies becomes truly global rather than merely Western in its outlook and assumptions, so that it acquires a new interconnectivity and critical reflexivity. We all know how far away we are still from this ideal, and how the power politics of knowledge production are a great inhibitor of a more egalitarian distribution of global equality in higher education and scholarship.

A critical global perspective reveals not only the European roots of the international study of religions as well as of most existing theologies, but also the painful connections between religions, imperialism and colonialism. For example, the whole so-called 'field' of religious studies, as historically constructed in its topics, methods and questions, is still often too much influenced by the earlier colonial perspectives in its perception of the 'religious Other' and an often 'exotic elsewhere', and also in some of the 'insider/outsider' debates in the study of religions.

## The challenge of religious pluralism and interfaith encounter

The recognition of the existence of religious pluralism in a global world has led to many new developments in both theology and religious studies. Historically, there was first the development of Christian ecumenism as a movement to bring about the reunion of the divided Christian churches to express the wholeness of the Christian faith and a shared worldwide mission. This ecumenism has found a strong institutional representation in the World Council of Churches, whose significance in creating a greater global awareness among Christians cannot be overestimated. An institutionally less concretely embodied, but equally important, idea is that of a truly *global* ecumenism which brings members of different world faiths more closely together through interfaith encounter and, more specifically, dialogue.

These developments, although often looked askance by scholars, are important not only in themselves, but in the new challenge they pose to the study of religions. In Christian theology, the theology of religions has developed into a field of considerable importance, but interfaith encounter and dialogue must also be critically examined in the study of religions. On closer examination it becomes evident that interfaith dialogue, as we know it at present, owes its birth and occurrence to secular society and its acknowledgement of religious pluralism, for such dialogue does not flourish in mono-cultural and mono-religious societies. Interfaith dialogue as praxis can be liberating, as it frees one from the boundaries and oppression of one's own standpoint and makes one discover the particular lens through which one's own tradition, whether religious or secular, has mediated the world.

I see the challenge of interfaith encounter and dialogue as one of promising potential for the further development of the study of religion without the need to give up any hard-won ground in terms of methodological advances. Our tools of analysis have to be ever more finely sharpened, but there is also a great need for synthesis and forward-looking vision. We need to go on wrestling with definitions of religion; we have to investigate the nature of the religious quest as an important dimension of being human; we need to go on building explanatory theories about the nature of religious language and experience, about the kind of constructs we have created regarding ultimate reality and transcendent foci – so many different ways of wrestling with God, human beings and the world, as traditional theology sees it. There are ever so many tasks and levels that different scholars need to engage in – and that students have to be made aware of – but these levels of study and conceptualization are not necessarily mutually exclusive as long as one does not dogmatically proclaim that there is only one correct way of doing theology and religious studies. If rightly understood and correctly practised, the diversity of themes, methods, approaches and interpretations cannot be anything but mutually enriching and supportive within the enterprise of advancing the study of religions in the widest, most comprehensive and mature manner.

## The challenge of gender insights

The challenge of gender insights is huge, and meeting it in the study of religions is an enormous task, at present largely incomplete. I shall not say much on it here since I have written extensively on it. At present gender studies, in religion as elsewhere, are in practice almost identical with women's studies, although this is slowly changing now. Yet in the canons of scholarship – in religious studies even more than in theology – there is often little recognition of women as agents and participants in their own right, especially not in the major literature surveys, histories and handbooks of the respective disciplines. Nor is the contribution of women pioneers in developing the study of religions generally acknowledged.

In the past, the role, image and status of women in different religions have occasionally been an object of enquiry for male scholars, but mostly in a descriptive, rather undifferentiated way. With women's full access to scholarly training and their greater participation in the academy, women themselves are now both subjects and agents of scholarly analysis. The growing number of women scholars in theology and religious studies marked by a gender-critical consciousness means that their research challenges some of the existing paradigms in both areas. More than an important paradigm shift is occurring – it is more like the shaking of foundations and a re-assembling of whole bodies of knowledge and their discursive practices, raising fundamental questions about the nature of all knowledge and all our methods of learning, teaching and research. As in many other fields, we are not simply dealing with a reinterpretation of texts and traditions, but with a complete re-positioning of bodies of knowledge, a re-arrangement and remapping of everything that relates to religion, society, and culture. This radical shift is not only about *what* we know, but even more about *how* we come to know, how we construct our knowledge, how we use and apply it. Women's research is thus moving from universality to particularity, from abstraction to engagement, and it includes a critique of objectivity as traditionally understood and practised, revealing all knowledge as morally significant, possessing an ethical and political dimension.

The feminist and, more recently, gender paradigm shift in theology and religious studies requires different research methodologies which elicit a more empathic involvement and personal concern in relation to one's studies. This in no way means the abandonment of the highest scholarly criteria and competencies nor the loss of objectiveness and critical assessment, but rather the application of these criteria within a different grid of complexity.

## The challenge of complexity

The challenge of increasing and accelerated complexity, understood as an integration of diversity without obliteration of differences, is probably the best way to sum up *all* the unprecedented challenges facing the study of religions today. This situation calls for a truly transdisciplinary collaboration among scholars. The impact of complexity remains often unrecognized, especially in the methodological discussions of religious studies, which sometimes reflect more of a contesting 'camp mentality' than a genuine commitment to seeking new insights and advances through working collaboratively together.

Georg Schmid in his book *Principles of integral science of religion*[8], which has perhaps not received the attention it deserves, has proposed a complex and differentiated methodology to deal with the *whole* of religion in an integral manner while clearly recognizing that the *reality* of religion – all that is intended in religious life and experience – cannot be really got hold of by either theology or religious studies. What characterizes the modern study of religion is, according to Schmid, the complex link between specific research on particular data with an integral reflection on the meaning of religion and the significance of particular data in a larger context, which today is a global one.

A powerful recognition of the implications of global complexity for situating ourselves and all our enquiries is Pierre Teilhard de Chardin's notion of the '*noosphere*', the worldwide layer of interthinking and interaction covering the globe, now so strongly 'embodied' or rather expressed through the virtual reality of the worldwide web. We are not only interdependent economically, politically, culturally and intellectually, but also at the religious and spiritual level. For Teilhard, religions have always been a central driving force in the development of human culture and civilizations, but far from considering religions as a phenomenon of the past, he regarded their contribution to our emerging world culture as absolutely essential. Teilhard was neither a traditional theologian nor a history of religions scholar, but a contemporary religious thinker passionately interested in the future of humankind and the flourishing of all peoples and the planet. His intriguing, but little known, theories about religion and culture are well worth studying, for they demonstrate among others that the human search for truth and understanding cannot be exclusively pursued by cognitive criteria alone, however important, but involves several other ways of knowing.

## Concluding reflections

To sum up, I have argued that the emergence of global awareness and globalization, the experience of religious pluralism and interfaith encounter, the implications of a critical gender consciousness and new gender practices, and the growth of increasing complexity in all areas of human endeavour, present four new dynamics that challenge theology *and* religious studies in several new ways, so that it is no longer enough to go on studying religion with our habitual theological and other skills by rehearsing established methodologies and problematics. Instead, we must acknowledge the newness of our situation of learning, teaching and researching, and attend responsively and responsibly to the critical questions arising from it. For Teilhard de Chardin this meant to develop new ways of *seeing*, enlarging one's vision – and some might even include here the power of dreaming to venture into the mystery of the unknown rather than being safe with the known. To *see more* means *to be more*, to live a fuller, richer, more rewarding life, and that includes intellectual life and vision, personal life and community life.

We are so familiar with the idea that it is necessary to preserve biodiversity for the continuation of biological and all other life. In analogy one can speak of what I, following Teilhard de Chardin, call the need for the preservation of '*noospheric* diversity', which includes the diversity of religious beliefs and practices that can nurture, empower, transform and heal human individuals and societies, and it also includes a great diversity of methods and approaches. Much is made by some scholars of Deleuze's and Guattari's plant-derived *rhizome* metaphor ('an underground root-like stem bearing both roots and shoots')[9] to contrast horizontal thought with *arborescent* hierarchies of knowledge, so that the multiple interconnections and proliferation of the former are privileged over the structured ordering of the latter.[10] I want to introduce yet another concept from the plant kingdom as a similarly helpful metaphor here, and that is the word '*pneumatophore*', described by the *OED* as 'an aerial root specialized for gaseous exchange found in various plants growing in swampy areas'.[11] I came across this expression when visiting mangroves with their many tangled roots in eastern Australia a couple of years ago, and I was so much struck by the symbolic significance of this word that I adopted it, since it can literally be translated as 'bearing or bearer of spirit'.

It seems to me that the most significant and exciting aspects of both theology *and* religious studies amid all our refining of concepts, critical questions and intellectual debates are those nodes, thoughts and connections that reveal themselves as *pneumatophores*, as bearers of spirit and life. The very fact of their existence, even if we only accidentally stumble on them at times, is a reassurance that knowledge can be more than a tremendous effort, planned and pursued solely by our will, by revealing itself as a *gift* that nourishes the human spirit, leading it to wisdom and surrender, to the abandon of all arrogance and vain claims. But this we cannot teach our students, they can only discover it for themselves. And many scholars seem to remain forever utterly insensitive to consider even the possibility of encountering such *pneumatophores* amid their teaching and research activities. Yet it is of considerable importance for our society, culture and politics that more people acquire a greater religious, but also theological and spiritual literacy and competence at a time when religion represents an increasingly influential part in national and international conversations and policies.[12] As scholars of theology and religious studies we have a responsibility to our different communities to help develop such religious literacy skills that can influence public attitudes towards greater openness, flexibility, and acceptance of diversity. In other words, I do not advocate a merely academic debate about the challenges and strategies of teaching both theology *and* religious studies in the same university department, but want to extend the reflections on our subject areas to wider social implications and participation by both teachers and students so that we create resources for much larger groups than ourselves.

If we can make a concerted effort to connect and interweave the many-coloured strands of theology *and* religious studies, as I have argued we must, then some unexpected new patterns of great strength and beauty may, hopefully, emerge. The future is always full of surprises!

## Notes

[1] *Discourse: Learning and Teaching in Philosophical and Religious Studies*, 5 (2), Spring 2006, 25.

[2] Pierre Hadot, *Philosophy as a Way of Life: Spiritual Exercises from Socrates to Foucault.* Oxford: Blackwell, 1995; see especially ch. 1 'Forms of Life and Forms of Discourse in Ancient Philosophy'.

[3] Shaul Shaked, 'The Science of Religion in Israel with Notes on Interlocking Circles of Tradition', in Gerard A. Wiegers in Association with Jan G. Platvoet (eds), *Modern Societies and the Science of Religions: Studies in Honour of Lammert Leertouwer.* Leiden: Brill, 2002, 258–271; the quotation is on p. 265.

[4] I have discussed some of these ideas in more detail in 'Is There a Future for Religious Studies as We Know It? Some Postmodern, Feminist, and Spiritual Challenges', *Journal of the American Academy of Religion*, 70 (21), June 2002, 365–388 and in 'Religion in a New Key: Global Perspectives and Encounters Challenging the Study of Religions', *Religion and Theology*, 3 (1), 1996, University of South Africa online; see www.unisa.ac.za/Default.asp?Cmd=ViewContent&ContentID=947 last accessed 28/08/2008.

[5] *Discourse*, 5 (2), Spring 2006, 75–98.

⁶  W. B. Eerdmans 2005.

⁷  'Globalization Theory and Civilizational Analysis', in *Comparative Civilizational Review,* 17, 1987, 20–30.

⁸  The Hague: Mouton, 1979.

⁹  *The Concise Oxford Dictionary,*1990, 1034.

¹⁰  See for example David Green 'From Tree to Rhizome: Pagan Spirituality, Science and Resistance in the New Millennium', in Ursula King (ed.), *Spirituality and Society in the New Millennium.* Brighton: Sussex Academic Press, 2001, 206–219; see also the article by l'Anson and Jasper quoted in note 5 above.

¹¹  *OED* 1990, 918.

¹²  See Madeleine Bunting, 'Faith Can Make a Vital Contribution to Both Democracy and Scientific Ethics', *The Guardian,* 19 June 2006, 29.

Chapter 10

# Interdisciplinary Theology
## Bridging the Theology/Religious Studies Divide

Shannon Craigo-Snell

## Theology and religious studies

A traditional definition of Christian theology as 'faith seeking understanding' can lead to sharp distinctions between theology and religious studies. For those who follow this Anselmic definition, theology begins from faith, involves confession of one's own beliefs, and speaks of God. Religious Studies is often understood in contrast: it does not assume faith, does not involve confession of one's own beliefs, and speaks of how other people speak of God. Religious Studies thus appears as a loose confederation of scholars and methodologies that investigate various communities, beliefs, practices, events, and texts that assert themselves as, or are perceived to be, connected to religion. In my own location – the perhaps liminal space of teaching Christian theology within the Religious Studies Department of Yale University – this traditional definition of theology, and the sharp distinctions it often supports, seem inadequate. In contrast, an interdisciplinary view of theology as performed visions of God renders theology and religious studies close-knit companions, integral to the humanities as a whole.

I understand theology as performances of visions of God, performances which happen in many genres and therefore require interdisciplinary study.[1] This circumlocution, 'performances of visions of God', is meant to avoid an expressivist understanding of the human person, in which someone first comes to an understanding of God and then expresses this in language or action. The discourse of performance emphasizes that ideas and worldviews not only produce culture, they are also produced by culture. A performance, such as a theological statement or ritual action, may express, form, reinforce, or resist a particular thought about God. Indeed, it may do all of these things and more. The language of performance also highlights the role of the audience. A performance does not have a singular or static meaning, but rather is open to complex processes of interpretation. A performance can be interpreted traditionally, against the grain, unpersuasively, with a hermeneutic of suspicion, charitably, in an unexpected framework, etc.

## Teaching theology in religious studies

In this chapter, I discuss how this interdisciplinary view of theology plays out in the classroom, speaking quite concretely about my classes, my students, and the work we do together. This is not because I am an educational expert, but rather because issues regarding the relationship between religious studies and theology are deeply connected to teaching. Attending to the practical and specific challenges of teaching shapes my own interdisciplinary understanding of theology.

During the first week each semester, I meet dozens of students who come with very specific desires and expectations. Some students come to my classes hoping to connect their new collegiate experiences with the church-centred life they led in high school. They are looking for a Sunday Graduate School that will shore up their beliefs against the challenges of an expanding worldview. They desire the shared affirmation of confessional Christian faith, granted validation within the walls of academia. Other students arrive eager for critical tools to help them dismiss religion – to quantify, classify, and neutralize the claims of faith. They want the intellectual authority of the academy to see through theological claims to the sociological, psychological, or anthropological issues behind them, such that religion is shown to be a smokescreen that is best not taken seriously.

Neither theology nor religious studies fulfils the desires such students bring. What my classes offer, instead, is the blunt reality that Christian talk about God permeates our world and has enormous influence on art, politics, economics, science, sociology, literature, etc.

The general aims of my courses are threefold: (1) to teach students to recognize theology around them, (2) to help them learn to analyse theology and (3) to foster the skills to make their own theological arguments.

## Seeing theology

My first task of the semester is to teach students to notice when theology is happening. If theology is not just direct propositional statements from those who profess faith, but any performance of a view of God, then theology is all around us. I try to teach students to notice when a communication – in any genre – is also intended or interpreted as a performance of a view of God. This is both structured into the syllabus and part of the moment-to-moment reality of the classroom. For example, in a course on Christian Understandings of Evil, we begin with Annie Dillard's *For the Time Being*.[2] This is a book that intersperses several different forms of writing, including: a journal about clouds, a natural history of sand, the writings of Teilhard de Chardin, a travel narrative of Jerusalem, and meditations on a diagnostic manual of birth defects. This text is deeply theological but not written in any standard theological or even academic genre. The book is so oddly structured that it serves to draw attention to issues of how different types of writing can convey theological perspectives. From there we move to Calvin, Barth and Schleiermacher, asking questions about genre and context for each. In some semesters, we then read Toni Morrison's *Beloved*, changing genre before moving on to philosophical writings on evil. The movements of the syllabus are intended to show theology happening in different ways. Class conversations then ask about theological views regarding evil in memorial services, greeting cards, television, etc. Together we analyse the theology of literature, political statements, and popular culture, all within a larger framework of traditional philosophical and theological texts.

In a year-long survey course on the history of modern Christian thought, the students read smaller bits of non-traditional theology genres, including Phyllis Wheatley's poems, Sojourner Truth's 'Ain't I a Woman' speech, The Declaration of Independence, some of Thomas Jefferson's comments on slavery, and so forth. I begin the section on Hegel by reading from Whitman's *Leaves of Grass* and discussing his views of America, threads that get picked up later on when we talk about Frederick Douglass, James Cone and Martin Luther King, Jr.

Also, students in this course make timelines, charting the lives of the authors of the class along with world historical events and major milestones in any other field of their choosing. English majors make connections between the novels of a particular time and place and the theology of the same culture. Psychology majors track changes in understandings of the human person in both fields.

This work surprises students, who begin to perceive theology happening all around them and to see connections between theology and other disciplines. It also raises difficult questions about the activity of interpreting various cultural performances as theology. How important is the performer's intention? Does it define the true meaning of the performance? Is it one factor among many? Is it inconsequential? Such questions are particularly pressing when the performance being read as theology might not have been intended as such, and when the performer and audience inhabit different cultural and religious locations.

Theology as performances of visions of God is a broad and generic view that is applicable beyond statements of Christian faith and useful for audiences and performances that are not Christian. However, this generic description of theology is derived, to some degree, from the specificity of Christian theology, and thus carries with it echoes of Christian thought (such as a loose assumption of monotheism) and Christian history (including political and cultural colonialism). In classes, students are excited about the possibilities of interpreting the national budget of the United States as a performance of a vision of God. Yet they wisely worry, would it be appropriate to interpret a Hindu ritual as a performance of a vision of God? The interpretation of a performance as theology requires – and draws attention to – the messy intersection of the performer, the context, and the audience. Each of these (performer, context, and audience) are deeply situated in webs of meaning that connect, overlap, and collide. A traditional view of Christian theology as 'faith seeking understanding' avoids some of these complexities. However, it can also mask them, or remain mute in response to a globalized world in which people of different cultural and religious backgrounds are constantly interpreting one another through multiple, and sometimes conflicting, lenses.

## Analysing theology

I try to teach students not only to see, but also to analyse many different kinds of performances as theology. In the humanities we learn to think clearly about subjects in fairly predictable patterns: we learn some historical background and some theoretical frameworks. We trace internal coherence and historical consequences. These patterns are familiar to students, and they bring them to bear on theology. The first questions asked about a theological statement are not personally prescriptive ('do you believe this is true?') but typically analytical ('what are the historical precedents and theoretical implications of this statement?').

Students are given a fair amount of freedom in terms of what they choose to analyse for their papers. They can write on the books we have read during the course, or write papers that analyse other theological performances. There is significant interdisciplinary work in these papers, as students bring skills from the humanities to theological performances, and ask theological questions about events and texts from various fields. They bring their particular disciplinary interests into the theology classroom in their choice of subject, and they demonstrate that theology plays a role in that subject.

For example, one student in a course on political theologies analysed the implicit theology in President Bush's first three major speeches after 9/11.[3] The student tracked explicitly religious language, along with assumptions about the role of human endeavors in shaping history, the reliability of human judgement, and the nature of power. The student then compared this explicated theology with traditional statements of Christian doctrine. The paper noted when the President invoked Christian language while making theological claims (assuming humans can locate evil with absolute accuracy, speaking of eradicating evil through aggression, discussing fighting evil without addressing the work of Jesus, etc.) that would be problematic in several mainstream Christian traditions. The paper did not argue that President Bush was a bad theologian or a bad Christian, but rather that there was a deep internal inconsistency in his invocation of Christian theology. In early 2002, this was a far more sophisticated analysis than was happening in public discourse within the United States.

Another student developed a theological and sociological analysis of the United States' war on drugs. This was a senior essay of some scope, so the student did a lot of research. Having amassed the evidence that while whites and blacks use drugs in similar proportions, blacks are more likely to be arrested, charged, convicted, jailed, and given longer sentences, the student then moved on to how Christian theologians describe sin. She argued that the racism of the US war on drugs fits within the Christian category of sin and, therefore, the first Christian response to it should be repentance. She looked closely at public policy and asked what Christians should be lobbying for if they take the idea of repentance seriously.[4] One of her recommendations for such lobbying was to grant broader authority to the United States Sentencing Commission.[5]

Other projects look at the performances in pop culture. One student compared and contrasted the views of evil presented in the Harry Potter books and the Left Behind series. Drawing on film theory and a body of work already done on Disney, another student argued that there is a religious structure to the role Disney plays in America, describing the rituals, icons, pilgrimages, and repeated exposure to mythic tales that are often crafted to include or mirror existing religious narratives. He then did a close reading of the theology implicit in *The Lion King*.

The arguments students offer in such papers are deeply theological. They are not credos ('I believe') but inquiries (what is the understanding of suffering implicit in this text). The structures point out incoherence, consequences, possible interpretations. They ask uniquely theological questions – they talk about God – and they draw upon theological frameworks and history. But they are also structurally quite similar to papers in other fields in the humanities.

## Performing theology

The final element of this interdisciplinary approach is that students are required to make their own theological arguments. If theology happens in multiple genres, it makes sense to a permit students to wrestle with the issues of the course in various disciplines and media. Many students opt to do creative projects instead of traditional papers. These creative projects come at the end of the course, after students have analysed various theological performances and after they have written papers in the style of traditional academic theology, where they attempted to persuade the reader with reasoned argument. At the end of the term, students not only bring the disciplines they are most interested in to the theology class in terms of facts (as they do with the timelines) or subject matter (as they do in their earlier papers) but also in terms of media.

They propose their own projects and we discuss the methodological issues involved. It is made clear that projects must engage themes and issues of the course. The students must make an argument. They need to ask specific questions and approach them with articulated methodologies.

This results in a wide variety of projects. For example, one small group in a course on Theatre and Christianity performed excerpts of *Waiting for Godot* as an Episcopal worship service. This was the launching point for a student-directed discussion about how and why Beckett ritualized the play through strict copyright regulations, about the theological themes of the play, and about the nature of language and ritual in forming the self. In that same class, another group performed parts of *Angels in America* as a miracle play cycle, making an argument about communal meaning making and the social construction of the holy.

Often students are able to make points and put forth arguments in other genres with far more precision and insight than they could muster in a theological paper. In the course on Christian Understandings of Evil, one student wrote a deeply moving short story about a woman's first day in heaven. She wakes up to the smell of fresh gingerbread, entering a paradise of sensory abundance and physical pleasure. This seemingly childlike conception of heaven is used as a foil for discussions that come later, when the protagonist reveals she was a comfort woman during World War II, kidnapped and repeatedly raped by Japanese soldiers. The narrative presents a paradox, making clear that there is no place for this former Comfort Woman in heaven. It can only be heaven if her experiences of torment are somehow erased or negated, but that pain is so much a part of her, if it were removed she would cease to be herself. When Jesus offers to relieve her of her sorrow, she fights back:

> 'No!' Jeehae exclaimed, abruptly jerking her hand away from His. She bolted to her feet, spinning to face Jesus. 'It may be awful, but it's mine. If you take this away from me, what else do I have? This is who I am; for the decades after my experience, my anguish consumed me. I have nothing – I am no one – without these memories.'[6]

Another student, who sketched endlessly during seminar discussion, proposed writing a comic book on evil. I was deeply sceptical. But he produced an incredibly concise ironic argument, in which a Devil tries to convince the reader that evil is created by human attempts to divide the world into good and bad. The comic book demonstrated a familiarity with several of the authors we read during the semester, offering an inverted analysis of their strengths from a Devil's point of view. This student later entered the comic book into an art show, finding an audience outside the classroom for his work.[7]

In a class on Political and Liberation Theologies, another student created an hour long video called *New Haven Jesus*.[8] He used various means in the video to build an argument. Beginning with footage of two poor neighbourhoods in New Haven, the student employed visual images to identify the people presently living there with Jesus. The video then shows edited interviews with three people of different religious backgrounds who are actively involved in work for social justice sponsored and supported by Christian organizations. The student explored the degree to which each person understands his or her work in the Jesus-centred, economic, and political terms of liberation theology. The first person interviewed, a New Haven native, spends hours each week involved in Catholic charities without making any explicit connection to his faith or to Jesus. The second person, a Yale undergraduate from a Baptist and Pentecostal background, articulates a Marxist view of the work of Jesus in terms of economic justice.

After showing edited segments of these interviews, the student added quotations from several sources, addressing unemployment among Latinos, Christian responses to capitalism, and American consumer culture. The video ends with quotations from Karl Marx, Gustavo Gutiérrez and the book of Matthew. The student arranged a showing of this movie at Yale and invited the whole class to attend. He provided programs that demonstrated his pride in his work and provided a frame for the video, including a thesis statement.

Two notes about facilitating this kind of interdisciplinary work: first, while students are encouraged to incorporate the insights, resources, and media of other disciplines in their theological projects, they are still required to articulate their ideas in the terms and frameworks of academic theology. The performances of *Waiting for Godot* and *Angels in America* were paired with directed discussion; all of the creative projects have verbal elements. The skills of traditional theological discourse add a new dimension to the work students do in other disciplines; and the work they do in other disciplines adds layers of perception, analysis and involvement to their theological work. Second, students must trust that the members of their audience are competent interpreters of theology performed in various genres. They only attempt subtlety and nuance if they believe it will be noticed, only make theological statements in other genres if they believe it will be interpreted as such. Consider how an image in the video of a boy riding a bike through an impoverished neighbourhood, arms outstretched, gestures towards an identification of the urban poor of New Haven and Jesus – both crucified. While the student who made the video was responsible for articulating a theological argument verbally, he also used visual images to perform a vision of God, trusting that the audience would understand.

In a classroom setting, this respect for the audience is built over time, through analysing performances together. It is also negotiated in discussion. One student was a classics major. For his final project in the Christian Understandings of Evil course, he wrote a series of eleven poems, based on the Ten Commandments and the commandment Jesus gives to the disciples to 'love one another as I have loved you'.[9] Each poem deals with the subject matter of the corresponding commandment, and also with Judas. While the first poem casts Judas in the traditional role of betrayer, each successive poem shifts this perspective slightly, until the final poem portrays Judas as a scapegoat, used by God for God's own purposes, betrayed by Jesus. The final commandment, for the disciples to love one another as Jesus has loved them, then has a chilling quality, uttered by the son of a

God who must bear the ultimate blame for every evil. While I could follow all of those points, these poems were also rich with allusions and echoes of other texts, with which I was not familiar. The student was aiming for an Ezra Pound level of intertextuality, within a classical corpus that I do not know well. We managed this difficulty with extensive footnotes that explain each allusion and its intended purposes.

## Interdisciplinary theology

An interdisciplinary view of theology opens the floodgates to such difficulties. Within a traditional theology classroom, a well-trained theologian can present herself as an expert, imparting knowledge. Within an interdisciplinary theology classroom, this is not the case. Students will bring in questions and answers from other fields and no one professor can be expert in them all. The theologian is a facilitator, inquirer, collaborator and catalyst.

Such teaching is one important role that a theologian can play in the humanities. The theologian brings a specific set of resources and skills into the broader conversations of the university, fostering theological questions in relation to various fields. This is a different role than that of master of a circumscribed field of theological discourse as 'faith seeking understanding', and it fits well within the context of a Religious Studies department in a secular institution.

Another reason an interdisciplinary approach works well within Religious Studies is that it does not uphold the traditional dualism between confessional and non-confessional statements. It blurs those lines in its subject matter, by seeing many events and texts that contain no explicit confession as theology, which can be interpreted as performances of visions of God. It blurs those lines in method, by inviting students to look at theological performances using the tools of the humanities, and to ask theological questions in other fields. And it blurs those lines in the media in which it is communicated. Students who write papers for their final projects do so in a context of theology as performance, wherein a theological stance can be performed provisionally and temporarily. They can inhabit a theological persona, or role, that may or may not be close to their own identity.

Students who choose creative projects can blur the lines further, since there are many artistic media in which the final product is clearly deeply related to the artist's own thoughts and concerns, without making a straightforward or simple claim on the identity of the artist. Students who produce creative projects can engage in constructive theology, talking about God, without claiming adherence to a particular set of beliefs. An interdisciplinary understanding of theology as performance allows students to occupy a space that is both specific and fluid, that is neither the objective observer existing in abstraction nor the firmly committed confessing believer. Is the view of the Comfort Woman an articulation of the view of the student who wrote the story? There is no way to know. The student articulated a substantive theological question and pointed out particular difficulties with traditional views, but she did not indicate her own personal stance. What about the author of the Judas poems – does he think God cannot be trusted? I do not know. He wrestled with theological claims and constructed a theological position. Even the budding sociologist who wrote about the sinfulness of the war on drugs – will she be off to lobby Congress to repent, was she exploring a point of academic coherence, or demonstrating the inconsistency of Christians who do not repent? I do not know.

What I do know is that all of these students learned to see theology in the world around them, to analyse it using a variety of means, and to make their own theological arguments. In so doing, these students were engaged in theology, in the context of religious studies as an academic discipline, and in a richly textured engagement with other fields in the humanities.

## Notes

[1] Throughout this chapter, I draw upon the multidisciplinary arena of Performance Studies. While I write explicitly about this field in other texts, I have omitted technical discussion of performance in this essay in order to focus more specifically on theology and religious studies in the classroom. Introductions to the field of Performance Studies can be found in Marvin Carlson, *Performance: A Critical Introduction*. New York: Routledge, 1996 and Richard Schechner, *Performance Studies: An Introduction*. New York: Routledge, 2002.

Further, I write that performances 'happen'. The use of this term is intended to connect to the broader literature on performance. 'Happens' evoke connections to elements the 1960s discourse of 'happenings', and it resists closure concerning the delineation of performance. Something that happens can be intended as a performance by the performer, interpreted as a performance by the audience, or both.

[2] Annie Dillard, *For the Time Being*. New York: Vintage Books, 1999.

[3] Chandler Poling submitted this analysis for Political and Liberation Theologies, Yale University, 2002.

[4] 'By no means do I mean to say that the Unites States government should enact a Christian practice of repentance. Christians in the United States, however, should recognize opportunities for repentance and lobby for corresponding

changes in policy.' Kathryn Banakis, 'Christ on Crack: A Theological Analysis of the Sin of Racism in the United States' War on Drugs', Senior Essay in Religious Studies, Yale University, 2003, 40.

5  Banakis, 41.

6  Tirzah Enumah, 'Overruled', submitted for Christian Understandings of Evil and the Power of God, Yale University, 2002, 17.

7  Quindlen Krovatin, *Lot the Diabolical Tot: An Illustrated Analysis of Evil*, submitted for Christian Understandings of Evil and the Power of God, Yale University, 2002.

8  Michael Montano, *New Haven Jesus*, submitted for Political and Liberation Theologies, Yale University, 2002.

9  Adam Brenner, '*The New Commandment*', submitted for Christian Understandings of Evil and the Power of God, Yale University, 2002.

Chapter 11

# Recent Developments in Theology and Religious Studies
## The South African Experience

J. Jarvis and C. A. E. Moodie

## Introduction

Both the cultural context and the peculiar history of South Africa provide particular nuances in developments regarding theology and religious studies in South Africa, making it an interesting case. The peculiarities of the South African situation do not, however, negate the more general significance of the South African experience for theological and religious studies in general. The dialectic between Christianity and African religious tradition, in a post-Apartheid and post-colonial situation, has impacted strongly on theology as a discipline. In addition, the presence of sizable and influential Hindu and Muslim minorities has been an important factor in the development of religious studies in schools, and hence also in the universities. All this has occurred in a period of less than 20 years during which South Africa has moved from domination by the 'Christian National Education' ideology of the previous government to a new dispensation underwritten by a constitution that is possibly the most radical in the world in its commitment to democracy and non-discrimination. On to this setting has been superimposed similar pressures to those that have affected the development of theology and religious studies elsewhere in the world. Taking this perspective as its point of departure this chapter reviews the general situation in theology and religious studies at tertiary level in South Africa and describes the development of religious studies in institutions in the Province of KwaZulu-Natal.

The present state of religious studies in South Africa, both in schools and tertiary institutions, grew out of the very peculiar context of segregation that prevailed before 1994. It has also developed in reaction to that previous context. The relationship between religion and education was deeply implicated in the previous political dispensation. The religiously based ideology of the previous government was directly expressed in its education system in general (Christian National Education – CNE[1]) and also shaped the manner in which religion was dealt with in school curricula. Since 1994 South Africa has engaged in a process of developing a new approach to religion in education in line with the values of its new democratic, secular constitution[2]. This has taken place in conjunction with the development of wider educational initiatives which have included the adoption of new national education policies and the development of new approaches to the curriculum at every level of education.

In the new school curriculum, after considerable debate and wavering in official positions, there is now a compulsory 'Religion Education'[3] component. This component falls within Life Orientation (LO)[4]. Reference will also be made in this article to the introduction of a new Religion Studies option in the Further Education and Training (FET) band[5].

While the values that inform the new dispensation in South Africa are democratic and steeped in human rights it is possible to draw parallels between the old and new dispensations with regard to their form even if not their substance. Reflection on this, perhaps unexpected, degree of commonality, may point to wider issues of relevance of religious studies in general beyond the special case of South Africa. In this chapter the main features of education and of religious studies[6] under Christian-Nationalism will be outlined, followed by a description of religious studies and its broader educational context in the democratic dispensation. Thereafter, some aspects common to former and current approaches will be highlighted with a view to their wider significance.

## Education and religious studies in Apartheid South Africa

All education in South Africa prior to the institution of the new democratic dispensation was required by law to be conducted within the parameters of CNE, described by its critics as not Christian, not national, and not education! CNE embodied the principles of the 'Christian-Nationalist' ideology of the National Party, which ruled South Africa from 1948 to 1994 (Ashley 1989; Christie 1989; Samuel 1990).

Even before 1948 CNE had a long history, going back to the reaction of the Dutch colonists against the imposition of a policy of Anglicization in education following the British occupation of the Cape of Good Hope during the Napoleonic wars. The Cape-Dutch resistance against this aspect of British imperialism was partly a cultural struggle but this was fused with a powerful religious element, in the form of the Calvinism of the Dutch Reformed Church (Malherbe 1925). Isolated as it was, at the Southern tip of Africa, this expression of the Protestant Reformation retained an archaic form. This was shaped by a mindset that derived ultimately from the Peace of Westphalia of 1648, which tied religious observance to a territorial principle. As a consequence religious observance, territory and membership of a national group were regarded in Christian-National ideology as aspects of one reality. This had profound implications for education in Apartheid South Africa and for religious education in particular. And, given the nature of the Apartheid system, this impacted significantly also on education across the different components of the country's population.

The principle of suffusion determined the most fundamental feature of religion within CNE. It was to exercise a determining influence across the curriculum. Although religious education was allocated a discrete slot within the curriculum, religion was not to be limited to the confines of a particular subject. It was required that the influence of religion should be pervasive (Rose & Tunmer 1975). The principle of suffusion is not an exceptional feature; this paper will go on to show how it applies in widely differing educational contexts. The exceptional character of the previous South African system lay in the nature of the values and beliefs that were to permeate the curriculum. For example, the role of history in the curriculum was, amongst other things, to show how God had planted Western civilization in the far south of Africa with a particular predestined purpose. The amalgam of religion and nationalism, which is evident in this example, was extended across all the subjects of the CNE curriculum (Rose & Tunmer 1975; Ashley 1989).

As might be expected, CNE required a specific approach in the case of religious education[7] itself. The style in which it was presented was authoritarian, deriving from the rigid form of Calvinism that constituted the 'Christian' element in CNE. In passing it should be noted that even the use of the term 'religious education', with its more expansive connotations, was largely confined to the single case of the 'white' education department in the Province of Natal, in which an 'English' influence retained some presence. At another level, and to a somewhat greater extent, this relative autonomy applied in the 'liberal' English-language universities – with implications for theology and religious studies in those institutions.

While some degree of autonomy was allowed in respect of English-medium schools for 'whites' in Natal, with even that coming under increasing pressure in the 1970s and 1980s, little deviation from CNE policy was permitted elsewhere in South African education. The Bantu Education

Act of 1953 removed control of schools for Africans from the churches, where it had previously resided (Rose & Tunmer 1975; Samuel 1990) and government control over 'Coloured' (mixed race) education also soon followed. CNE policy was enforced without regard for cultural or religious differences, although the situation was less clear with regard to the 'Indian' population, comprising a Hindu majority and sizeable minorities of Muslims and Christians (with denominational backgrounds generally far from Calvinism).

Until the 1960s repatriation to India remained a preferred though impractical option for dealing with the 'problem' of people of Asian descent. In practice, government domination was extended over 'Indian' schools, which had largely been founded by local communities. But religion remained a more difficult matter to bring under control compared with other sections of the population where, despite opposition outside of the Dutch Reformed Churches, a Christian majority could be relied on, in a statistical sense at least, for the implementation of CNE. The situation in this regard changed in the 1980s, when the control over education was devolved, to separate 'Coloured' and 'Indian' administrations as part of a last, determined effort to reform (and maintain) the Apartheid regime in the face of mounting pressures. In the case of 'Indian' education this led to the institution of the subject 'Right Living' in the school curriculum in place of religious education. This reflected the reality of religious diversity in 'Indian' schools and was also a portent of future developments in post-Apartheid education.

## The principle of suffusion in education in post-1994 South Africa

The foundational values of the new constitution of the Republic of South Africa are enshrined in the general, cross-curricular outcomes to which all South African education, in all forms and at all levels, must now be directed. The aims of the constitution are presented at the beginning of the introduction to the Revised National Curriculum Statement (RNCS) (RSA Dept. of Education 2003a), and are reproduced in the 'Statements' for each of the learning areas in the General Education and Training band (GET)[8] and for the FET subjects (cf. RSA Dept. of Education 2003b). The values that are expressed in these aims are therefore central to the school curriculum as a whole but they are especially important to Life Orientation (LO) and hence also to 'Religion Education' which is accommodated in LO. The LO Learning Outcome pertinent to religion education requires that

> [t]he learner will be able to demonstrate an understanding of and commitment to constitutional rights and responsibilities, and to show an understanding of diverse cultures and religions.

The listed aims of the constitution include unity, democracy, social justice, human rights and the improvement of *the quality of life of all citizens and the freeing of the potential of each person* (RSA Dept. of Education 2003b: 1). This encompasses a broad range of more utilitarian educational and vocational concerns. But there is an explicit commitment to go beyond vocational and economic considerations and to emphasize what might be called 'ideological' values and the social transformation to which they are intended to lead.

The notion that the school curriculum is not supposed to promote a particular religion has not been without criticism on the grounds that this makes it a value neutral curriculum. Husain and Ashraf (1976), in their discussion of the nature of Muslim education, criticize the educational approach of the modern West specifically on this account. They advocate an approach in which the values of Islam pervade the whole curriculum, instead of a situation in which schools in Muslim countries have tended to offer a largely Western form of education, with Islamic religious education included by way of a supplement.

The criticism of the West, in this particular respect at least, is overstated – education in France or the Unites States of America, for example, could not easily be categorized as value-free – but the point is underlined that we should not be surprised that the transformation of South African education has seen a move from one 'ideological' orientation or values-perspective to another. What we must ask in relation to the aims of this chapter is how this perspective impacts on the understanding of the place of religion and the approach to the teaching of, or about, religion that follows from it. Over the past several years a rather tortuous path has been followed in South Africa in this regard, although the issue of religion in education has now been settled in South Africa's RNCS (2003a).

## Religion Education in the 'new' South Africa

The transition from 'old' to 'new' constitutional dispensations necessarily involved a radical shift in relation to religion. The pre-1994 constitution of South Africa had commenced with the words, 'In humble submission to Almighty God . . .', and from 1948 this had provided the framework for the domination of Calvinist Christian Nationalism. The new constitution provides for a secular state with recognition of the right to freedom of religion. In the original new National Curriculum Statement (RSA Dept. of Education 1996) religion was omitted altogether, on the presumption that religion could not appropriately be included as a part of secular state education. An extended and vigorous debate ensued. An example of what emerged in this debate can be seen in a submission to the RSA Department of Education by the South African Council of Churches (SACC 2003). The opinions of the SACC are significant in view of its history of outspoken opposition to Apartheid and its strong connections with key figures in the new government. The SACC submission did not seek to promote the kind of religious instruction approach that had characterized South African education previously but it expressed concern about the neglect or disregard of religion in the new school curricula. While the SACC submission took issue with aspects of a draft policy statement published by the Department of Education (RSA Dept. of Education 2003c) it expressed support for its *tri-fold emphasis on religion education that is educational, that explores diversity, and that stresses common values of equity, tolerance, multilingualism, openness, accountability and social honour.* In paragraph 6 it went on to state the following:

> We further endorse the adoption of a cooperative model of religion education that does not attempt to impose a particular religion on learners. . . . We applaud the Policy's recognition of the need to acknowledge the relevance of religion to all educational disciplines and in all stages of human development . . . to produce well-rounded and responsible citizens.

The SACC submission came near the end of a long process in which a range of alternatives to the initial omission of religion from education had been mooted in discussions of the Department of Education and various interest groups. Amongst these alternatives was the option, implemented earlier in Australia, of delegating responsibility for religious education[9] to clergy (or denominational representatives) for a specified period in the school timetable. This, in its own way, amounted to another version of the Department's abdication of responsibility for the issue.

The current policy for Religion and Education (2003) is the result of nearly 10 years of researching and consultation. In September 2003, the final National Policy on Religion in Education (RSA Dept. of Education 2003d) endorsed the acceptance of religion as an essential component of the curriculum. It was followed by the publication of National Curriculum Statements on 'Religion Education' and 'Religion Studies' (RSA Dept. of Education 2005a; 2005b). Both titles, it must be noted, avoid the use of the word 'religious', on account of its association with religious instruction and religious education from the pre-1994 dispensation. The titles also underline the point that it is not part of the purpose of state education to make people religious but to educate them about religion.

The Religion Education document outlines a comprehensive and well-balanced approach to education about religion but there are serious problems surrounding the place that it has been allocated in the curriculum. The time allocated to LO in the curriculum amounts to about 2 hours per week and in this time all the learning outcomes (covering the personal, physical and social development of the learners) need to be addressed. Given the fact that the publication of the LO document pre-dated that of the Religion and Education policy by about 2 years, it may be argued that Religion Education has been superimposed on the existing LO framework. The counter-argument, if the Department of Education were to be pressed, would doubtless be that what is presented in the Religion Education curriculum statement is not an *ex post facto* add-on but rather an explication of what was inherent from the start in the concern with the understanding of diversity within the focus on Social Development. If this position is accepted, the question arises as to why religion has been granted so restricted a place within the new curriculum as a whole with the practical result likely to be the effective nullification of what the Religion and Education Policy (2003) sets out to achieve.

Religion Studies represents a new initiative in the FET phase of secondary education (Grades 10–12), replacing the previous subject, Biblical Studies. As an FET elective subject the outcomes state that the learners should be able to demonstrate knowledge and understanding of a variety of religions. In Grade 10 the emphasis is on religions found in South Africa, in Grade 11 the focus is widened to include Africa and in Grade 12 religions throughout the entire world are explored. Learners should also be able to reflect critically on the interrelationship between religion and society and analyse, relate and systematize universal dimensions of religion.

Religion Studies, as a full-fledged subject for the National Senior Certificate (NSC)[10], has a much firmer foundation in the curriculum, albeit only in Grades 10–12, than Religion Education. But its place as an elective alongside subjects such as History, Geography and Art has yet to be translated into practice. Judging from experience with other subjects, whether or nor religion studies is offered in schools will depend very much on the interest and will of individual school managements to include the new subject in the school's curriculum offerings. Pragmatic considerations such as the availability of teachers for the subject are liable to count heavily in this regard. At this point there is a vital connection with developments in universities regarding theology and religious studies.

## Theology and religious studies in South African universities

Religious studies[11] at South African universities has gone through a difficult time during the past 5 years. In some cases departments closed, in other cases departments merged with other disciplines or were severely affected by rationalization. No new departments of religious studies have been instituted at any South African university. By contrast, in neighbouring countries such as Botswana and Lesotho, departments of religious studies have continued to flourish.

The link between the future of religious studies and teacher provision will be outlined in this section but a consideration of changes in the status of theology in South African universities will serve to lead on to this issue. In short, theological studies in South African universities have suffered pressure and erosion in recent years, although the effects of this have not been uniform, as will be seen in the case of University of KwaZulu-Natal (UKZN) and its constituent institutions. The pressures have been largely financial in nature and have coincided with a shift to a neo-liberal economic approach on the part of the new government as it acceded to power. Of the four liberal universities the University of the Witwatersrand (Wits) and Rhodes University have closed their theological faculties. Rhodes University was for decades the premier training institution for clergy of the 'English' churches, and the closure of its theological faculty is therefore of great symbolic significance. Apart from financial problems in the university sector, brought about by diminished state subsidies and increased costs, the ability of churches to bear the costs of university education of their prospective clergy has impacted on universities in terms of reduced student-intake.

Recent developments in UKZN and their preceding history in the institutions from which UKZN was constituted in 2004 provide an illustrative example of the situation of theology and religious studies in South Africa as a whole. The institutions that merged to form UKZN were the University of Natal (NU),[12] one of the four liberal 'English' universities that managed to maintain some degree of autonomy and international recognition during the Apartheid years, and the University of Durban Westville (UDW), originally founded in the 1960s as an Apartheid institution for 'Indian' South Africans although by 1993 it had a majority of African students.

In the case of UDW, until the end of the 1990s the university supported a Faculty of Theology as well as departments of Religious Studies, Islamic Studies, Hindu Studies and Hindu philosophy in the Faculty of Arts. Before the formation of UKZN, UDW had amalgamated all of these into a School of Religion and Culture. In addition to other factors already mentioned, a more utilitarian or mercenary outlook on the part of students who increasingly desired marketable qualifications contributed to the demise of these departments.

Trends at NU, prior to its amalgamation with UDW, tended to run counter to developments at UDW and other South African universities. Prior to the mid-1980s NU had no theological faculty but it had long maintained departments of Biblical Studies and Theology on one of its campuses, in Pietermaritzburg (UNP). The courses taught by these departments served the needs of prospective ministerial candidates, some of whom went on to complete a BA degree as a prelude to studies for the postgraduate Bachelor of Divinity degree at Rhodes University. By the 1960s, though, the Department of Theology had metamorphosed in all but name into a highly successful Department of Religious Studies – success being measured in terms of the very large numbers of students who included courses in 'theology', and even majored in it, without any intention of seeking ordination and, indeed, very often without any religious commitment[13]. In many ways UNP provided an example of what a thriving department of religious studies might be.

By the mid-1980s, in conjunction with a German Lutheran funding initiative, a full Faculty of Theology had been established at UNP. Since then, despite recent restructuring which has reduced theology to a school within a broader faculty, theology at UNP has continued to thrive. It has in effect very largely taken the place once occupied by the Rhodes University Faculty of Theology. While theology in the other 'liberal' universities was closed down or collapsed into schools of religious studies, at UNP it thrived. This may be attributed to an innovative spirit which saw the Faculty move away from a eurocentric ethos and a restricted role of clergy-provider to mainstream churches. The UNP centre now has extensive links with the rest of the African continent and 'theology and development' is a phrase which characterizes its work. It now forms part of the School of Religion and Theology of UKZN. It has links with other associated institutes, such as the Centre for Constructive Theology and the Catholic seminary at nearby Cedara, but more especially the UNP centre has strong links with the Lutheran, Anglican and Evangelical Houses of Study, which are located near the campus. There are currently proposals to move the present Methodist theological college from Pretoria and constitute it as yet another associated House of Study.

The new school, of which the previous UNP Faculty of Theology is part, has a second centre in the city of Durban, which largely incorporates the work of the previous UDW School of Religion and Culture, although religious studies is also represented on the Pietermaritzburg campus. To a large extent the two parts of the new School of Religion and Theology operate separately and serve a different clientele. The theology section has a secure role both in undergraduate education for ministry and in its extensive postgraduate and research programmes. The situation with regard to religious studies at UKZN is indicative of tendencies at South African universities in general, where disciplines that are not immediately associated with career openings and marketability have come under pressure in the last decade as government and students look to economic return as a measure of the worth of university programmes.

Whether policies at school level will throw a lifeline to religious studies at university level remains to be seen. In the case of UKZN it must be noted however, that any training of pre- or in-service teachers to facilitate either religion studies or religion education has to take place through consultation with the Faculty of Education. It is in this Faculty, in the School of Social Science Education, in the LO discipline that religion education (and possibly religion studies) is situated. It is hoped that collaborative teaching can take place, whereby members of the School of Religion and Theology can contribute to the training and development of especially religion studies teachers. To date the KwaZulu-Natal Department of Education and Culture (KZNDEC)[14] has done nothing to market Religion Studies as a subject and so there is no demand for this subject at tertiary level. If the subject is successfully marketed and several schools offer the subject in grades 10–12, the need for Religion Studies to be offered at tertiary level would become a reality and this could impact positively on the collaborative relationship referred to above.

With regard to theology, the success of UKZN stands out amidst the erosion of theological studies at most South African universities, although there are other exceptions, including the University of South Africa (UNISA), the University of Stellenbosch (US) and the University of Pretoria (UP). US and UP are both former 'Afrikaner' universities. UNISA, with a worldwide reputation for distance education and a total student enrolment of more than 130,000 boasts of about 1,200 part-time students in the School of Religion and Theology. US has responded to the new dispensation with new courses that emphasize diversity and human rights.

UP presents an especially interesting case study in transformation. It was previously a stronghold of hard-line Afrikaner Nationalism and CNE, and boasted two faculties of theology which operated separately from each other, each exclusively serving two different Dutch Reformed denominations. Theology at UP has reinvented itself as a single faculty which has attracted denominations such as Presbyterianism and Methodism. This has helped in overcoming the anathemas of the Apartheid. That these denominations, previously at loggerheads with Afrikaner nationalism and its CNE policies, now send African students to UP, and that they are welcomed and indeed sought after by UP, is an eloquent indication of the demise of CNE and of transformation in South Africa. But amongst other factors underlying even these developments are the financial and economic pressures that have had so wide an influence in the universities and the country as a whole.

## Conclusion

The Association for the study of Religions in Southern Africa (ASRSA) has been in existence for almost 30 years. ASRSA has its own accredited journal, *Journal for the Study of Religion in Southern Africa*, and annually holds a conference to which academics from theology and religious studies departments from all the Universities in South Africa and neighbouring African countries are invited. Two longstanding members of ASRSA served on the now defunct, Standing Advisory Committee on Religion in Education and contributed together with others to the formulation of the Policy for Religion and Education (2003). ASRSA has recently elected a member from the US Faculty of Education (whose field of expertise is religion education and human rights education) to its Executive Committee. It is hoped that the new Policy for Religion and Education (2003) and the NSC subject, Religion Studies will afford the opportunity to promote the study of religion at tertiary level. ASRSA could well be the vehicle used to foster future collaboration between Faculties of Education and those of Theology and Religious Studies.

# Notes

[1] CNE embodies the principles of the 'Christian-Nationalist' ideology of the National Party which ruled South Africa from 1948–1994.

[2] The Manifesto on Values, Education and Democracy (2001) supports the South African National Curriculum Statement (2002) and provides teachers with an understanding of the collective Human Rights Values in the South African Constitution (1996).

[3] Religion education slots into the social development aspect of LO and focuses specifically on the demonstration of an understanding of religious diversity in South Africa. Inter alia the following 'topics' are investigated: religious symbols, holy days and religious festivals, diet, clothing, scriptures and oral tradition, the contributions of religious organizations to social development, discussion on the contribution made by religions to promoting peace.

[4] Life Orientation (LO) broadly comprises three areas of learner development: personal development, physical development and social development.

LO is a compulsory part of the school curriculum for Grades R (Reception class)–12. In the GET in the foundation phase (Grades R–3) the focus is on Life Skills. In The GET Intermediate phase (Grades 4–6) and in the GET Senior phase (Grades 7–9) LO is one of eight compulsory learning areas. In the FET (Grades 10–12) LO is a compulsory subject which learners need to pass in order to finish school with their National Senior Certificate (NSC).

[5] FET – Grades 10–12.

[6] Religious studies used here to cover both studies at tertiary level and at school level (both Religion Education and Religion Studies) collectively.

[7] Religious Education was a compulsory school subject under CNE, also known by names such as 'Bible Education', 'Scripture' and 'Religious Education'.

[8] GET – Reception class to grade 9.

[9] 'Religion Education' is referred to as 'Religious Education' in Australia.

[10] Final school leaving certificate.

[11] Note that at school level the subject is called *Religion Studies* and at tertiary level *Religious Studies*.

[12] NU included the Campus in Pietermaritzburg, also known as University of Natal, Pietermaritzburg (UNP).

[13] In the previous situation in South African universities it was the norm to 'major' in two fields in initial degree studies, and many UNP students combined 'theology' with another major subject, such as Mathematics, Geography or English, which they regarded as the mainstay of their career preparation.

[14] In the Western Cape the Education Department has introduced Religion Studies into at least 30 schools and so there is a demand for the subject to be offered at tertiary level as part of the Bachelor of Education degree.

# References

Ashley, M. (1989), *Ideologies and Schooling in South Africa*. Rondebosch: SATA.
Christie, P. (1989), *The Right to Learn*. Johannesburg: Ravan.

Husain, S. S. and Ashraf S. A. (1975), *Crisis in Muslim Education*. Jeddah: Hodder and Stoughton.

Malherbe, E. J. (1925), *Education in South Africa (vol 1: 1652–1922)*. Johannesburg: Juta and Co.

Rose, B. and Tunmer, B. (1975), *Documents in South African Education*. Johannesburg: A. D. Donker.

RSA Department of Education (2003a), *Revised National Curriculum Statement*. Pretoria: Department of Education.

—(2003b), *Revised National Curriculum Statement: Life Orientation*. Pretoria: Department of Education.

—(2003c), *Draft National Policy on Religion in Education*. Pretoria: Department of Education.

—(2003d), *National Policy on Religion in Education*. Pretoria: Department of Education.

—(2005a), *National Curriculum Statement: Religion Education*. Pretoria: Department of Education.

—(2005b), *National Curriculum Statement: Religion Studies*. Pretoria: Department of Education.

SACC (2003), *Submission: Draft Policy on Religion in Education*. Cape Town: SACC.

Samuel, J. (1990), *Education: From Poverty to Liberty*. Claremont: David Philip.

Chapter 12

# The Place of Theology in Iranian Universities

## The Challenges of Teaching Theology in Modern Iran

Mohammad Sadegh Zahedi

Islamic Studies in Iranian universities has several branches of which theology is just one. Under the heading of 'Theology' comes theology, jurisprudence, Quranic sciences and the history of Islam and Islamic civilization. In this case, theology is an academic field of study and students are required to pass several units to get their BA. They may then continue their studies in theology to obtain their MA and PhD. Theology in this instance is a professional field of study and is usually taught in humanities schools. In addition to this, theology is taught in Iranian universities at a more general level as a compulsory course for all students. Each student must pass some units in theology regardless of what they are studying, whether medical science, engineering, social science or humanities.

In this chapter I will examine the common features of theology at both its professional and general levels. To provide an understanding of the situation of theology in Iranian universities and the challenges of teaching theology, it is first necessary to explain two key terms which are very common among Iranian scholars: 'Traditional Theology' and 'Modern Theology'. It seems to me that having a clear understanding of these two concepts will help to clarify what is meant by 'theology' and show some of the difficulties of teaching theology in Iran today.

## What is traditional theology?

There are three main theological schools in the history of Islamic theology: the *Mu'tazili*, *Ashari* and *Shiite* schools. *Shiite* and *Mu'tazili* theologies are on the one side and *Ashari* theology on the other. To place a general label on these schools I should say that *Ashari* theology is faith-based and

the two others reason-based. *Shiite* theology has been the most accepted
and prevalent theology in Iran for centuries. The most well-known book
in *Shiite* theology is *Tajrid-al-Eteghad* (Summary of Beliefs) written by
Khaje Nasir al-Din-e Tusi in the thirteenth century. This book has been
the main textbook among Shiite theologians since it was written and it is
still the main resource for teaching traditional theology in Iranian universities today.

After the death of Khaje Nasir al-Din-e Tusi, several commentaries were
written on his work, one of which became famous. The book was written
by Allameh Helli, one of Tusi's students, under the title of *Kashf al-Morad fi
Sharhe Tajrid al-Eteghad* ('Making the Intentions of Tajrid al-Eteghad Clear').
Students read *Tajrid al-Etaghad* with the explanations of Tusi's apprentice.
It seems to me that analysing this book, including its contents and method,
would help us understand the general features of traditional theology.

The book is in two parts: philosophy and theology. Almost two-thirds
of *Tajrid al- Eteghad* has to do with peripatetic philosophy. The author discusses essence and existence, form and matter, substance and accident,
necessity and contingency . . . and after these philosophical discussions
he begins talking about God: the existence of God, God's attributes and
other theological subjects. He seeks to prove the existence of God by way
of the contingent-necessary argument and he grounds his theology in his
metaphysics, which of course is peripatetic metaphysics. This metaphysical
basis can be seen in his other theological discussions in the book. I will
explain the changes that have happened in modern theology regarding
this metaphysical foundation.

Tusi's approach is apologetic and most of his arguments are *a priori* and
in my view axiomatic. He uses definitions and metaphysical principles to
explain and prove the truth of theological beliefs. He tries to show the
truth of his claims and the falsity of other claims. Most of the discussions
take place through what might be described as an internal discourse. When
he refers to other views these views belong to Muslim theologians you will
not find the name of a non-Muslim theologian in the whole of the book,
and there is little about other religions. This points to the fact that the discourse of the book is theologically internal.

Because the author lived in the thirteenth century, naturally we should
not expect to find anything about modern philosophy, modern epistemology or modern thought in his book. The book is based on a scholastic
worldview and its epistemology and methodology are scholastic. From this
we can see that the theological subjects and problems in his book are very
much of its time. Some problems which were important at that time may

not be important today, just as there are many new theological problems which scholars encounter today which are not found in the work.

By describing Tusi's book in this way I do not seek to marginalize it since, as I mentioned before, it is still a textbook in traditional theology and is taught in Iranian universities. This is only an attempt on my part to give some background to traditional theology in Iran. Now we turn to take a look at the situation of religious studies in contemporary Iran and to what is called 'Modern Theology'.

## Modern theology and religious studies in contemporary Iran

For more than 100 years Iranian scholars and thinkers have been acquainted with modern philosophy, and this acquaintance has grown more and more in recent years and this is also the case with modern science. Thus 'modern philosophy' and 'modern science' are not new concepts for Iranian scholars; however, the term 'modern theology' is a new phrase that emerged only two or three decades ago. It was first used by Abdolkarim Soroush and it has become a common phrase in contemporary Iranian theological discussions ever since.[1] Modern philosophy has been taught in Iranian universities for several decades – before and after the (1979) Islamic Revolution, but since the Revolution it has received more serious attention. The story is somehow different, however, for theology and religious studies. During the past three decades theological and religious studies have undergone remarkable development in Iranian universities and research centres. Many instructors and researchers are working on religion and various religious subjects. Theology and religious studies had never before occupied this place in Iranian universities. After the Islamic Revolution religion came into the centre of theoretical and practical considerations in Iran. This in turn has brought many questions concerning the relationship between religion and other subjects such as politics, economics, sociology, law, culture and so on. Furthermore, Iran has experienced the development of pure theological studies in recent years. In order to explain this more fully I will divide developments in religious studies over the past three decades into two categories: 'internal religious studies' and 'external religious studies'.

### Internal religious studies

In short, internal religious studies involves rethinking religious and theological ideas, including ideas about the nature of God, faith, revelation, miracles, immortality, evil, creation and so on. With internal religious studies, theologians try to find satisfactory responses for new theological issues by referring to religious texts. I will explain how modern philosophy and religious studies have influenced these studies.

### External religious studies

The development of external religious studies is concerned with the relationship between religion (especially Islam) and various subjects such as politics, economics, education, law and so on. Sociological and psychological research on religion should also be added to these subjects. For example to determine the relationship between religion – Islam – and politics, some central questions are: Does religion have any political content? What is the role of religion in politics? How should religion engage in politics? For another example, concerning the relationship between religion and economics, the main question is: What does religion have to say about economics, if anything at all? And regarding law and legislative systems, the relationship between religious law and common law is an important question. I do not intend to go into details about these various problems, but I will describe the situation of religious studies and the factors which have played a main role in these studies as follows:

During the past three decades in Iran, academic studies and research on modern philosophy have been developed rapidly in two directions. First, there is analytic philosophy and its various branches such as philosophy of science, ethics, philosophy of logic, epistemology and philosophy of religion in particular. Before the Revolution there were no courses on these subjects but now certain universities in Iran offer MA and PhD courses in these fields. Second, is continental philosophy. Philosophers such as Kierkegaard, Nietzsche, Sartre, Heidegger, Gadamer and many other continental philosophers are generally known to Iranian scholars and some of their books have been translated into Persian. Since the Revolution, Iranian theologians have taken the contributions of modern philosophy seriously and the influence of modern philosophical theories on religious studies in Iran cannot be ignored.

In addition to modern philosophy, the works of modern Western theologians have had an impact on religious studies in Iran. This is a completely new development that has taken place over the last two decades. Prior to this time, theologians such as Paul Tillich, Dietrich Bonhoeffer, Karl Barth and Rudolf Bultmann were mostly unknown to Iranian theologians. But now some of their main texts have been translated into Persian and their views are being discussed in theology classes. Also other contemporary theologians and religious philosophers such as John Hick, William Alston, Alvin Plantinga, Richard Swinburne, Gabriel Marcel, and Martin Buber are known to Iranian scholars today. Their works have been translated into Persian and Iranian instructors teach their ideas to their students. These different ideas are considered to be modern theological views and Iranian theologians find new problems, new methods and new answers in these theological discussions which are not devoted to Christianity alone and could be considered by Islamic theology too. This movement has resulted in a significant outcome in that it has opened Islamic theology's doors to other theologies to the extent that theological discussions in Iran are no longer just an internal discourse. Iranian theologians have found that there are a number of areas which are common to different theologies. Therefore, comparative studies of religions are now an active movement in religious studies in Iran.

Religious studies in Iran involves a wide range of activities. Now religion is considered not only by theologians but also by other specialists such as psychologists, sociologists, lawyers, political scientists, etc. So the literature of religious discussions in Iran is full of various topics with different approaches. To this literature we should add several translations of psychology of religion, sociology of religion and also philosophy of religion. I will explain how this growth of various translations and writings has caused great difficulties for teaching theology.

## The challenges of teaching theology

As I mentioned before, for years Iranian students were taught – and still are taught – what is known as 'traditional theology'. But teaching theology is no longer as easy as it was in previous generations. Because of the wide range of topics and books in religious studies which are considered 'modern theology' in Iran, theology has come across a new situation and its teaching entails several challenges which I divide into two groups: the challenge of choosing theological content on the one hand and choosing teaching methods on the other.

### Choosing appropriate theological content and texts

Almost all theology instructors believe that traditional texts are no longer appropriate for teaching in universities, because they are written on the basis of an ancient epistemology and methodology. Also traditional texts do not refer to many theological issues which are important today. One difficulty of teaching theology is that an appropriate text on Islamic theology based on modern epistemology and methodology was not accessible. For example, as I mentioned above, the formal theology in Iran has been Shiite theology for many years. But, how can we define Shiite theology today? Another problem is that the definition and parameters of Shiite theology are not as clear as before. There are many theological problems which are completely modern and do not have any historical background in Shiite theology – or even in Islamic theology generally. What should an instructor teach as Shiite theology today? And there are other challenges, which I list below:

- Although there have been various interpretations of Revelation in the history of Islamic thought such as philosophical, mystical, and orthodox, we have encountered new interpretations of Revelation influenced by modern thought in recent years. Some of these are not consistent with traditional beliefs. The difficulty is to develop a consistent system incorporating the traditional and new ideas.

- It seems the boundary between theology and religious studies is too ambiguous in contemporary Iran. Religious studies with its various approaches is considered 'modern theology'. For instance, there is no clear line between philosophy of religion and theology. Sometimes it is not clear if what is taught has a theological basis or is just a theory in philosophy of religion. For example, consider the theory of religious pluralism. Is it a theory in theology or in philosophy of religion? This ambiguity makes it difficult to choose an appropriate text for teaching theology and not anything else instead of theology.

- Can a theology instructor teach in his/her class the views of other theologians from other religions at least when there is a common subject between them? Suppose an instructor wants to explain what faith is. Can he use Paul Tillich's view about the ultimate concern of man? Or should he just refer to Khaje Nasir al-Din-e Tusi's view that faith is a firm true belief – or cite other Muslim theologians? We can put one 'why' in front of any answer to this question. It seems to me that we will have a mixed theology or, if you like, a 'salad bowl' of theologies in future.

- Religion in contemporary Iran is facing different challenges. One challenge involves social–practical issues in society. Sometimes, social problems are used as counter-examples for religious theories. Of course, some theologians try to separate a theory from what is happening in action to show that practical problems do not show the falsity of religious theories especially in the realm of social subjects.

## Methods of teaching

In addition to the challenge of choosing an appropriate text for teaching theology, another problem is how a theology instructor should teach theology today. This is more of a concern when he or she wants to teach traditional theology. Traditionally, theology has been taught as an apology. No belief was true except what a theologian believed and he was trying to defend his belief and show the falsity of other beliefs. The truth was determined *a priori* and the main duty of a theologian was to show the truth of his belief. So it seems that theology was like an ideology. But now, because of the situation I described, that method does not hold weight in theology classes. Most of the students do not attend the class with prejudice. They want to know the truth and they criticize every belief they encounter, regardless to which theological school the belief belongs.

I mentioned that Shiite theology is regarded as a reason-based theology. But the rational method – to prove or to disprove something with an argument – is no longer esteemed in theology classes today. Students expect more than proofs and arguments in a theology class. They are searching for a positive feeling with regard to religion. Other theological approaches may be more useful such as phenomenological, pragmatist, existential and semantic approaches. But the problem is that these approaches are not well known by theology instructors in Iran.

The main question for both theology instructors and students alike is: What is the goal and benefit of studying theology? This question is asked more frequently, at the general level where the course is obligatory. Should a teacher in a theology class try to develop students' religious knowledge or should he try to improve or promote their faith? Could these two goals be reached with the same method? The difficulty is that in a theology class you have a variety of students with different wishes and requests. Students ask why they should learn theology. What is its use in life? It seems to me that in this atmosphere we should move toward an applied theology like an applied ethics.

New teaching theories stress that the best way of teaching involves the critical method. Students should learn to think critically and be taught how to critique. Now, the question is how we can employ the critical method in a theology class and stress religious faith at the same time? In fact this is a problem which concerns the relationship between faith and criticism. Many instructors think the critical approach will make religious faith weaker but it seems that without critical thinking, the justification for religious beliefs will remain unsolved.

## Conclusion

In this chapter I have described the situation of theology and religious studies in Iranian universities. Although the formal education has been traditional theology, since the Revolution and especially during the two past decades, a new movement in theological studies has arisen in Iran. This new movement is influenced by modern philosophical and theological debates, and many Muslim theologians are trying to re-organize their theological discussions in Islamic theology. This re-organization involves considering new questions in theology, trying to find new answers to theological questions and developing new methods in theological education. In this regard, the works of other theologians from other religious traditions have proven to be very useful. The new generation of theologians in Iran is developing new texts on Islamic theology taking into consideration the matters mentioned above, but they are still at the beginning of the journey. Also in the case of Iran, determining the relationship between religion and other social institutions is being taken more seriously. As for theological education, although I explored the Iranian experience, it seems to me that in some aspects, the challenges are not local but universal. As far as Iran is concerned, I think that theology has an undetermined situation in contemporary Iran. There are many theological discussions, but no theological school has arisen. We may expect to see different theological schools with different theologians in future.[2]

## Notes

The term 'theology' can be translated in two ways in Persian: Theology in its restricted meaning is called 'kalam' and in its wider sense 'elahiyyat' which contains kalam and other branches of Islamic Studies such as Quranic sciences and Islamic jurisprudence. In this chapter when I use the term 'theology' I mean the restricted sense or kalam.

[1] Although the phrase 'modern theology' has been used before, what is considered modern theology today in Iran goes back to the works of Soroush.
[2] Theological studies in contemporary Iran are between tradition and modern thought. In this regard it seems to me that it is like early Islamic thought when the new theological schools were rising.

# Bibliography

Ahmad Naraghi (1999), *A Treatise on Understanding Religion*. Tehran: Tarh-e No.

Ali Ojabi (1996), *Modern Theology in Coexistence with New Ideas* (selected papers). Tehran: Andisheye Moaser Institute.

Allameh Helli (2003), *Kashf-al Morad fi Sharhe Tajrid-al Eteghad*. Qom: Jameaye Modarresin (Theological Instructors' Association) Publishing.

Baha al Din Khorramshahi (tr.) (1996), *Religious Studies* (selected translations), Tehran: Institute for Humanities and Cultural Studies.

Hassan Ali Akbarian (1998), *An Introduction to Knowing the Territory of Religion*. Tehran: Institute for Islamic Culture and Thought.

Hossein Kalbasi (2005), *Philosophy, Theology, Religions, Mysticism* (collected abstracts). Tehran: Institute for Humanities and Cultural Studies.

Islamic Propagation Office, Qom Seminary (1995–2006), *Naqd va Nazar, Cultural, Theological and Social Quarterly*, various volumes. Qom: Islamic Propagation Office of the Islamic Seminary of Qom.

Mahmoud Khatami (2003), *Phenomenology of Religion*. Tehran: Institute for Islamic Culture and Thought.

Religious Studies Association in Iran (2002), *Religious Studies in Contemporary World* (collected papers). Qom: Ehyagaran Publishing.

Religious Studies Association in Iran (2003), *Globalization and Religion* (collected papers). Qom: Ehyagaran Publishing.

Chapter 13

# The Bible
## Fringe or Hinge?

### Hugh Pyper

In the debate over the relationship between theology and religious studies, biblical studies often seems to be overlooked. This is of some concern to me as the Head of the only dedicated Biblical Studies department in the United Kingdom and as such one that I have given some thought to. Is biblical studies a peripheral adjunct to the debate, liable to be squeezed out as the competing claims of a variety of religious traditions, texts and methodologies clamour for space? Or is it, as I will hope to argue, a potential pivot point, a place where the history, the methods and the concerns of both theology and religious studies meet, and thus a vital resource where the intersection of the two disciplines is inescapable and a place where the issues involved in giving each their due can be most directly tackled? Is it inevitably a fringe subject, or could it act as the hinge between the two thus as the basis for a more coherent approach to the curriculum in Theology and Religious Studies departments?

## The Bible as fringe

The Bible constantly risks being marginalized in theology and religious studies curricula in Great Britain, not through any programmatic intention on anyone's part, but because local decisions about curricular development and staff appointments have responded to the perceptions of local priorities. The decline in the number of A-level candidates who have had the opportunity in the course of their studies to undertake any sustained engagement with the Bible is part of the changing environment which means that there is a reduction of the perceived demand for biblical studies. A particular interpretation of philosophy of religion and ethics has moved to the centre of religious education curricula. This is both because they are seen as relevant, a term which will be examined more closely in what follows and, frankly, because they demand relatively little subject-specific training on the part of the teacher, who may not be a religious specialist. Without denigrating the importance of such studies, it remains true that most teachers could chair a debate between students on euthanasia with some preparation, but not all would feel able to explain the development of Sufism or the synoptic problem.

This goes along with a commendable urge both at school and university level to expand the curriculum beyond the core disciplines of traditional Christian theology to embrace a wider range of religious traditions and methods of study. The time available for religious studies teaching, however, does not expand to encompass this, so decisions have to be made. There is a strong pressure to opt for what can be defended as relevant and what can be taught by the widest range of staff as student/staff ratios rise and as the case for any appointment has to be made in an increasingly competitive university environment.

## The Bible and theology departments

One might think that in the spectrum of university department in the United Kingdom, it would be among the more theologically oriented departments that biblical studies would find a refuge. Yet even there the Bible, and especially the Old Testament, can find itself increasingly construed as remote from the core interests of students. I have heard this put, as an argument that proceeds along the following lines:

We have to teach ethics to be perceived as relevant and to accommodate what prospective students want and expect. As a theological department, we could justify teaching practical and contextual theology as a way of satisfying this need and to entice students away from the attractions of the Philosophy Department. An argument could be made that practical theology depends on an understanding of systematic theology. This might possibly induce us to consider biblical theology. That might mean that there is a place in the provision for a New Testament specialist, and they occasionally remember that some knowledge of the Old Testament might be of use to their students, so a case could grudgingly be made to have some teaching of the Hebrew Scriptures. However, if posts are hard to come by and resources stretched, the Old Testament is the most dispensable of our disciplines.

Allowing for some satirical exaggeration, this is not an unfair analysis of the situation on the ground. This problem is compounded by the sometimes uneasy relationship between the disciplines of biblical studies and theology. I cherish the memory of a certain very eminent Orthodox systematic theologian lecturing a class of students among whom were fairly traditional Scottish Presbyterians, one of whom was driven to exclaim at one point 'But, Professor, the Bible disnae say that!' The reply was a weary wave of the hand and the striking phrase 'Please, do not bore me with the text!' Biblical studies is far from a simple handmaid of theological studies and to rely on theological justification for its significance is to appeal to a sometimes lukewarm champion.

The problem with the text becomes all the more fraught because any respectable university level teaching of the biblical texts requires at least some familiarity with the original languages. Finding room in a syllabus for Greek and Hebrew, even at introductory level, and finding someone prepared to teach it, is an additional hurdle that has to be faced. What has to give in the curriculum to create the space for languages?

A final problem in incorporating biblical studies into a theology programme could be summed up in the two questions: whose theology and which Bible? Does the programme encompass Catholic, Protestant and Jewish theologies, let alone Mormonism and the whole range of less familiar Christian approaches? Again, the Bible leads inevitably into areas beyond the strictly theological, in particular into the study of archaeology and ancient history and of ancient religious practices. How much of that can be justified?

By suggesting that Biblical Studies is thus pushed into a fringe position, I am not suggesting that there is programmatic hostility to the Bible or that decisions are not made with regret. What I am suggesting is that this is a consequence of starting at the 'ethical end' of the disciplinary range in terms of practical theology. I want later to suggest that starting from the biblical end may in fact help solve some of these problems.

## The Bible and religious studies

In religious studies departments, the Bible is equally likely to be at the fringes. The commendable desire to encompass the range of human religious experience means that the biblically based traditions have to take their place among other religious traditions. Moreover, for understandable reasons, there may be a residual felling that Christianity, and to an extent Judaism, has a privileged status culturally in any case so that true equity demands some redress of the balance. Postcolonial paradigms suggest that the Bible is very often a cause of problems and has been used to repress and supplant other forms of religious expression. All these considerations will tend to lower the priority accorded to teaching biblical studies. Even where Christianity forms part of the curriculum, there is a tendency to succumb to the same pressures as in theology departments and to concentrate on the ethical and the phenomenal, rather than the textual. The same issues over language also exist, heightened by an understandable argument that if Greek and Hebrew are to be taught, why not Arabic and Sanskrit, to name just two potential candidates? Indeed, why should the biblical languages have any priority?

In both models, I suggest, the Bible and biblical studies end up at the fringe of the curriculum, and thus are vulnerable when funding, posts and space on the timetable are vulnerable. Yet perhaps we can turn this position to the advantage of biblical studies. As we debate the relationship between theology and religious studies, and whether this is a competitive or cooperative one, we have hit here on a common factor. In curricula designed round either discipline, the Bible is driven to the edge.

What would happen, however, if we moved the margin to the centre? It might then be that the Bible and indeed particularly the Old Testament/ Hebrew Bible could provide the unifying element from which both theological and religious studies could radiate and where the common interests and points of contention between the disciplines could be most clearly and helpfully articulated for students. From its common status as the fringe of the disciplines, biblical studies can offer to act as the hinge that joins the two disciplines in a highly flexible way.

## The Bible as hinge

The very fact that here is debate and discomfort over the terms Old Testament and Hebrew Bible shows that this text is a point of articulation of different paradigms and modes of understanding. Is this text part of the scriptures of Christianity, or of Judaism? Is it a scriptural text, or a historical document that in complex ways bears witness to the religious life of the ancient Levant, or a cultural phenomenon that informs the politics and culture of Europe and thus is at heart of the complex and clashing identities that characterize the postcolonial and postmodern world?

The answer is that it is all these things and more. The methodological debates that characterize the divide between systematic and dogmatic theology, biblical theology, the history of the ancient Near East and the study of religions have their roots in debates over the Bible. It is not simply an act of Western or Judaeo-Christian hubris to place this text at the centre of these debates. It is where they started, and for sheerly pragmatic reasons of its global reach and its vital role at the centre of the methodological debates, it cannot be ignored. The one text can be and, importantly, has been subjected to the entire range of reading strategies that theology and religious studies can offer. For all its importance, the same cannot be said of the Qur'an, for instance. Could we unify the theological and religious studies enterprises in a unified department by starting students with a biblical text and then showing them how a systematician, a literary critic, an anthropologist, an archaeologist and a historian of religion would read it?

My own experience of teaching the Bible in a mixed department of Theology and Religious Studies bore in upon me the fact that much of what I was teaching fed into and drew on the methods of my religious studies colleagues, but that the almost universal assumption by others was that the bulk of my teaching was somehow related to theology. Of course there was an inescapable theological element, but this was by no means dominant. I would submit that it was in those classes that students got to experience most clearly the tensions and synergies between the theological and religious studies components of their degree. They learned to appreciate the problems and possibilities in using texts for interpreting the religious systems of the ancient Mediterranean. They had object lessons in how one should proceed to interrogate sources against their biases, both in the text itself and in the commentary literature upon it. They learned that the same text had been interpreted by Jewish, Christian and secular readers with rather different consequences and so to interrogate the hermeneutics of their sources. The issues of communication, translation and intercultural understanding were inescapably brought to their attention.

They also learned that the Bible has been misused as a powerful but misleading model for the role of texts in religious systems. The Bhagavad Gita is not the Bible of Hinduism, but the history of how Western scholars of religion have interpreted and sought to codify non-European traditions shows that model inappropriately applied. They learned that the Bible is a contested theological resource, and that orthodox Christian theology is one immensely rich interpretative tradition derived from it, but only one of several. They learned too how to criticize the inanities of much public theology and that appealed overtly or covertly to biblical myth and slogan.

I am not here suggesting that the whole curriculum should be reduced to biblical studies, but that the conscious foregrounding of the Bible as the 'common fringe' of both theology and religious studies is a way to bring the two disciplines together and to provide a 'point of articulation' which allows students to see the relationship between the range of courses they may be taking in a theology and religious studies degree.

## A brief polemic and a position

In his recent book, *The End of Biblical Studies*,[1] Hector Avalos accuses academics who practise biblical studies of being in the business of preserving their own privileged hobby by making spurious claims of relevance for an antiquated and positively malign body of material. While the call to be accountable for the privilege of an academic career needs to be heeded, the charge of irrelevance needs to be contested, and not be spurious claims either. On the contrary, irrelevance needs to be reclaimed as a virtue, especially when 'relevant' has become a code word for 'contributing to the national economy' or 'supportive of the latest cultural fashion'. Relevant to whom, in any case? The sacrificial laws of Leviticus can be an excellent pedagogical tool for questioning our criteria of relevance and getting across the message that the most unlikely things have been or are of vital concern to people. The Bible may be irrelevant, but it is also inescapable in any consideration of theology and religious studies.

Biblical studies also allows us to find an anchor point in the current theoretical maelstrom. It is an unusual discipline in that its focus is on an object of study, not a methodology. In the face of the competing and confusion range of methods that a student of theology and religious studies has to encounter and assimilate, the facticity of the text of the Bible offers a point of return and of stability, even as a stable point to begin to question the origin and authenticity of that very text.

For all these reasons, then, I would urge anyone considering the problems of constructing a coherent degree programme that includes both theology and religious studies to at least consider using the biblical text and the range of methodological option in biblical studies as the hinge to hold the two strands together. The Bible as an object of theological enquiry and a datum for religious tides can allow students to take a stereoscopic view of their studies, bringing the possibility of deepening their understanding of both disciplines and gaining a depth of focus on how and why human beings engage with a religious dimension of life.

## Note

[1] Avalos, H. (2007), *The End of Biblical Studies*. Amherst: Prometheus Books.

# Index

Note: Page numbers in italics denote illustrations.